SOWBELLY

SOWBELLY

THE OBSESSIVE QUEST FOR THE WORLD-RECORD LARGEMOUTH BASS

Monte Burke

DUTTON

DUTTON
Published by Penguin Group (USA) Inc.
375 Hudson Street, New York, New York 10014, U.S.A
Penguin Group (Canada), 10 Alcorn Avenue, Toronto, Ontario, Canada M4V 3B2 (a division of Pearson Penguin Canada Inc.); Penguin Books Ltd, 80 Strand, London WC2R 0RL, England; Penguin Ireland, 25 St Stephen's Green, Dublin 2, Ireland (a division of Penguin Books Ltd); Penguin Group (Australia), 250 Camberwell Road, Camberwell, Victoria 3124, Australia (a division of Pearson Australia Group Pty Ltd); Penguin Books India Pvt Ltd, 11 Community Centre, Panchsheel Park, New Delhi - 110 017, India; Penguin Group (NZ), Cnr Airborne and Rosedale Roads, Albany, Auckland, New Zealand (a division of Pearson New Zealand Ltd); Penguin Books (South Africa) (Pty) Ltd, 24 Sturdee Avenue, Rosebank, Johannesburg 2196, South Africa

Penguin Books Ltd, Registered Offices: 80 Strand, London WC2R 0RL, England

Published by Dutton, a member of Penguin Group (USA) Inc.

First printing, March 2005

10 9 8 7 6 5 4 3 2 1

Copyright © 2005 by Monte Burke

 REGISTERED TRADEMARK—MARCA REGISTRADA

Library of Congress Cataloging-in-Publication Data

Burke, Monte.
   Sowbelly : the obsessive quest for the world record largemouth bass / Monte Burke.
     p. cm.
   ISBN 0-525-94863-5 (alk. paper)
   1. Largemouth bass fishing—Anecdotes.   I. Title.
   SH681.B89 2005
   799.17'7388—dc22

                                                               2004028973

Printed in the United States of America

Set in Adobe Garamond with Univers
Designed by Daniel Lagin

To Heidi and Hansell

CONTENTS

The fish sees the bait, not the hook; a person sees the gain, not the danger.

—Chinese proverb

SOWBELLY

PREFACE
The Optimists

I n the spring of 2003, I approached my editor at *Forbes* magazine with a story idea about the chase for the world-record largemouth bass. It wasn't immediately an easy sell. I wasn't going to uncover some seedy corporate scandal or analyze some brilliant new marketing scheme. And the somewhat obscure endeavor of a few obsessive fishermen surely wouldn't move any markets. But the chase had all of the elements of a good story, so I gave it a shot anyway. I pitched it like this: A collection of very dedicated people—entrepreneurs, really—are actively pursuing a lofty goal, using their wits and an incredible amount of hard work. At stake was the possibility of great triumph, as well as the risk of utter failure. The plot thickened with the colorful, mysterious, and daunting history that had to be overcome. It helped, too, that at the time an $8 million bounty lay on the head of the world-record bass—money put up by a Tampa, Florida, outfit run by a used-car salesman and a real-estate developer.

I'll admit that I had more than a little self-interest in this story. I have been a fisherman all my life. I grew up in the American South, in North Carolina and Alabama, where fishing for largemouth bass is both a predominant pastime and an industry like, say, skiing in Austria or window shopping in New York City, where I live now. In North Carolina my family lived on a farm. Behind the house, down a gentle slope of horse pasture, lay a blackwater pond full of plucky bass. After my father, Donald, patiently taught me how to fish, I spent an inordinate amount of time tossing lures into its dark water, sometimes even hooking into a wriggling, green-sided largemouth bass. One summer I used a miniature remote-control boat—outrigged with a 6-inch rod tip, 4 feet of monofilament line, and a spinning lure—to troll the pond. I hooked and fought bass from a lawn chair on the shore.

When my father died of cancer in 1989, we moved to Alabama to be closer to my mother's family. I was seventeen years old, an awkward and self-conscious teenager, devastated by my father's death. Fishing was one of the few things that I believed I did well—largely thanks to my father—so I did it often. Luckily for me, my grandfather, whom we called Toots, had a bass lake in Alabama that was just a twenty-minute drive from our new house in Birmingham. He named the lake Tadpole. I fished that lake nearly every day during my last summer before college, and it became a bridge that connected my past with my future.

And I haven't stopped since. Fishing—especially for largemouth bass—was just something you did in our family, a stubborn stain on our genetic code that, like freckles, hasn't been scrubbed out through subsequent generations, though it missed a few of us. Neither my mother nor my youngest brother cares much for the sport. But for me, as it had been for my father and grandfather, fishing was a necessity, though why I love it and continue to pursue it with such passion is as mysterious and beguiling as the black water in that North Carolina farm pond.

So I thought that maybe by hanging out with these world-record-bass chasers—even though they obviously had taken what was for me merely a passion to the much higher level of obsession—I could shed some light on this mystery of mine. My inquiry, I believed, was perhaps similar to the way a pathologist studies the brain of a madman to determine the roots of lesser mental illnesses.

I didn't tell my editor any of this. But I did say that all fishermen, every time they cast a lure, dreamt of catching the biggest fish. And the world-record bass was, for reasons both mythical and absolute, the most sought-after prize of them all. I thought, however quirky, that this was a story the readers of the magazine would enjoy. My editor leaned back in his chair in an office that overlooked Fifth Avenue and thoughtfully rubbed his goateed chin as the idea dangled in front of him. Then he bit.

The article was published in *Forbes* in the summer of 2003, my contribution to the canon of fish tales. But something happened during the research and writing of that piece: I found myself falling in love with the stories of this small group of individuals who have distilled what they want out of life to the single act of catching the world-record bass. The result of that love is this book. The stories within, I believe, are more than just tales of catching fish. They are about what we humans will do, what we will gain, and what we are willing to sacrifice, in attempting to reach a goal. They are stories about life.

And one story gave birth to all the others included here.

On the rainy morning of June 2, 1932, a poor twenty-year-old farmer from Telfair County, Georgia, decided it was too wet to plow his fields, so he went fishing. A few hours later on Montgomery Lake, an oxbow of the Ocmulgee River, George Washington Perry caught and kept a 22-pound, 4-ounce largemouth bass—the largest ever landed in recorded history. We know very little about George Perry and his fish. None of the eyewitnesses to his catch are alive today, and only a few stories published about his fish actually use Perry as a primary source. As such, plenty of people doubt that the event ever really took place. Yet the International Game Fish Association (IGFA), the keeper of all fishing records, still recognizes Perry's bass as the world record to this day, and it is notable as much for its staying power as for the mysterious circumstances under which it occurred.

Perry's story is also the element that bonds together the rest of the characters in this book, all of whom I spent a year traveling the United States and beyond tracking down. Their stories make up the strange and lively tale of the chase for the new world-record largemouth bass, that mythical, as-yet-uncaught fish that some of its more fervent pursuers have affectionately dubbed "Sowbelly," for the swinelike girth it will most certainly possess. I started in California, wended my way through Texas to rural southern outposts in Mississippi and Georgia, and even traveled to the forbidden island of Cuba. I interviewed historians, biologists, con artists, detectives, and fed-up spouses. I fished with some of the best big-bass anglers alive. Along the way, I met a taciturn LAPD motorcycle cop named Bob Crupi who came within a hairbreadth of besting George Perry's record and finally exorcising the demons that lie buried deep within his soul. I hung out with Mike Long and Jed Dickerson, the de facto heads of two competing fishing posses, whose increasingly tense turf battles take place in suburban San Diego on a tiny lake that harbors enormous bass. I visited Bill Baab, the world's leading authority on the story of George Perry's fish, and the story's most tenacious guardian.

In Texas, I met biologist Allen Forshage, the head architect of that big-thinking state's complex and very expensive plan to grow the next world-record bass in a laboratory. I spent a week in a shack with Porter Hall, an Alabaman who has lost his marriage and daughter in his thus-far futile pursuit of the world record, but who believes he's finally found the magic bullet: to grow the damn thing himself in his private pond in Mississippi. I contacted fame-seeking con artists who were caught with lead weight stuffed into the bellies of their bass. And in Cuba, I spent time with the thoughtful Samuel Yera, for whom the chase lives most vividly in his curious mind.

Each of these characters had one thing in common: They were all chasing the ghost of George Washington Perry.

George Perry lived in a more innocent time, before our age of technology and stringent rules and media consciousness made records the objects of ravenous desire. His fish remains an anomaly in our modern era, which is remarkable for its unsentimental attack on records of all kinds. Whether it's from improved fitness, advanced technology, illegal supplements—or some potent combination of the three—the significant feats of the past continue to fall. Roger Bannister's 3:59-minute-mile mark has been lowered by sixteen seconds since 1954. Bob Beamon's historic long jump stood for twenty-three years until Mike Powell bettered it by two inches in 1991. In baseball, Lou Gehrig's consecutive game streak set in 1939 was broken fifty-six years later by Cal Ripken, Jr., and Roger Maris's 1961 single-season home-run record has been twice topped, first by Mark McGwire in 1998, then again three years later by Barry Bonds. Even important fishing records, like those for brown trout (1992) and Pacific Blue Marlin (1993), to name just two species, have fallen. Part of the hubris of our age is the belief that we can always do things better than we once did. But Perry's record, almost three-quarters of a century later, remains unbroken.

In order to qualify for an all-tackle (using up to a 130-pound test line) world-record catch today, fishermen must go through a somewhat tedious process. The IGFA requires the following: that the fish is weighed on an IGFA-certified scale in front of witnesses who must be shown the actual tackle used to catch the fish; that the fish is 2 ounces heavier than the previous record; and that the angler mail in a photograph showing the fish, the tackle, the scale, and the angler with the fish. For the more important records, like the largemouth bass, the IGFA reserves the right to administer a polygraph exam. The certification process is not fail-safe, which has compelled more than a few to try to cheat it. But in general, it weeds out the imposters. In January 2004, a controversial pending world-record bass caught by a woman named Leaha Trew (whom you'll meet later in the book) was thrown out for not meeting the standards.

The irony, of course, is that Perry's fish would have never qualified today. Neither a photograph nor a mount of his fish exists. No one knows for sure the make of the rod and reel he used to catch it. And no one ever subjected him to a polygraph test. Perry did nothing more than weigh the fish on a postal scale in front of a few witnesses and send the measurements in to a *Field & Stream* magazine fishing contest.

Then he took the bass home and ate it.

His nonchalance was completely understandable: In 1932, the record was no big deal. His bass wasn't officially recognized as the world record until two years later, and only became the IGFA's standard when *Field & Stream*'s records were transferred to that organization in the 1940s. The conspiracy theorists have always debated the authenticity of Perry's catch, a din that only grew louder when he died in a plane crash in 1974, taking all of the secrets of the world's most hallowed fishing record with him to the grave.

But since 1932, the importance of the record has grown immensely, corresponding with the incredible rise in popularity in the United States of the largemouth bass, which has unequivocally become America's fish. How and where to catch the next world record has been a perennial favorite story of the nation's outdoor periodicals like *Field & Stream, Bassmaster, Outdoor Life,* and *Sports Afield* since the 1970s. And the heightening fixation on the record has had a strange effect on a handful of bass fishermen: It has turned them into record chasers, individuals who play out their passion in relative obscurity, known primarily only to others who are in pursuit of the same scaly grail, on the lunatic fringe of the $12-billion bass industry.

The true record chasers have no rabid fans cheering them on, no million-dollar national tournament tours to compete in, no television shows to host, no lucrative sponsorship deals to sign. And as four notable modern anglers—Bob Crupi, Mike Long, Jed Dickerson, and Porter Hall—know all too well, unless you break the 22-pound, 4-ounce mark, you earn no riches. And even that money exists more in the theoretical realm than the actual one. The outdoor press often repeats that the angler who breaks the record will reap at least $1 million in endorsement money, but not if that angler happens to be using the wrong rod or reel, or the tackle companies deem him not marketable. Every so often, a magazine will put up prize money, but it's usually closer to $10,000 than $1 million. The Big Bass Record Club was offering $8 million to any member of its organization who caught the biggest bass in the world, but it folded in 2003 due to a lack of new members and the untenable burden of heavy insurance premiums.

That's not to say that fame and money can't be made in bass fishing. Denny Brauer, a tournament angler from Missouri, appeared on a Wheaties box in 1998 and has made almost $2 million in career tour earnings and another $1 million in endorsements. Together the CITGO Bassmaster and the Wal-Mart FLW tours have minted a dozen millionaires, and enabled another five hundred or so anglers to make bass fishing a full-time career. And then there are television personalities like Roland Martin, who can be found five days a week on the Outdoor Life Network kissing bass before he drops them back into the water, his hair bleached blond from the hours in the sun and his shirt festooned with as many sponsorship patches as a NASCAR driver's Nomex suit. Even a hybrid of the two types of bass celebrity has been created. In 2004, a bass tournament angler was featured on the reality show *The Bachelor*. Plenty of individuals have become famous and made very comfortable livelihoods from simply catching bass. But no one has ever made a living from pursuing the world record (though some, as you'll see, have *spent* a fortune in doing so). And what's ironic to record chasers is this: Most of the fish these famous bassers catch are . . . well . . . small.

There's a reason for that. Truly huge bass are extremely rare. Lets say, for argument's sake, that the 11 million frequent bass anglers in the United States each catch five bass a year (a gross undercalculation that doesn't take into account bass anglers in other nations or the tens of millions of bass caught by the 33 million other freshwater anglers in the United States). Most of these bass will weigh between 2 and 3 pounds. In 2003, there was one bass caught in the world that was officially 20 pounds or more, one of only twelve such fish on record since 1923. That means, at the very best, your annual chance of catching a 20-pounder in the United States alone is 1 in 55 million. That's what statisticians call an outlier. You are far more likely to be struck by lightning or become a U.S. Senator than catch a 20-pound bass. There just aren't that many around.

But fishermen in general rely on an almost theological faith— "Faith that the water that you are fishing has got fish in it, and that you are going to catch one of them," as the novelist and noted fishing bum William Humphrey once wrote. Fishing is the sport of optimists. Every cast into the unknown water world is merely an expression of that optimism, and thus no guarantee of some connection with another living being. The world-record chasers have taken this faith a step even further. They are perhaps the fishing world's biggest optimists, in pursuit of a bass that, statistically speaking, may not even exist. Each of these anglers believes somewhere deep down that catching the world's biggest largemouth bass will get him or her something—personally, financially . . . each has his or her own reason.

And to get there, they've each turned this pursuit into an obsession. Susan Orlean wrote in *The Orchid Thief* that once people become adults, they view obsessions about seemingly inconsequential things—like flowers or big bass—as a bit naïve. But very rarely in this world does someone achieve the absolute pinnacle of his or her profession without some sort of obsession. For these record chasers, that fixation has manifested itself in various ways. Some things have been irretrievably lost: Edenic innocence and purity and even the enjoyment of a sport that most fell in love with as children. But others have been gained: notoriety among peers, a profound faith in the unknowable and, perhaps most significantly, a sense of purpose in an otherwise chaotic world.

But here's one thing that gnaws at the gut of each and every one of these record chasers: Anyone could break it. Whereas you or I will never top the single-season home-run record in baseball, we *could* land the next world-record bass. An eight-year-old on his or her first fishing trip is just as likely to pull off the feat as someone who has spent a lifetime on the chase.

And yet this dedicated collection of individuals persists—casting, retrieving, and hoping for that one fish.

The question is, Why?

It is sadder to find the past again and find it inadequate to the present than it is to have it elude you and remain forever a harmonious conception of memory. —F. Scott Fitzgerald

CHAPTER ONE
Why Settle for the Small Ones?

B ob Crupi circles the busy block in Van Nuys twice on his Kawasaki 1000 before settling on the best vantage point: the parking lot of a 7-Eleven. He shuts off his bike, leans it onto the kickstand, and sits and waits, chin resting on his hand, eyes darting to-and-fro behind his dark aviator sunglasses, searching for patterns. His quarry is predictable: The hookers working the circuit, flaunting their wares in hot pants and skintight sweaters. The shifty small-time drug dealers in their shabby green army jackets. All anxious, trying to make eye contact with passersby or people in cars, as attuned as auctioneers to the tip-off of a subtle nod. It's six-thirty on a spring evening that's whitewashed by the dry southern California sun, still hours away from setting. But he knows they will be out soon, working the cars constantly emptying and refilling these streets that run by the seedy hotels and fast-food restaurants and under the wires that coil like black ivy around the telephone poles and traffic lights. The daylong heat and sun always makes them lose patience, makes them careless. Their urge overpowers them, is insatiable. And eventually, it will drive them onto the streets in broad daylight and into the world of

Motorcycle Bob. All he has to do is sit and wait. Just be patient. "If you're in the right spot," he says, "it's only a matter of time."

He knew some of them by name—at least by their street names. The hookers: Precious, Sweetness, Chocolate. The dealers: Smiley, Casper, Ricardo. They all played the same game every day, in the same place, with the same players apprehended, arrested, and back on the street a few hours later. They might as well make it legal, Bob thinks. But it's not, and probably never will be, and anyway, he has a job to do. You have to follow orders.

That's the number-one rule for a cop. He grimaces when he thinks back to Compton in 1992, when he watched that order crumble, driving by slowly on his bike as the looters smashed store windows and pulled out the TVs, the VCRs, the liquor. They dropped things as they skipped away: Walkmans, loaves of bread, and bottles that fell from overfilled arms and popped into so many shards on the asphalt. Greedy fuckers. The orgy of looting. They scurried right by him without even a glance or the slightest hesitation. He was powerless to stop anyone. "We could have smoked a bunch of those shitbirds while Reginald Denny was getting his brains bashed in," he says. Cops like to go in and do their business, but when you tie their hands behind their back, well . . .

But you have to follow orders. And that's what Bob is doing now. Following orders. Scanning the streets of Van Nuys, looking for patterns.

There. He sees one. First of the evening. She's swinging her hips, working the sidewalk, close to the traffic, bending down occasionally to look into car windows. Bob waits until the right moment. Don't want to strike too soon. Wait for them, make sure they're hooked well, then strike hard. She stops. A single white male, his head on a swivel, is in a green Buick that's braking for a stoplight. She leans over into the open passenger's-side window. They talk, exchanging street code ("You a cop? Show me your dick."), then her head pops up, a quick surveying glance. She opens the door and gets in. The john drives slowly, one eye on the road, the other sizing up his new companion. That's all Bob needs. He twists the ignition key, firing up the Kawasaki, and pulls the bike upright and forward off the kickstand. He flips on the flashing blue-and-red lights and cuts quickly across traffic, maneuvering in the narrow spaces between the cars until he's behind the green Buick. They both pull over to the curb. Bob leaves the lights on and gets off his bike, standing up to his full ursine height, arching his back and straightening his belt buckle. He has a body that looks capable of inflicting serious pain. His light brown police shirt is pulled tight over his casklike torso. Fading blue ink from his tattoos spills out from the short sleeves that partially cover his burly sunburned arms. On his forearm, a wild boar rides a largemouth bass like a rodeo cowboy. Bob's hair is short and brown and edged with gray, like the tip of a lit cigar. A trim brown motorcycle-cop mustache forms a crescent above his top lip.

He approaches the car slowly, fingering the billy club that swings at his hip. Hookers are generally less dangerous than drug dealers, who have taken wild shots at him, but he still has to be careful. Step out of the car, he says, hands on the hood. He is, as always, as straightforward as a lead pipe. The john says he was just giving the woman a ride, though he's cloudy on the details of their exact destination. Yeah, she says, he was just giving me a ride. Bob asks them both for identification. Neither has any. She gives a name, made-up of course, then turns to let him put the cuffs on. She knows the drill. The john is not so compliant. I was just giving her a ride, man. Driving without a license, Bob says, and soliciting a prostitute. You have the right to remain silent. The man resists and pulls away. Gonna be a shitbird, eh? Bob grabs the man's right arm and twists it behind his back and yanks it toward his head, hard, sending a shot of pain up the man's elbow. The man gasps. The cuffs go on, tight. Bob radios a black-and-white to transport them to the station.

The evening has begun. It will go on like this—the stalking, the arrests—until his shift is over at 3 a.m. and the younger men on the force ask him out for a drink. They go to blow off some steam, to let loose the nervous energy held so tightly during the shift. But Bob has no tolerance for that anymore—the antics of the young officers, the case of beer hidden in the alleyway, the false bravado of the stories from the night. Bob is in the zone now. He knows that this is his big opportunity, his chance. He knows where the damn fish is, knows how to stalk it, how to hook it and land it, knows what this will all mean. So he punches out at the station and jumps back on his bike, the wind peeling away the stresses of work with every mile gained on the dark highway home.

He tiptoes into the modest ranch house, pulls off his shiny black motorcycle boots, and takes off his uniform. He peers into his bedroom at Trish, his wife, sound asleep, her face lit by the blue light of the digital clock that reads 3:33. He passes the kids' room. His six-year-old daughter and five-year-old son are under the covers in their beds, sleeping peacefully. He doesn't know them at all—doesn't know what their favorite foods are, the TV shows they watch, what they do after dinner, if they are happy and well-adjusted children. He feels a sharp, quick pang of hurt in his stomach but fights it off. This is his opportunity and he must seize it. He is good at what he does. Very good. But what separates him from the others, above all, is his dedication. And that, of course, comes at a cost. It always does.

Outside, the Chevy pickup sits on the street, hooked up to the trailer and the bass boat, ready to roll. He checks one more time to make sure everything is in place. His checklist consists of two anchors, a depthfinder, and a twelve-pack of Diet Pepsi. No food. Don't want to have any unusual scents on your hands. The bass might pick them up. Three rods, all black graphite. He runs his fingers over the 8-pound test monofilament line to check for nicks, then double-checks the knots that attach the size-two bronze hooks. The drag on the reels is set perfectly: not too tight, but not loose enough to give on the hookset. He is meticulous about his gear. No secrets exist to catching big bass. You just can't make stupid mistakes. He checks the minicooler full of live crawdads. He does all of this now so he doesn't have to think about it later on the water, where he will sit from sunup until sundown. In the zone.

Bob starts the pickup and drives twenty minutes through the sleepy, dark world to the Castaic Lake Recreation Area. He's the first to arrive, as always. He noses the front bumper of his truck up to the gate and turns off the ignition. He leans the driver's seat back and folds his arms over his brawny chest. Then the best big-bass fisherman in the world falls into a deep sleep for two and a half hours, dreaming of a fish known to the locals as "Sowbelly." When he awakes, he'll employ the same vigilance he exhibited hours earlier on his beat—his pursuit of justice never ends. By all rights, that record fish should be his. He's fought the good fight, crossed all the t's and dotted all the i's. He upheld his own system.

From 1988 until the Northridge earthquake of 1994, this is how Bob Crupi lived his life.

Bob Crupi had come within 4 ounces of breaking the world record in 1991, when he landed a 22-pound, 1/2-ounce bass on Castaic Lake near Los Angeles. It was one of two fish he had on the top-ten list of the biggest largemouth bass in history. No one in bass-fishing circles had heard from Bob in nearly a decade, but most assumed he had never stopped trying to catch the world record, especially after coming so tantalizingly close. So I gave him a call. A gruff voice on the other end of the line said, "This is Bob Crupi."

I flew out from New York to Los Angeles late on a Tuesday night in July of 2003 and drove forty-five minutes north on eight-lane Interstate 5 to Castaic, a truck-stop town littered with gas stations, strip malls, and strip joints. A couple of eighteen-wheelers were pulled over on the off-ramp, their yellow-bulbed night-lights tracing the borders of their trailers as the drivers slept in their darkened cabs. My motel room, a dingy, overpriced flea-bag right off the exit, sounded like I-5, and not a river, ran through it. I didn't sleep a wink.

The next day, in the gray light of 6:00 a.m., I stood outside of a Shell station across from the motel, holding a large cup of coffee, shivering a bit in cool morning air. A Suburban attached to a bass boat, with a license plate on the trailer that read DBL DGT, pulled up in front of me. I opened the door and got in and shook hands with fifty-year-old Bob Crupi. Apparently impervious to the chill, he was wearing long black shorts and a sleeveless black T-shirt that showed off his big arms and tattoos. The interior of the truck was spotless. A stuffed lion stalked me from the dashboard. Bob and I exchanged some pleasantries. I could tell right away he didn't really like talking to journalists. We annoyed him.

Bob and I had agreed in a phone call the previous day to fish the lagoon portion of Castaic Lake, the reservoir in the scrub-covered desert hills above Los Angeles where Bob had landed both of his near-record fish. The man-made reservoir is the last link in a chain of reservoirs that hold precious Colorado River water meant to slake the insatiable thirst of the San Fernando Valley. The upper portion had been ruined as far as big largemouth bass went because of the introduction of striped bass (or "stripers"), which outcompeted largemouth for food. And the city of Los Angeles had ordered a drawdown of Castaic in 1995 to check for damage to the dam after the earthquake the year before, and with that had destroyed some of the best bass habitat. But as far as anybody could tell, no striped bass inhabited the lagoon, and Bob said he'd seen "what would be the world record swimming in the lagoon on more than one occasion." I was excited. I was going hunting for the world-record bass with Bob Crupi, the man I had first read about in an outdoor magazine when I was a teenager, the only man ever to land two bass of more than 21 pounds. Granted, July was not the best month to fish for big bass, but they would be in there and, well, you never knew.

Five minutes into the drive, I asked Bob a question about his pursuit of the world record. The muscles in his jaw clenched tight, and his face turned red. He was simmering. I thought he was thinking about his answer. His silence made me nervous. I started to stammer a bit, trying to clarify my questions. When he answered, his voice rose well above mine. "I'm not after this goddamn record anymore. I'm done with the whole fucking thing."

"Well," I said, as calmly as I could, "let's just go after it just for today, OK?"

"You're the client," he said, shrugging his shoulders.

We pulled past the gate at the state park and backed the boat into the water. Bob jumped in and threw me the keys to the truck. "Park it right over there," he said, motioning to the barren lot. We were the only ones there. I guess he was right about July. I parked the truck and warily eyed the stuffed lion on the dashboard. I walked quickly back to the dock, leaped into the boat, handed Bob the car keys, and we were off.

Maybe fifty yards from the dock, Bob moved the boat with the electric motor in gradually diminishing circles while eyeing the depthfinder, which showed a few small green blobs ("Those are fish," he said) and a severe dropoff on the lake's floor. It was, he said, a good spot for big bass that lie in wait to ambush their prey. He finally shut off the motor and let out one anchor from the front of the boat. I let out another anchor from the back. We'd employed Bob's now-famous double-anchor technique, cribbed from other anglers during the glory years, an example of just how hard he had studied his craft. The two anchors held the boat absolutely still, negating any swaying effects that a slight current or breeze might have on the boat and his line in the water. "You want to sit the bait," he said.

Bob opened a bucket, took out a crawdad, and hooked it just behind the head. The crustacean raised its pincers, protesting mildly. Then Bob cast maybe thirty feet from the boat, letting the line out until the crawdad settled on the bottom of the lake. He flipped his bail and held the monofilament line in his fingers. I followed his lead. He told me to watch the line, to look for the sudden jerks that would signal that the crawdad felt imminent danger and was using its powerful tail to try to swim away from a big bass. If the line started to move, he explained, you held on and waited until it went straight. That meant that a bass had taken the bait. You had to wait until you were absolutely certain it was hooked. And that was when you were supposed to strike.

The sun was already out in full force in what would be an excruciatingly hot southern California day. Bob opened up the first of many Diet Pepsis and sat silently, chin in hand, looking out from behind his dark polarized glasses, as if he could see through the mystery of the dark water. We sat like this, in the exact same spot, for twelve hours straight. Neither of our lines ever moved, once.

Robert J. Crupi, it could be said, was born to break George Perry's record. On June 2, 1953, exactly twenty-one years after the world record was set, Bob was delivered into this world in Brooklyn, New York, the son of Salvatore and Viola Crupi. When he was ten years old, his father moved the family to Los Angeles to take over the management of a five-and-dime store. But Bob brought something out west with him from Brooklyn: the burning desire to be a cop. His maternal grandfather, Christian Schultz, was a member of the New York City Police Department, a tightly wrapped man who frequently brought his job home and treated his family like the street criminals he stalked on his shifts. Bob hated the powerfully built, bitter old man—hated his guts because of his propensity to ruin a Thanksgiving gathering or Christmas dinner by getting drunk and yelling at Bob's father. The old man would even, on occasion, threaten to hit Bob's mother and even Bob. They all cowered in his big presence. But something about the air of authority that his grandfather carried with him intrigued young Bob, especially when the older man was wearing that crisp blue uniform, that shiny badge and holstered gun. Nevertheless, Bob hated him. Even at a young age, Bob had a heightened sense of what he perceived to be right and wrong. And he decided very early on in life which side he wanted to be on.

The move to California, out from under the grime and menace of New York and his grandfather and into the sun-sweet land where dreams were reborn, invigorated the Crupis. They were happy. While his parents ran the store, Bob spent every free moment of his childhood on the rivers and reservoirs, fishing. Something about the sport intrigued him, though he could never say exactly what that was. But it made him joyous, unbelievably so, to bring home a stringer of bass or trout for his parents. He even convinced them to buy him a four hundred-gallon tank, which he put in the garage. He filled it with lake water and a few big bass. He would sit and study his pet bass, watching them swim for hours and experimenting by dropping in live crawdads and golden shiners to see which bait the bass preferred. His friends played other sports—football and basketball—and excelled at them. Bob was always good at catching fish. And the more he caught, the stronger his urge became to catch even bigger ones, to be the one at the dock at the end of the day with a stringer that included at least one fish that was larger than any of the ones that the grown-ups in boats had brought to shore.

In 1975, Bob graduated from the police academy and lived with another cop in the Sunland area of Los Angeles. He started working on the force in a patrol car, and he found police work exhilarating. Young cops, they say, are like children: They don't know enough to be afraid. The car chases, the stakeouts, the drug busts, even the light duty of traffic patrol were immensely satisfying. He had found the perfect methodology for carrying out his black-and-white vision of the world. There were law-abiding people and there were shitbirds and there was no in-between. He even enjoyed some of the off-duty fun, hanging out with the others after the shift, unwinding with more than a few beers, chasing women who loved the uniforms in a much different way than Bob had when he was a kid.

But Bob never strayed too far from bass fishing. He spent his days off and his vacations on Castaic Lake and noticed that at the docks he still had the knack for hauling in the biggest fish. While other fishermen would show up with a stringer full of 3- to 5-pound bass, Bob would walk over at the end of the day and slap down a 12-pounder with an authoritative *thump* on the dock, his one fish that he had spent the whole day hunting. To Bob, the world of fishing—his passion—was as black and white as his job: There were big bass, and the rest were pretty useless. The scale told the story, settled the debate. "Why settle for the small ones?" he was fond of saying.

Turns out, Bob Crupi was not the only left-coast transplant who made good. Largemouth bass are not native to California, but like oranges, they have taken very well to the Golden State. As the story goes, Orville Ball, the San Diego lakes superintendent; Rolla Williams, a writer for the *San Diego Union*; and Ray Boone, who played baseball for the Detroit Tigers, went fishing one day in 1958. According to Orville, Ray started talking about his fishing exploits during spring training in Florida. "He said that these damn three-pound Northern-strain bass in these reservoirs were no big deal compared to the eight-pounders he caught in Florida," recalls Orville, now eighty and retired in Washington state. "That got my curiosity up." Orville contacted the world's leading ichthyologist at the time, Professor Carl Hubbs of the Scripps Institution of Oceanography, and confirmed that Florida-strain bass had the potential to grow bigger than their northern cousins. In 1959, Orville convinced the county to import some pure Florida bass to Upper Otay Lake near San Diego. To prepare the reservoir, the state put in rotenone, a toxic chemical, to kill all of the fish in the lake, which included northern bass, bluegills, and catfish. They wanted the new bass to start with a clean slate. In the spring of 1959, twenty thousand bass fry arrived via a National Guard training flight from Florida. But that first batch was contaminated with Ichs, a parasite, and had to be destroyed. A year later, twenty thousand new fry came from a hatchery near Pensacola, Florida, and were planted in the lake and, eventually, all over the state. The thinking was they would make a nice addition to the state's other game fish and take well to the state's newly constructed reservoirs built to handle California's ever-expanding population in the 1950s and '60s. Little did they know *how* well.

A few years after the initial stockings, wildlife biologists began to notice something strange. Like some of the female humans who inhabit California, the bass disappeared for a while, then turned up with a part of their anatomy unnaturally enlarged. The adult bass being caught in the state had the same head-to-tail lengths as their Florida kin, but their weight was uncanny. These bass had bellies that would have made Nell Carter seem svelte—so big that some of the fish appeared to be almost circular in shape. The biologists noticed that just six or seven years after a reservoir was stocked, bass would grow to 10 to 15 pounds, a size that largemouths in their native state of Florida would be lucky to reach by age twelve. Sure, the long warm-weather season in southern California and clean reservoir water made a nice habitat for the bass, but their sizes made no rational sense to the biologists, so they started looking for a reason. Then it dawned on them: The largemouths were eating another Fish and Game Department project.

Since the 1950s, for recreational anglers, the department had been stocking thousands of pounds of rainbow trout, California's native fish, in the same reservoirs as the bass. The big bass were gobbling up these one-pound protein treats like they were food pellets and growing to abnormal sizes. "We knew that the fish had the potential to grow larger, but we didn't know how large," says Orville, the Godfather of big bass in California. "And we didn't think they would eat the trout. But it's a good feeling whenever you plant something in the garden and a beautiful thing comes up and blooms. It tickles me to death."

Just fourteen years after that initial stocking, California bass began an attack on the record books that hasn't ceased. In 1973, Dave Zimmerlee landed a 20-pound,15-ounce fish in San Diego's Lake Miramar that became the world's second-largest bass and the California state record. It was the first 20-pound-plus fish caught since George Perry's, forty-one years earlier. Raymond Easely beat that with a 21-pound, 3.5-ounce fish from Lake Casitas, a reservoir near Ojai, seven years later, and the second California gold rush was officially on. When his friend and sometime rival Dan Kadota caught an 18-pounder from Castaic Lake in 1988, Bob Crupi knew his time had come. His lake—the one he had studied for years and knew inch-by-inch—was bearing fruit.

In 1988, Bob made his full commitment. Bass fishing became for him something more than a passion. It was more akin to breathing. He was always the first in line at the parking lot at Castaic, always the last off the water. He spent every nonworking waking hour on the water, observing, trying new techniques, watching for patterns. He cobbled together all of his vacation days so he could take the month of March off, the time of year when the big bass went on the spawning beds and were at their most vulnerable and, because of the eggs, which can add up to two pounds in weight, at their heaviest.

The days all blended together in a sunburned California dream. At the dock, the motor would *pop-pop-pop* until it caught a gear, then Bob would gun his boat across the reservoir to his spot, circle it a few times with the quiet electric motor, eye the fishfinder to make sure he was on at least one big fish, then double-anchor, bait his hook, cast it out, and sit and bake in the hot sun. For hours, for days, for weeks.

Every fish could be caught. They all made mistakes, made themselves vulnerable. You just had to be in the right place at the right time. He called these places his "confidence spots." If he knew a big fish was in the vicinity, he had no reason to move. For anything. He carried a white bucket on the boat that served as a Portajohn. He would drink one Diet Pepsi after another. Visualizing his crawdad slowly making its way along the rocky lake bottom, Bob stared hard into the water trying to clear his head of any other thoughts. Every once in a while, though, he would find himself thinking about the money, the talk shows, the product endorsements that were sure to come when he broke the record. How it would change his life. How he knew he could do it. But he would banish those distractions as quickly as they came and would refocus even harder on the bait below. He wasn't doing this for the fame. This was about hard work and sacrifice and a world that if it were at all just, would reward him with what he so desperately desired.

Though he worked all night and got only a few hours of sleep, Bob never felt tired on the lake. He was always on point, always focused on the water before him, on the monofilament line he held between his fingers. He watched the line for anything unusual, any jumps or twitches that might signal a bass. Bob mostly fished by himself. He didn't need help from anyone else, and anyway, he wasn't interested in anyone tagging along. He didn't mind being on the water for so long every day all alone. In fact, he quite liked it.

His techniques on the water were not unique. The use of two anchors he learned from Dan Kadota, who had himself learned it from some commercial fishermen in the Pacific. Crawdads? Sure, some guys used rubber imitation trout or live golden shiners, but most of the two-dozen or so people on the lake on any given day were using the crustaceans. Everyone knew that bass loved them ("Maybe it's a Southern thing," said Bob). Perhaps the only technique that Bob used that was different was the 8-pound test line. That was far lighter than most people were willing to go. But Bob felt that big bass were warier, and anyway, he could land big fish on 8-pound test, no problem.

But what separated Bob Crupi from all of the others was something else. Like a great natural athlete, he had all of the physical tools. But to be the best, you have to possess the intangible. For Bob, the intangible was his ability to deny basic human nature, to fight off the boredom and loneliness, to resist the urge to change his tactics if they didn't produce immediate results, to become comfortable with being uncomfortable. "I don't think he was any better at it than a handful of other people," says Porter Hall, who chased the record on Castaic at the same time as Bob. "The thing that separated Bob was that he was there all day, every day. Always the first on and last off. Damn did he fish hard. He just out-worked everybody else." Porter remembers only one day when Bob left the lake early. As Bob motored by on his way to the dock, Porter asked him why he was leaving. Bob looked irritated. He explained that he had to go pick up his kids from school. "Nobody's fault but my own," Bob said, shaking his head in disgust.

By the late 1980s, southern California was abuzz about Castaic, about the huge bass that had been seen swimming in the lake: a fish of well over 20 pounds, possibly even a world-record fish. And, all of the locals said, if anyone was going to break that record, it would most likely be that crazy motorcycle cop.

Around this time Bob's fishing began to take a toll on his family. His wife, Trish, had given birth to a daughter in 1987. A year later she had a son, and Bob was at the hospital for the actual birth, but had shed the sterilized garments and was back on the water within an hour. Bob was rarely at home, and even when he was there it was either to pick up the bass boat after work or to get a few hours of sleep before reporting back to his job. He saw the kids or his wife only in passing as he blew through the house, rushing to get onto the water or onto his bike. Trish began to complain that she was raising Bob's two children all by herself. Bob hired a nanny, but Trish said he had missed the point. But still, Bob couldn't stop fishing. It wasn't just the world record anymore, not the fame and money that would supposedly follow it, not the esteem and jealousy that it would certainly inspire in other anglers, his competitors. It was something else altogether, something he had no easier time explaining now than he did when he was a kid. It was an obsession that bordered on addiction. "It gives me a high to catch big bass," Bob said. "It comes from doing something that's not average." In some eerie way, Bob had unwittingly become just like the johns and druggies he arrested every day while on patrol. His wife first threatened him with divorce in late 1989.

Then on March 9, 1990, Bob announced himself to the big-bass world with a bang. His fishfinder had picked up a huge bass that hung tight to the lake bottom at Trout Point. A year earlier a fisherman had hooked and lost an 18-pounder in that same spot. He knew that this could be it: the fish that he had spent two years pursuing. He double-anchored his boat and, two hours later, hauled in a huge bass—his biggest ever. He brought it in to the dock later in the day and had it weighed on the postal scale, which wouldn't make it official, but would give him an idea of what he had on his hands. Just for a moment, he allowed himself to dream about the world record or, at the very least, the state record. His heart sank. The scale was reading just over 21 pounds—off the world record by a pound and change, and even below Easely's record for California. Bob took the fish into town to have it certified anyway (it was part of a five-fish stringer that weighed 72 pounds, 1 ounce—a state record that still stands today). He wanted to make it official. The 21-pound, 1/2-ounce fish was the third-largest bass in history. He hoped that it would help justify all of this fishing to his wife. And, maybe more importantly, to himself.

Then Bob Crupi experienced something that he had never gone through in his thirty years of fishing: a slump. He suddenly had trouble locating big fish and sat over spots that felt fishless.

And even when he did hook big bass, they somehow threw the hook or broke the line. He even began to feel tired during the day, losing his concentration, something he never thought was possible. He was miserable and began to question if all of these sacrifices he had made at home and at work were for nothing. A slump was nothing to be ashamed of. Even premier athletes like baseball players went through periods when they couldn't produce. Most of the time they just fought their way through it. But Bob knew, also, that some of them never recovered; their confidence was irrevocably shaken. He worried that he had lost his edge, maybe forever.

In the beginning of 1991, Bob hit his nadir. He had gone too many fishless days. He needed a break. His wife was set to attend a seminar, a David Del Dotto "get-rich-quick-from-real-estate" conference that was being held in Irvine. She pleaded with him to go with her, to take time off and maybe, just maybe, save their marriage. With no other place to turn, Bob decided to go. The other anglers on Castaic—Dan Kadota and Leo Torres—couldn't believe what they had heard. Big Bad Bob Crupi was leaving the lake just as it seemed ready to spit out the world record. Now of all times? But Bob, ever sure of himself, dismissed their comments, left Castaic with his wife, and headed for Irvine.

The trip was just what Bob needed. He didn't listen too hard to Del Dotto's real-estate ramblings, but enjoyed the time off the water. He spent hours by the pool, relaxing, not thinking about fishing. At night he and Trish would go out to dinner, either with other conference attendees or by themselves. They were getting to know each other again. Bob was softening up, enjoying his first real time away from bass fishing in ten years.

One morning he went down to the hotel lobby to pick up the paper. He flipped to the sports page, and there on the front were two brothers, Mike and Manny Arujo, smiling, holding two fish, one 14 and the other 18 pounds, caught at Castaic Lake. Bob was incensed. He knew every other fisherman on the lake, but who the hell were these two, and how the hell did they catch those fish? He went back up to the hotel room and started pacing. "Pack up, honey. We're going home."

Bob was back on the lake the next day, but something still didn't feel right. He fished, without any real success, for the next two months. But he knew if he just kept at it, something would happen. And something did, on March 5, 1991 . . . just not to Bob. Mike Arujo, one member of the sibling duo that no one had ever heard of, who had only been fishing the lake for three months, landed a 21-pound, 12-ounce bass, smashing Easely's state record with a fish that was a mere 8 ounces from Perry's world record. Bob was devastated. A newbie had caught a spectacular bass after just ninety days on the lake. Bob had been on the chase for years with little to show for it. All of the hours, the stress, seemed for naught. He went home that night prepared to tell his wife that he was done, that he had given up the chase. "Fuck it, I thought. It wasn't worth it," he said.

Here for the first time was the crack in the fortress wall that had always been so stone solid. This was the sign, he thought, that he should quit. He'd go back on duty and forego the rest of his planned month off. He expected Trish to be relieved, to want him back for the sake of the family, to be happy that he had decided to quit. But what she said shocked him: She told him to get back out there and catch a bigger fish. For better or for worse, the Bob Crupi that she had married wouldn't give up right now, not when he had come this close. She appreciated the time and attention he had given her lately and knew that he loved her. But now it was time for him to get back on the lake. "Then the light just went on," Bob said.

He was on Castaic the next morning. Once again, Bob was

first in line and first on the water. He fished hard, relying on his old instincts, his old determination. "It all felt right," he said. Did it ever.

On the morning of March 12, 1991, Bob had a hunch. Some big bass had been caught a few days earlier at Old Shithouse Cove (named for the floating Portajohn that was once there). While waiting by the gate, he'd made the decision to spend the day on the cove. He moseyed his boat up to a spot by a sunken tree that provided excellent cover for a big bass and ran the quiet electric motor.

A dozen or so other boats dotted the water that morning, scattered in some of the other big-name spots, like Elizabeth Canyon, Trout Point, and Red Rocks. Bob didn't know if the Arujo boys were there that morning, and he didn't care anymore. Thinking about them was only a distraction. He stopped and double-anchored. He opened the bait bucket that held maybe thirty crawdads that he had hand-selected from the secret creek behind his house. He waited for one to catch his eye. He liked the crawdads with what he called "daditude," the friskiest, most pugnacious of the group. A little brown crustacean reached up to Bob's hand as he lowered it into the bucket. There he was. Bob grabbed it on the back and impaled it with a hook behind its brain.

It was eight o'clock on a bluebonnet morning. He pitched out the crawdad and let it settle onto the shallow, rocky bottom. Almost immediately, the line started to move in quick spurts. He put his reel in gear, took out all of the slack, and waited. The line jumped sideways—a sign of a strike. He reared back, bending the rod almost in two. The fish ran hard, smoking a bunch of line from his reel. He knew right away that the fish was about the same size as the 21-pounder he had caught almost exactly a year before. He worked the bass to the surface, careful not to put too much strain on his rod and the 8-pound test line. The fish kicked its tail on the water and pulled out some more drag. Slowly, Bob got it to the surface again, and this time he reached for his net. He worked the fish in, inch by inch. Three minutes after he had hooked the bass, with its mammoth distended belly, it was safely in his livewell. "I knew it was another big fish, but I didn't think right away it was the record," he says.

Instead of motoring straight to the dock and the postal scale that was stowed in the park office, Bob calmly rebaited his hook and took another cast. He caught a 6-pounder, probably the male partner of the fish in the livewell. He let that one go. He made a few more casts before he got curious. He wasn't thinking about the world record, but maybe, he thought, this fish would put Arujo in his place and break his lake record—no small achievement. Bob took it into the docks. The postal scale read somewhere around 22 pounds. At that point Bob knew he had the state record, and potentially even the holy grail that he had sought for three years now.

He took the fish to a local liquor store with an official, certified digital scale. The man behind the counter photographed the fish, took its measurements, and acted as the witness. The fish was absolutely gigantic, with a belly the size of a bowling ball. Eggs were dripping out of its stomach. Bob draped it over the scale. He first saw the numbers "22" flash on the digital readout and thought for a moment—just for a moment—that this was the fish. Then he saw the ".01" that followed. He was short by just under 4 ounces. If this fish had eaten maybe two more bites for breakfast, Bob would have beaten Perry's world record. A call was put in to the State Department of Fish and Game to come and certify this fish as the unchallenged new state record. No one was in the office. A message was left. Then Bob thought about the thousands of eggs that this female bass was carrying and decided to drive it back to the lake. He got into his boat and went back to Old Shithouse Cove. He held the fish in the water for maybe five seconds, then it shook free with a kick of its giant tail. And with that, only the second ever recorded bass of over 22 pounds in the world disappeared into the depths forever.

Bob left the lake and went home. Even before he could tell his wife about the fish, the phone started to ring. Writers from *Sports Afield, Outdoor Life, Field & Stream,* and the *Los Angeles Times* asked him the same questions.

"No, I never thought about keeping the fish," Bob answered, politely at first.

"It was full of eggs."

"I hoped that it would grow bigger in the next year or two."

"I'm a cop."

"No, I don't believe in George Perry's record."

He started to get agitated almost right away.

Bob wasn't prepared for what would happen next. He had always been a solitary man, on his bike and on the lake. He was naturally a bit surly, not a talker, never speaking any more words than were necessary to get him through the day. He wasn't accustomed to all of this attention, all of the questions. The media bothered the crap out of him. He was like Ted Williams in that way. He just wanted to do what he did so well in a vacuum. For Williams, that meant hitting a baseball. For Bob, it was catching big bass. But the press kept hounding him relentlessly. Calls came in from New York, Miami, even Japan, at all hours of the night. He let the answering machine pick them up, then deleted them immediately. Reporters showed up at the docks in the morning, hoping to get a comment, barging into his personal space. They wanted to know what kind of rod and reel he was using, wanted to know all about his techniques. They wanted to fish with him, to watch him do his thing, to study him like a lab rat. "I was doing things my own way and didn't want to divulge anything," Bob said. He refused to cooperate, so they started printing preposterous rumors and falsehoods they'd obtained from anonymous sources (he'd killed a man while on duty; he'd cheated and used live trout for bait; he'd illegally used two rods).

But the media wasn't the worst problem he had. Suddenly, Castaic was packed full of boats. In the parking lot, license plates from Alabama, Kentucky, and New York were sprinkled amidst the blue-and-gold California plates. On the water, other anglers spied on him with binoculars, watching his every move. "I can't tell you how many people have seen me take a piss in a bucket," he said, still irritated twelve years later. Little groups of anglers, gossiping like ladies at a tea party, would suddenly get quiet when he walked by them at the gate in the morning. Men like Mike Arujo bad-mouthed him at tackle shows, saying he was a cheater. Other anglers started calling him "Bob Crappy" behind his back. Bob didn't do himself any favors with his guarded, secretive, and snarling ways.

Porter Hall, after considerable nagging, even fished with Bob a few times but never felt comfortable in his presence. "Bob's a cop and has this shell around him," he said. "I don't know if he considers anyone a friend. He and I had respect for each other, and I enjoyed fishing with him. But he doesn't want any real friends."

The park service boats, maybe picking up on the things that other anglers were whispering, started motoring by him on the water, eyeing him closely, kicking up wake into his double-anchored boat and screwing up the natural movement of his bait. When Bob got on a good bite at a certain spot, other anglers would horn in and ruin the action. A group of gypsies in johnboats, pontoon boats, and every other type of watercraft imaginable anchored up around him for a week at Mud Point, one of his honey holes, and their anchorlines and general commotion spoiled the spot. Even his employer seemed to get in on the act. When Bob hurt his back during a big bass tournament in Tennessee, he went on disability. A month into his rehab, his doctor told him to start some light exercise. So Bob of course went fishing. He caught an 18-pound, 9-ounce bass that made the papers. The LAPD launched an investigation for benefits abuse. Internal Affairs found him not guilty. But Bob's world had suddenly shrunk to an uncomfortably small size.

A few months later he'd finally had enough of the allegations and called Ed Zieralski, a respected outdoor writer at the *San Diego Union-Tribune*. Bob wanted to exonerate himself, wanted the truth to be out there. He granted Ed an interview, fully disclosing all of his methods. The story appeared in mid-1991. He even began to answer some of the calls from the television folks, but soon found out that talking to the press was a mistake. They all wanted to film him, have him haul their photography boats. They wanted him to pose with a fish in a certain way, to read from asinine scripts. But he was giving them something for nothing. He found no upside in cooperating with the media. They didn't make him any money, and he didn't want the fame. And it all took away from what he would rather be doing: chasing the world record. He stopped granting interviews altogether by the end of 1991.

But he persevered, fishing under this microscope, in his zone, for three more years. Other anglers, like Porter Hall from Alabama, John Collins from Ojai, and Bill Sansum from San Diego, imitated his tactics and made names for themselves on the lake. Even Orlando Woolridge, the former NBA player, fished the lake. The scene at the gate every morning had taken on the character of a Grateful Dead concert. Some fifty trucks, each trailing a bass boat, would sit in the early morning darkness. Groups of anglers gathered in small huddles, bleary-eyed, drinking coffee over small campstoves, talking about how they were sure Sowbelly was swimming in the depths of Castaic. Every morning the line in front of the gate crackled with anticipation that this could be *the day*. And when the siren sounded, they took off and jumped in their trucks like the start of a Le Mans auto race and jockeyed for position at the boat ramp and on the lake. At nightfall, they went home for a few hours' sleep, then turned right around and headed back to line up at Castaic. But no one ever came close to Bob's fish.

Then in January of 1994, an earthquake registering 6.7 on the Richter scale rocked nearby Northridge. Everyone in the fishing community took it as a good sign. This was the near-cataclysmic event, they thought, that would stir up the big bass in the lake. Nature was indicating that she was ready. The year turned out to be one of the most popular on the lake. But the fish numbers and sizes inexplicably went down. Then in 1995, the city of Los Angeles, fearing that Castaic's water was about to burst through and flood the San Fernando Valley, drained the lake down 130 feet to check the dam for any earthquake damage. And later that year, someone landed a striped bass, signaling an irreversible invasion of that voracious species. And Castaic's magic run was over, just like that.

Bob told me all of this during our long and uneventful time together on the water. He seemed strangely distracted that day. Some of his gear had fallen into disarray. His seat cushions were coming apart at the seams, and the Astroturf-like rug on the bottom of the boat was shabby and peeling at the edges. When he talked to me, I noticed that he'd put his rod down behind him, leaving the bail on his reel open, unconcerned with holding or even watching the line. He didn't seem to really care about fishing at all.

Many people I had spoken to before my trip had warned me

about Bob. They said he was a bitter man who had become hardened by the fact that he had come so close to the record and the
riches, but had ultimately failed. There is no award for second
place in this race. The whole chase thing and the near miss did
seem to have taken its toll on him. He talked very openly about
how it had almost destroyed his marriage and his family. "I missed
the first five years of my kids' lives," he said. His children hate
fishing as a result, and you get the feeling from his stories of their
insouciance that he has very little moral authority at home,
whether it's a result of his own guilt or just the simple fact that he
was absent for a bit too much of their childhood.

And it's true that he didn't realize too much gain from the
number-two fish in history, at least in monetary terms. He sold a
few T-shirts and a few thousand copies of his video, *Bodacious
Bass*. He garnered a few tackle sponsorships that entitled him to
free rods for life. But the one consistent moneymaker has been his
guiding business. His fame has allowed him to book trips whenever he likes and charge an exorbitant fee of $650 a day. But it's
pretty clear that Bob doesn't really like guiding all that much and
that the money doesn't make it any better. His temperament and
methods don't fit very well with guiding clients, a garrulous job
that requires sublimation of one's ego. Hunting record-size bass is
a solitary endeavor or, at best, one shared by two like-minded individuals with the same end goal and a steadfast agreement on the
best means to get there. Clients talk too much. They get bored
very easily. They have to pee all the time. They lose their concentration. They don't listen to him. They want to catch the 5-pound
bass—considered trophies in most parts of the world—that
breach around the boat all afternoon ("Little shitbirds," Bob calls
them). And they ask him questions about his fish, which makes
him clench his jaw and turns his face red and raises the volume

in his voice a decibel or two. To Bob, it should all be reduced to the simplest of terms: A man. A method. A fish. The rest is just bullshit.

And anyway, he's sick of the whole chase thing, as he frequently reminded me on our trip. "I don't believe in Perry's record. There are way too many holes in the story," he said. "But I want all of this to be over and done with. I'll go down and buy whoever gets it a round of drinks. I had my fifteen minutes of fame. I just hope whoever gets it works hard for it."

Bob is not an easy guy to feel sorry for, and what I felt that day for him was not exactly that. But as other boats gunned by us without so much as a glance, and two kayakers just blithely paddled by, I found myself wanting to yell out, "Do you know who this is? This is Bob Crupi, dammit! He was once the best big-bass fisherman alive!" But I didn't. Bob has a good life. He still has his family. He still does pretty much what he wants to do, saving up guiding money for trips to Africa to hunt elephants and dart rhinos (He's still a predator who likes to hunt for the biggest things around). And he's at the age where he can retire from the force at any time and live comfortably for life. The stresses of his job have started to wear on him. Just before we fished together, he had worked overtime as Los Angeles was put on orange alert due to the threat of terrorism.

But I did find myself that day wishing he would enter the race again—for his own sake, maybe. He was, in a sense, still an underdog to this legendary world-record bass and the mythical qualities that had surrounded it in the almost seventy-five years since its capture. And I did start to wonder, given his venom for the press, why he had agreed to our time on the water, to be subject to my niggling questions. And toward the end of the day, as the sun started to fall behind the scrubby hills of the Angeles National

Forest, he did steer the conversation back to the record, with no prompting from me: "You know, when I retire, I'm going to hunt and fish full-time," he said. It was like he wanted to get in his final words, ones that he had been thinking about since my first questions in his Suburban some twelve hours earlier. "If a lake turned on somewhere and wasn't too far away, if there was another opportunity, I'd be a fool not to try again."

We finally gave up a little after six. He pulled the boat up to the dock and I went to fetch the truck. The other cars had been long gone, and with good reason. We hadn't even had a bite. I started up the engine and looked again at the stuffed lion on his dashboard. We cinched up the boat, and Bob drove me back to my motel.

"Thanks, Bob. That was fun," I said as I got out of the truck. And it had been fun for me. I had just spent the day with Bob Crupi on a lake he said (and I believed him) the world-record bass was finning around in, somewhere. Though he'd been a difficult, taciturn interview and we hadn't caught a thing, I did have a good time. And I couldn't shake the last words he'd spoken on the boat—what seemed to me to be the ones that broke his hardened carapace for only a brief moment like he was a tight fist about to unclench—the ones about the "opportunity." Most of us only get one in our lives if we're lucky. But out here in California, you never knew.

"No, it wasn't that fun," Bob said. "It's fun when you catch big bass." There it was, in black and white with no room for gray. There were big fish and there were shitbirds. There were those who abided by the law and those who broke it. Bob just wanted to go about doing his job and keeping order in the universe—on the streets and on the water. A certain purity came from his law-and-order view of the world, and he was certain that he was on the right side of things. With that, I closed the doors of the truck. And then the lion in winter drove his bass boat off into the California horizon.

When I got back to my office in New York, I had three messages on my machine. Two were from other record chasers in California. Both asked the same thing: Was Crupi still after the record? Both sounded worried.

Big bass fishing is an attitude sport. If your life is in turmoil, so is your bass fishing. If you've got your life together, your bass fishing picks up. —Bill Murphy, from *In Pursuit of Giant Bass,* the bible of big bassers

CHAPTER TWO
The King of San Diego

I t's inevitable. That's what they say about Mike Long. The tall, imposing, athletic redhead with a booming, deep-chested voice, he's the one who will break the record. It's just a matter of time. He's studied the hardest, he's the fittest, he wants it more than anyone else. He's in the right spot: the heat of the world-record chase has moved from Castaic Lake 160 miles down I-5 to his home turf, the dozen or so reservoirs surrounding San Diego, which boast seven of the top fifteen largemouth bass ever recorded. He has an advantage with his network of other fishermen and Fish and Game officials, contacts who clue him in when a lake is getting ripe—a privilege no other record chaser enjoys. He's caught more big bass than anyone, ever, a number he can recite off the top of his head: 301 bass over 10 pounds, forty-one over 15, six over 17, six over 18. And that one over 20: the golden bass that put him in the pantheon and cemented his reputation, the one he had patiently waited fifteen years for. In the newspaper and magazine stories and on the television shows, they all describe him with the same phrase: "the best big-bass fisherman alive, period."

Mike likes the recognition because, in his head, he knows they are right about him. He's not afraid to say it himself. There is no one better. Sure, he feels a lot of pressure, but most of it is pressure he's put on himself, pressure he's yearned for. He is the top dog, which means everyone is trying to knock him down. He likes that, in a way. It keeps him focused; it provides the motivation. But the pressure is a double-edged sword. With it comes a cost, both mental and physical. Even on days when he doesn't feel like it, he has to drop everything and go fish a lake if it has produced a fish in the high teens, if it's "hot." He has to catch a big fish seemingly every week to keep his name in the paper, to keep that edge on his competitors. He can show no weakness.

It gets to him, though. His stomach is a stormy sea of acid that tosses and turns. And staring deep into the water, concentrating with every fiber in his body on one spot for hours on end, takes its toll. He has a bit of a temper when he goes home at night after a bad day on the water. Everything seems to hurt a bit more now. He burned out once, eight years ago, and quit fishing for a while. The chase had become an overwhelming burden, the fishing no longer fun. But challengers have arisen now, like that kid Jed Dickerson and his buddies, the trio that actually outworked him last year, spending two hundred days on the water. They're all after his crown. But what they don't realize is that their efforts just stoke his fire even more.

He's reluctant to admit it, but he wants the record more than anything. He truly believes that he is the one who will break it, that he deserves it somehow. And when it happens, then and only then will the pressure lift. So he can't quit now. He's worked too hard, come too close. If he stays with it, keeps getting up at 3 a.m. to get out on the water, keeps fishing almost forty hours a week, he knows it will happen. It's inevitable.

In the winter of 1999, seven of the best big-bass anglers in the world gathered on the banks of Castaic Lake to take part in a photo shoot for an *Outdoor Life* magazine story called "World-Record Bass Cult." Most of the heavies at the time are in the picture—Bob Crupi, Porter Hall, Mike Gash—standing together in two loosely configured rows, all holding up replicas of their biggest fish, all sporting black sunglasses and tough-guy expressions. In the top left-hand corner of the photo is a strapping young man who was a relative newcomer to the scene at the time, just beginning to establish his reputation on the reservoirs near San Diego. That man was Mike Long. At some point during a break in the shoot, Bob Crupi, who by then was beaten down by the burden of the chase, took an invisible crown from his head and, in a theatrical gesture made in front of the other anglers and cameramen present, placed it on top of Mike's, anointing the young man as the new king of big bass. Mike, flattered but also confident in his rightful ascension, beamed with pride.

"It's yours," Crupi said. "And you can keep the damn thing."

Michael Christopher Long, 38, has lived all of his life in the town of Poway, a swelling strip of San Diego suburb tucked just over a desert mountain, some thirty miles from the sea. I drove to meet Mike one evening in early April of 2004 at his one-story ranch house—a left, then a right turn from the Taco Bell—the only house on the block with a bass boat in the driveway. He greeted me at the door and beckoned me in to take a seat. His wife, Debbie, his two kids, and his best friend and fishing buddy, John Kerr and his wife, Amy, were glued to the large-screen television set flickering in front of them. They were watching a rerun of a Hank Parker fishing show on the Outdoor Life Network, which, as luck would have it, featured Mike. Bass after wriggling bass was yanked out of the water and into the boat and fawned over by both guest and host. Hank Parker, in his inimitable Southern drawl, kept heaping praise on "Mac Lawng" for his unbelievable big-bass prowess. On camera, Mike was quiet and seemed a little uncomfortable. "These fishing shows are funny," he said as we watched. "They make it all look so easy. But it's actually pretty hard work and a lot of pressure to catch those fish on demand while the cameras are rolling."

Mike may be the only world-record chaser with some modicum of fame outside the small world of the record chase. He has appeared on a half-dozen other TV fishing shows. He has fished with various members of the San Diego Padres, comedian Robin Williams, pop star Nick Lachey, and even the lead singer of the heavy-metal group Iron Maiden. Every year, his big-bass workshop at Fred Hall's Fishing Tackle and Boat Show in San Diego is jam-packed with admirers. In a drawer in his living room, he keeps a big black book stuffed with his magazine and newspaper clippings from the last ten years. He's on the cover of a dozen magazines, including *Bassmaster, Field & Stream,* and a Japanese magazine called *Crazy Bass.* In each instance, he's holding a gigantic, potbellied bass, one hand on the fish's bottom lip and the other cradling its stomach.

His house is a shrine to his passion. The four mounted bass on the wall of his dining room are so big they each need heavy screws set into the framing studs to keep them from crashing to the floor. Their shiny, hard plastic bodies are contorted sideways, held forever in the pose of a powerful swimming motion. They are part of his collection of twenty mounted fish. Hanging on the living-room walls, in lieu of paintings or family pictures, are several large photos of Mike, wading hip deep in a lake somewhere, holding bass dripping with water and smiling fondly into their huge, gaping mouths. It's as if Mike were a prized high school athlete whose devoted mother had decorated the house with the trophies, pictures, and awards from her son's starry athletic career.

Mike was born the son of a real-estate agent. Poway was smaller then and not the sprawled suburbia it is today, the victim or beneficiary, depending on your viewpoint, of the unbelievable real-estate development boom in southern California that started in the late 1980s and shows no signs of slowing down. He was five years old when his maternal grandfather took him on his first fishing trip, into the High Sierras. One day his grandfather sent Mike down a creek by himself to fish, to get out from underfoot of the older men on the trip, the serious fishermen. Mike came back to camp toward evening with a mess of trout on his stringer, each of which weighed over a pound. The older men had only caught smallish fish. "My grandfather said I had a gift," Mike says. "He told me it was like I put my head in the water when I fished." Mike uses the phrase to this day to help him maintain his focus on the water.

In high school, as it turns out, Mike did excel at athletics. He was the starting wide receiver on the football team, a surfer and a snowboarder, and one of the best junior milers in the country— even an Olympic aspirant. He ran a sub-four-minute mile in 1985 while winning the California, Arizona, and Nevada regional high school title. But he wilted in the swampy humidity of Baton Rouge, Louisiana, at the Nationals and gave up the sport and any dreams of college or further competition. But he still looks and carries himself with the confidence of an athlete. Mike is 6'5" and an in-shape 230 pounds. He possesses a body that's an anomaly in the bass-fishing world, where most folks tend to be paunchy and out of shape, looking a bit like a bass themselves. Mike even dresses the part of an athlete. His daily fishing getup consists of

Nike cross-training sneakers, Nike sweatpants, and a long-sleeved T-shirt, all worn with freedom of motion in mind. With his red hair and goatee, blue eyes, and athletic build, he bears more than a passing resemblance to the baseball player Mark McGwire. "Athletics have helped me in fishing," Mike says. "You need endurance when you work a fish for eight straight hours in the blazing sun. It's like running track. I visualize the finish line, then go as hard as I can. A lot of guys come out here and they're overweight and they don't feel good. You have to have that endurance to catch fish."

Mike's athleticism is apparent on the water. When he hooks into a big bass, he becomes a hurdler, highwire walker, and juggler all at once. He swings back on his rod to set the hook, then, with one eye on the fish, tiptoes backward in the boat quickly to retrieve his net. With one foot he steps on the trolling motor to guide the boat safely away from the bass. Then he reaches down to scoop the fish into the net with one hand as he holds the rod in the other.

Athletics have also instilled in him a highly competitive edge. "I've always been the best at everything I've done," he says without a trace of modesty. And he'll do whatever it takes to win. Some years ago, burned out from the world-record chase, he took a year off to race mountain bikes competitively. He was known on the circuit as "the sandbagger," because he refused to move up to a division with a higher talent level. He stayed in the beginner division, well, because he was winning most of the races. This competitive drive, combined with his desire and size, intimidates other anglers. "A lot of people are scared of him," says John Kerr. "They just stare at him in awe and follow him around." Renowned lure maker and friend, Jerry Rago, adds: "Every once in a while he shows his competitive side and tells you he'll kick your ass. And you know he means it."

Once out of high school, Mike became a laborer for a construction company, laying house foundations by pumping concrete through a hose. He then worked for a landscaping company, then as a framer for five years, then an ironworker. All strenuous jobs that kept him in shape and kept him busy for an honest forty hours a week. "It was tough," he says. "I couldn't really sneak away ever." But in 1996, he became a desk jockey as the project manager for a construction company, a job that allowed some freedom. "Now I'll list a job, make sure the prices are sent out, and order the material," he says. "Then I'm free to do what I want to do," which, since 1996, is hunt the biggest bass in the world, sometimes up to five days a week.

On a beautiful, seventy-degree spring morning, Mike and I drive to San Vicente Reservoir, one of the twenty clear canyon lakes fed by water from the Colorado River and managed by San Diego County. Mike likes to go to San Vicente to unwind and relax. The lake is less regarded by big-bass anglers because it contains relatively small fish. Because of this, and the fact that the lake is large (1,000 surface acres) relative to neighboring waters, Mike feels like he has the freedom to fish there without everyone watching his every move. Like Bob Crupi, for the last few years, due to his growing reputation, any trip Mike takes to a smaller, hot lake of the moment is greeted with intense scrutiny by fellow big-bass anglers, who watch his every move through binoculars and brazenly motor up beside his boat to either ask a question or try to poach his spot, figuring if Mike is on it, it has to be good. The unwelcome attention has led Mike to use some unorthodox means of concealing his identity on the water, like donning a Gene Simmons–style wig. But on San Vicente, other anglers generally leave him alone to practice new tactics and test out his lures. Perfectionism, after all, demands hours of practice. He's like a pro golfer playing a less demanding course to work on a specific part of his game.

To Mike, each lure has its own personality, and he'd like to get to know exactly what that is before he puts it to the test. He'll take a batch of a certain lure, say, his Mission Fish or Castaic swimbaits—six-inch soft plastic baits meant to imitate a trout or some other forage—and throw them, one by one, into the water to see how they swim as he reels them back to the boat. He'll then dry off the lure and take a waterproof Sharpie pen and number the lure one through five, with "1" being the lure that swims the truest and does what it's supposed to do. If the lure has a tendency to veer to the left as its swims, he'll put an "L" next to the number, say, a "3L." Same idea goes for any lure that runs to the right, or perhaps dives a bit deeper than the others. "I do this so when it's crunch time, when I'm on a big bass, I'll be confident in knowing exactly what that bait can and can't do," he says. "That's something a lot of people don't do."

Most people aren't as meticulous as Mike is *off* the water either. In a log that he keeps at home, he records all of his catches of bass over 10 pounds, plus any bass of that size from local lakes that he hears or reads about someone else catching. He writes down the lake, the date, the time of day, the temperature and weather conditions, the barometric pressure, the moon phase, and the lure used to catch the fish. For his own catches, he writes down the exact weight and measures the girth of the bass around the breast, middle, and anal areas. He notes the characteristics of the fish. How healthy are the fins, the eyes, the tail? Do any distinctive markings stand out, like a black dot? Then he pulls three guitar-pick-size scales from just behind the pectoral fin of the fish and puts the scales on a slide card where he can count the rings, like those in a tree, to get a reasonable estimate of the age of the fish.

He's planning on importing all of his historical data into an Excel spreadsheet someday soon, but for now, it's all contained in a big black notebook, the pages worried over and yellowed at the edges.

When we get to the lake that morning in early April, a Fish and Game officer at the dock and a few other fishermen, who are backing their boats into the water, say hello to Mike. They all seem thrilled to see him. Mike jumps from the dock into his state-of-the-art 21-foot-long Ranger bass boat, tricked out with a 225-horsepower Mercury outboard motor, a depthfinder with GPS, two aerated livewells, and a foot-operated trolling motor on the bow. He moves the boat slowly out of the "no-wake zone," then pushes on the throttle, bringing the nose of the boat on plane as he approaches seventy miles an hour on the water. His cheeks flutter from the force of the wind. He circles around a bend, then eases the boat to a stop near the shore, grabs his rod, and pops down the trolling motor, which he works with his foot while he leans back onto the high chair in the front of the boat. He looks, from afar, like a great blue heron slowly stalking its prey. He stands there, motionless, staring down deep into the clear water, where you can see the bottom at thirty feet, looking for the telltale signs of bass on the lake's floor, the cleared-off rings of sand among the green vegetation that signal a bass bed.

In the spring of each year, female and male bass "come shallow" as they say, and, with considerable effort, clear off a roughly three-by-three-foot area with their fins and powerful tails. The area they clear, the "bed," will serve as the spawning area for the fish, a clean surface where the female will lay her eggs and the male will swoop in and fertilize them. With careful stalking—the boat must be quiet and should cast no shadows over the fish—an angler can see the male and female lolling about near the bed, waiting for the urge to spawn or protecting the nest after the deed is done. The female, when she's ready, will hover over the nest, then contort her body in a sideways shudder as she shoots out the eggs. Then nearly simultaneously, the male will rush in and spray his semen on them.

Generally speaking, male bass act as if they prefer Rubenesque women. The more fit and aggressive males will pair up with the most voluptuous females, which sometimes outweigh their suitors by a factor of five. The male has a very specific job: to fertilize the eggs and guard the nest afterward from bluegill and cannibalistic bass. After the actual spawning, the female will sometimes hang around the bed, but she is more skittish, fleeing the area at the first sign of danger. The male, however, will sometimes even go so far as to protect the nest from the mother of his progeny, nudging her away from the nest if she comes in too close.

Just before the female is about to spawn, her body turns a different hue—almost glowing—the color of a watermelon rind. Bed fishermen, as they're known, look for fish like this, because it is at this moment when the female bass is at her biggest, laden with up to two pounds of eggs, and is also the most vulnerable to being caught. The females tend to get a bit cranky when they are about to spawn and snap at anything that annoys them. Thus, a well-placed lure, perhaps shaken annoyingly at her nose, will sometimes elicit an angry strike from the bass that is at the peak of her largesse, which is the reason every bass on the top-25 list was caught between January and June, roughly the period of the spawn.

In a more genteel time, bed fishing was frowned upon as an unsporting practice. Dr. James A. Henshall, a Cincinnati-based fishing biologist who wore Teddy Roosevelt–style spectacles and a big bushy mustache twirled upward at each end, wrote about fishing for bass on their beds in his 1881 treatise, *Book of Black Bass*:

Their anxiety and solicitude for eggs and young, and their apparent disregard for their own safety at this time, is well-known to poachers and pot-fishers, who take advantage of this trait and spear or gig them on their nests. I have known, also, some who call themselves anglers—Heaven save the mark!—who take the bass at this time in large numbers, with minnows or crawfish.

Henshall would no doubt be appalled to know that nowadays, most who call themselves "anglers," especially those who are after the world record, specifically target these fish on the bed. It's a fairly recent development. Just ten years ago, most anglers fished like Bob Crupi, with live bait that dawdled in some spot down deep, unseen. But that's changed, in large part because of the big-bass mania that Crupi's fish helped ignite.

The reason that the record chasers go for the spawning bass is that those big females, overpowered by the urge to procreate, sometimes only show themselves once a year, during the spawn. And their egg-weight can make the difference between a 19-pound fish and one that challenges the record. Targeting a species during the mating season is commonplace in the world of hunting and fishing. Salmon and shad fishermen only really get a shot at catching those species when they leave the ocean and run up freshwater rivers to spawn. And big buck deer are most vulnerable to hunters when they are "in the rut," that is, turned on and crazed by their insatiable lust. People for the Ethical Treatment of Animals (PETA) and other like-minded groups might not like the practice, but bed-fishing advocates like Mike Long point to studies done by biologists that claim that as long as a female bass is properly released, she'll still be able to complete her spawn. And, well, they say, everyone else is doing it.

On the water, Mike slowly guides the boat near the shoreline, still searching. He comes upon a big bed near some lake grass, but the female scoots away, spooked by the boat. The male stays defiantly behind, suspended in the water, slowly flapping his pectoral fins. Generally, Mike won't fish for the male. They don't grow as big as the females (4 pounds is considered a huge one), and if you catch the male off the bed, the female often won't come back for the rest of the day. But the male does serve a purpose to bed fishers, as sort of another lure. He's the one you want to agitate, to make swim around in tight circles, causing a commotion that the angler hopes will pique the interest of the female and bring her back in. After waiting ten minutes or so without seeing the female, Mike decides to go ahead and fish for the male, for lack of anything else to do. He wants the practice. He casts out a small white jig, which plops into the water and comes to rest in the center of the cleared-out ring. A perfect cast. The male immediately charges in at the lure, zigzagging around it, obviously pretty pissed-off that an intruder has entered his love nest. Mike gives the tip of his sturdy black graphite rod a few shakes that are conveyed down the line, causing the white rubber legs on the jig to periodically billow out, then contract. This action finally is too much temptation for the male. In one swift motion, he turns on the lure and devours it. Mike sets the hook with force. The fish—maybe a pound or two, considered a tiny one by California standards—wriggles free just as Mike gets it near the boat. Later he would land one male of that same size, and lose another at the boat. But as he'd already reiterated a few times, today is just practice.

But even in practice, Mike strives to be perfect. He's run his finger up and down the lines of each of his six rods, checking for nicks invisible to the naked eye that might break on a big fish. He's retied the lures to the ends of those lines. His boat is immaculate and well-organized: the net hung over the driver's seat out from under his feet, the unused rods stowed in a compartment under the floor of the boat. There's not an empty drink bottle or any other trash in sight. He's applied a few coats of sunscreen to his fair skin, and is wearing wraparound polarized sunglasses and a wide-brimmed camouflage fishing hat on his head. "Too much sun can make you looney," he says. "When you get dehydrated and overheat, your brain doesn't work as fluently as it should." And he has everything he could possibly need stowed onboard: Pepto-Bismol, PowerBars, toilet paper, Gatorade, first-aid kit. His every move seems to have been rehearsed a thousand times. This preparation is what separates him from nearly everyone else.

"I'm always ready to go," he says. "I need to be able to concentrate and focus, to get all the distractions out of the way, because this is really all about patience and waiting for your turn. The more you do something, the more it becomes part of the fiber of who you are. If you fish all the time, it becomes part of your memory and subconscious."

Says friend John Kerr: "What makes Mike so good is that he pays attention to the details. He has a barometer at work, he watches the trees and listens to the sounds of the frogs and crickets in his backyard that signal that the bass are on the bed. And he puts in the time. People don't realize the time and commitment and effort he puts in." Ironically, this kind of diligence is expended in the pursuit of a hobby or to what most people would consider recreation. I'm not certain Mike is at all aware of how others outside of his tight circle of fellow bass maniacs might perceive him.

From that first fishing trip with his grandfather, Mike realized he had a talent not only for catching fish, but for catching bigger ones than anyone else. When he was a boy, he would sneak out of his house, not to drink or raise hell, but to fish, walking five miles to the lake with his fishing rod. He grew up fishing the lakes around San Diego, diligently studying the water and practicing the sight-fishing methods. So in 1996, when he finally landed that job that allowed him some freedom, it was no big surprise that he initiated an assault on the area's lake records—the 14-pounder at Cuyameca, the 16-pounder at Sutherland, the 17-pound, 8-ounce at Vail, and the 18s at Poway and Mission Viejo. No other angler even owns two lake records in the area. Mike is arguably not only the best big-bass fisherman in the world, but also one of its best bass anglers in general, as the biggest bass are generally older and wilier, and thus harder to seduce. Still, outside of the big-bass world, and despite the press, he's a relative unknown in the angling world. Bassmaster tourney anglers reel in $1 million in prize money, and TV personalities lead cushy lives off camera, but they have less talent. "It kills me that the tourney guys aren't as good," Mike says. "And the TV guys gnaw at my gut. They're full of shit." Mike says he's thought about getting a TV job, but he doesn't think he's host material. "I don't have the right look or the right voice," he says. Plus, a TV show where the host goes weeks or months without catching a fish probably wouldn't fare too well.

Still, there has been some notoriety such as the countless magazine and newspaper articles written about him and the TV shows mentioning his exploits. The Japanese worship Mike Long, or as they call him, "My Lon." In Japan—where big-bass fishing has begun to approach the feverish level of a fetish—he is known and adored by more people than he is in his own country, much like Jerry Lewis is in France. The Japanese TV networks have sent crews over to film him fishing. A few years back, a magazine sent a photographer, writer, and an interpreter over to record everything he did. They followed him around everywhere, photographing him eating dinner and sitting on his couch watching TV. They wanted to see where he slept. "If I picked my nose, it was *click, click, click,*" he says. They wanted to get to the essence of what made Mike tick, to tease out his secret like he was an alchemist with the formula for producing gold. They even asked him what kind of underwear he wore. They showered him with gifts like expensive rods and reels. After three full days, the Japanese were exhausted from their long trip and crazy work schedule. On their last night in town, Mike took them to a strip club. They were all smiles on the water the next day. But Mike says they left without getting to his core, without cracking his code. "It's hard to fit what I see into words or pictures," he says. "I don't know how to explain it. It just is."

And there have been some financial rewards, money that comes in handy, a nice supplement to his middle-class life in Poway, where his wife has to work part-time as a teacher so the family can get by. He's won a number of regional tournaments, making $10,000. And beginning in 1999, he won the Big Bass Record Club's largest fish of the year award three times in a row when that organization was still in business, racking up $78,000 in prize money. But the club was both a boost and a bane to the big-bass scene, according to Mike.

The BBRC was the brainchild of Mickey Owens, a real-estate developer, and Bill Currie, owner of Bill Currie Ford, one of the largest new- and used-car dealerships in Florida. Both men realized that bass fishing was a huge industry in the United States and figured there had to be a way for them to get a piece of the action. Their conversations would always inevitably turn to the chase for the world record. They'd read in the outdoor press about the obsessed anglers across the country who were after the fish, about the dollar signs that were supposedly attached to its capture. There,

Owens and Currie saw their opening. "The world record is the ultimate, the big one, the holy grail," says Owens. "I turned to Bill and said, 'We ought to start us a club.' " So they did, in 1998, naming it the Big Bass Record Club. With the backing of the insurance giant Lloyd's of London, Owens and Currie started soliciting members across the country. The idea was simple: join the BBRC for an annual twenty dollars, and be eligible for $5 million should you catch the biggest one of all time. To further entice bass anglers who lived in places like Minnesota and Iowa—which have plenty of bass, but compared to California, Texas, and Florida, relatively small ones—they handed out checks ranging from $10,000 to $50,000 to the member who caught the biggest bass in his respective state. Things went very smoothly for the first five years. With little paid publicity, word of the club got out. The membership by 2003 had ballooned to 10,000, and the prize money for the world record had risen along with it, to $8 million. But just as Owens and Currie were about to start an ad blitz to attract more members and jack the money up to $10 million, they were forced to shut it down, ironically, as you'll see, due in large part to Mike.

Mike says the extra money was nice, but the BBRC's influence on the bass world was mostly detrimental. "People started to chase the fish because of the dollar signs they saw. When the BBRC came along, ethics and morals went out the door. There were fish snagged, caught at night. A lot of evil things were done. Guys just came out of the shadows," Mike says. "It just wasn't pure anymore. Like sports in general—in football and baseball—you have to go to the college level to find purity, because of the dollar signs. It was tough on me because I was doing everything legitimately." Mike had to pass polygraph tests for some of his BBRC fish to be accredited. Other anglers had their applications denied, either because they declined to take a lie-detector test or because they fabricated the size of their fish, something Mike says he would never even think about doing. He's a perfectionist with his morals as well.

Mike swears that while he'd like the money, it's not the reason he's after the world record. He says it's something else, something to do with another buck—as in being the biggest buck in the pen. "There are guys out there talking so much smack, saying things like 'You don't know how to fish,' and stuff like that," he says. "It's not the money or the notoriety for me. It's about being the biggest dog." It was a sentiment that I kept running into over and over with these big-bass fishermen. It wasn't the size of their wallets, their looks, or type of cars, but the size of their bass that determined their standing in this niche of the broader world. Perhaps the same type of thing goes on in other settings. On Wall Street, for instance. It struck me that that this particular impulse may have something to do with our modern age, when, if you're not in the military fighting against terrorists or if you're not a professional athlete, there are fewer and fewer ways for men to size themselves up against other men. This exercise in ego is an instinct still extant in our species, stronger in some than in others. Most fishermen will admit to always wanting to be the one who has the biggest fish at the end of the day. The big-bass fishermen have just taken this impulse a few leaps further, with the world record being the ultimate smackdown.

And Mike's confident, despite the increased attention on the fish, that he's the one who will eventually break the record though some self-doubt does creep in. "A lot of people say I'm the favorite to catch the world record, and yeah, they're probably right," he says. "But I think someone else will find it before I do. I won't be the guy who gets to break the record after the long dry spell." He reckons the next world-record holder will be like Mark McGwire, who broke Roger Maris's thirty-seven-year-old single-season home-run record in 1998. But Mike likens himself to San

Francisco Giants slugger Barry Bonds, who put the record out of reach three years later. "When it's all said and done, I will break the world record too," he says.

But Mike emphasizes that he's not after the record every day he's on the water. "If I see a blood trail, I know I'm on the quest again," he says. "But if I don't see the patterns, I try to relax. I feel like you can beat yourself up trying to chase the ghost. It can ruin you. It's there, for sure, but half the time it's just a ghost."

And the record chase has taken its toll on him. "Peer pressure is a tough thing," he says. "You care about what your friends think. When people keep telling you that you are going to break the world record, it puts pressure on you, so you have to go out and try on the days when you really don't want to." The pressure he feels has manifested itself physically. On occasion Mike comes down with migraine headaches on the water, presumably from being in the sun too long and staring into the water so intensely. And last year, he developed a much more troubling problem: a stomach condition that creates acid that catches in the back of his throat. The condition has recently gotten so bad that he has developed a form of esophageal cancer and has trouble speaking for a few days after a severe bout with the reflux.

And even though we're on San Vicente, the lake where Mike thinks he can get away, he can't seem to outrun his fame. As Mike fishes over a bed, a heavyset angler named Anthony, who barely fits into shorts that reach down to his calves, motors his boat over to us. As he talks, he stutters nervously, like a little kid meeting his idol.

"Hey, Mike," Anthony says while flapping the front of his shirt to get air to his skin. "I saw you on TV last night." His boat bumps Mike's. "Hey, is that a Megabass rod?" Anthony asks. It is, the $500 rod that's considered to be the best on the market. Anthony asks Mike if he can hold it, and Mike obliges, not exactly peeved about the intrusion, but not overly ecstatic, either. "Man, that's cool," Anthony says as he gives the rod a wiggle. "So, you caught any today?"

"A few," Mike answers, then makes a cast off the front of the boat. Anthony sits there for a moment too long before finally getting the hint. Mike shakes his head as he motors away.

Being Mike Long these days is not easy. But his stature does provide him with some perks.

A few days later, I head to Lake Jennings, five miles east of El Cajon. The reservoir was built in 1964 for drinking water, and is surrounded by hillsides that bear the scars of the 2003 forest fires in the area, with melted cacti dotting the blackened desert sand. The dock was left unscathed, as was the sign that greets all anglers, reading:

Bare Feet
High Heels
Prohibited
On Dock

On this early morning, during the best time of the season to catch big bass, the lake is completely devoid of boats or any other activity. That's because it's closed. But for Mike Long, John Kerr, the photographer Dusan Smetana, and the lure-maker Jerry Rago, it's open today, thanks to a little-known and almost never exploited clause in the bureaucratic county code. For $300, you can do a photo shoot for a major publication and have the lake to yourself on a day it would normally be closed. Dusan, who photographs for many outdoor magazines, wants to take some shots of some big bass and sell them to *Field & Stream*. Mike Long will fish on closed days a few times a year, often at the best lakes in the area. It's a privilege that seems to be extended to no one but Mike, and it's one that inspires the envy and anger of many other anglers, because on off days you have a great shot at catching big bass. On a normal day, Lake Jennings would have more than a hundred boats jockeying for spots on its eighty-five surface acres. Today, there will be exactly three boats, meaning the fish will suffer less harassment in general from anglers' lures and loud boat motors, and thus will be more likely to be comfortable and show themselves. No one will compete for the best spots on the lake. Mike, John, and Jerry can cover every inch of shoreline, stopping only for the largest fish. Even areas that are always roped off to angling for one reason or another—too close to the dam, or perhaps a spawning area—are available today. It's akin to getting in early on an initial public offering of a hot stock: You're not guaranteed to hit the jackpot, but your odds are increased and certainly are better than those who aren't afforded the privilege. And it raises a few ethical questions: What if Mike or John were to catch the world record, or even the lake record, on an off day? "It would be uncomfortable, but we've earned it," Mike says.

I jump into the boat with John Kerr. John and Mike have been best friends and fishing buddies since the sixth grade. For Mike, John is one of the few people in the world in whom he can truly confide, who understands his unique situation, who he can trust fully. Although they are best friends, John and Mike could not be more different. John is the yin to Mike's yang. John is a wiry thirty-six-year-old, with short reddish hair he covers with a white Ranger Boats baseball cap. He is shorter than Mike, maybe 5'9", and slighter, looking young enough to pass for a college kid. John is like the little brother of the duo, and he happily lets Mike do all of the talking. He is naturally a very shy man, diverting his eyes and mumbling almost inaudibly when he talks to anyone he doesn't know. Their methods and preparation differ as well. John is the messier of the two, sort of an absent-minded professor–type. He'll sometimes go a whole day on the water so full of intent and concentration that he'll forget to take a sip of water or a bite of food and wonder why he feels like passing out face first on the dock at the end of the day. He often has to be reminded to take off his down jacket—necessary to fight the chill of the early morning—well after the southern California sun has turned up the heat to furnacelike levels in the afternoon. His four rods are messily splayed about the boat, the tips of a few of them hanging perilously off the side. Remnants of old lures—plastic shad baits and ripped-up rubber salamanders—lay scattered on the floor of his boat.

But John more than holds his own on the fishing end. He's primarily a tournament angler, participating mainly on the local San Diego circuit, where the modest purse money helps pay the bills more than chasing after the world record. He's been pretty successful, too. In 2003 he won the U.S. Open on Lake Mead. The prize included the boat and motor he's using today, the Ford truck he hitches those toys up to, and $50,000 in cash. Mike has lately begun to join him in some of the tournaments, and they've become a formidable duo, winning almost everything they enter. Even their names, they like to think, evoke fear in the hearts of their fellow tournament anglers. When read together, "Long-Kerr" sounds like "lunker"—the universal name for big, badass bass.

Though Mike garners almost all of the attention, John doesn't seem to mind. In fact he seems to prefer to avoid the spotlight. "Sometimes the pressure is too much on Mike," he says. "It gets to the point where he feels he has to be on the water all the time. It gets to him emotionally." John's just happy to fish. "Me? Obsessed? Yeah," he says. "If I could, every free moment, I'd be fishing." As it turns out, John has to work like the rest of us. He's a bulk manager at a local grocery store, earning enough of a salary to feed and house his wife and five sons. But John, in his own quiet way, is a dark horse in the race to catch the world-record bass because of his connection to Mike and his talent. Indeed, if he didn't spend so much of his time fishing in tournaments, where the time constraints don't reward the patience needed to hunt big bass, John might be the front runner. "I'd put some money on John, for sure," says Jerry Rago. "He's just as good as anyone else out there. Just quieter about it." Quiet, but he's after it too, when he has the time. And he understands what's at stake, describing it with all of the blunt wit of Gertrude Stein: "The world record is so important to so many people," he says. "That's why it's so important."

It's a pleasure to watch John ply his craft. His cast, called a "pitch," is a thing of effortless beauty. As he gets ready to make the cast, he holds the lure in the long, slender fingers of his left hand. He holds the rod with his right hand, his thumb on the open-faced spool to keep his line from backlashing. Then he "pitches" an underhand toss, starting the rod tip at 6 o'clock and ending the motion at 11, letting go of the lure at the precise moment that the line tightens on it. It's all done with the grace of a bullfighter pulling his red cape away from a charging bull, the control of a yo-yo artist, and the accuracy of a champion horseshoe thrower. His target is tiny, a spot with maybe a three-foot radius some twenty feet away. And he didn't miss all day. With his lure settled on the bottom of the lake, he focuses on the small spot in the water, his entire body tense and inert except for his right hand, which shakes the rod tip to give the lure down below some movement.

He is a bit more talkative than usual, perhaps because with his concentration down deep he does not have to look me in the eye. He works the trolling motor with his foot, his eyes forward, always scouting. He stops when he sees a promising fish and repeats the whole thing over again. He does this for hours. Sitting behind him on the boat, I am almost lulled to sleep by this rhythmic casting and working of the fish.

But the peacefulness of the day is shattered when John suddenly swings back on a big bass that he'd been stalking for half an hour. But instead of going tight, the lure comes sailing out of the water. He's missed it. "Shit," he says as his face turns red. He starts breathing heavily through his mouth as if he's just crossed the finish line in a sprint. But watching him more closely, I see that the heavy breathing is more a manifestation of the seething frustration he feels inside at the missed opportunity. "That was a big fish," he says.

His near miss has suddenly woken me up as well, and I stand as John guides the boat back to a place where he had marked a big fish earlier. This time it only takes a few casts. He lifts back with a violent backstroke, his glinting black rod pulled into an arc. He has this fish hooked, and he gives the rod a short pump, then does a few lightning-fast revolutions of the reel to gain line. He does this over and over, horsing the big bass in, trying not to let her get her bearings. If he gives her even a second to figure out what's going on, she'll gain the upper hand, diving deep or running for cover, seeking out a downed tree where the line can become tangled and snap. Anglers like John love these big bass because they seem more intelligent than smaller fish, like they've been hooked before and know how to get loose. It all adds to the challenge.

"Don't come up, don't come up," John starts repeating under his heavy adrenaline-generated breaths. The big she-bass does anyway, breaking the glassy surface of the lake ten feet from the boat, her bulky black back to us, full of fury for having been unceremoniously yanked from her matrimonial bed. In the air for only a split second, she gives a huge shake of her head, all massive white mouth and pinkish gills. She is absolutely enormous. "Grab the net!" John yells at me, his shyness suddenly gone. I oblige, and with a lucky scoop, 15 pounds of glistening female bass are brought aboard the boat. John is smiling now, a wolfish grin. He picks her up for a second and admires her incredible girth. Her stomach is impossibly large. It seems that if she were to take just one more bite of food, she just might spontaneously burst into a bloody, fleshy mess. Her distended eyes are the size of half-dollars, big frightened-looking, jet-black pupils encircled by brown. He puts her in the livewell, which is barely big enough to contain her, and turns on the water and aerator. The photo shoot, for which John will later change his shirt and don a red-and-white number crammed with the logos of his tournament sponsors, now has its female model. It's hard for me to imagine that a fish would have to weigh 7 pounds more than this behemoth to break the record—7 pounds, nearly one-third larger.

John stops for a moment to check his lure and line for any damage, then takes a deep breath and puts his foot back down on the trolling motor. He had just spent three hours fishing with only a near-brush with success. Then came the moment—the hookup, the battle, the netting, the dumping of the fish in the livewell— which had taken maybe thirty seconds all together. But this is what makes it all worth it, makes him want to get up at 4 a.m. to come back out tomorrow—and the next day and the day after that—to do it all over again. It makes him now step on the trolling motor with more force to get to the next spot even faster, more deter- mined to catch another big bass (which he will). He's still pushing audible breaths through his mouth, but they're coming more slowly now, in a more even cadence. "You question your ability when you lose one. But when you catch a big one, you're back on top," he says. "That thirty seconds is like a crack-pipe hit, it's just a rush. That moment when you get her into the net, that's the moment you wait for. There's such relief." He pauses to light a Marlboro Light 100. "You won, and she didn't."

The drug analogy may be right on, but it seems like it could even be something larger, more cosmic than that for these guys, like T. S. Eliot's "still point in a turning world." It's the moment when this big and confusing and busy earth stops for a second and gives you a glimpse of something absolute and controllable, something ripe with hope and optimism and potential.

But all silver linings come with a dark cloud. And it was John Kerr who first found the bass that would become San Diego's most famous and controversial fish of all time.

Lake Dixon is a small drinking-water reservoir in Escondido that's filled with crystal-clear Colorado River water. Up until 2001, it had been the secret honey hole of Mike and John's, a body of water so small (seventy-five surface acres) and featureless, it seemed unlikely to produce big bass. But Mike and John had been following Dixon for almost twenty years. They knew that almost 35,000 pounds of trout were planted there each year ("No one feeds their bass as well as we do," says lake ranger, Jim Dayberry). They watched as the bass grew over the years, from 5 pounds, to 10 to 15. "Dixon matured in front of our eyes, and we got better with it," says Mike. A time occurs in a reservoir's life when it becomes ripe for the taking. Dixon, they knew, was there—full of big bass, possibly even the world record. Mike had caught an 18-pounder there earlier that spring, but didn't tell anyone. He and John knew that if he had brought that fish in to the dock to be weighed, it would have been splayed all over the sports section of the newspaper and the fishing Web sites, and the bass-crazy hordes would have swiftly overrun the lake. And it would all be over, just like that. Nothing killed a lake faster than a few big fish in the news.

John first saw the bass on a Saturday in April 2001. She was guarding a big area near the shore. John drifted over her a few times, trying to figure out the best way to approach the fish. But when he finally got into place, finally figured out his plan of attack, the wind kicked up, turning the lake's surface from a perfectly smooth window into thousands of tiny shards of opaque glass. He called Mike in a panic. It was absolutely one of the biggest bass he'd ever seen. The next day, John had to work, but Mike went out to Dixon. The bass was nowhere to be found. He went back out the day after that. She was still gone. But he had a blood trail, enough of a sign to make the huge push they'd been waiting so patiently for. He went out the next three days in a row, but she never showed herself.

On Friday, April 27, while John was stuck at work again, Mike went back to Dixon. He motored the boat over to a flat as the sun came up and noticed that many males were in the area. The consorts were there, but where was the she-fish? He finally saw her, a big black shadow moving slowly near the lake's bottom. The fish swam lazily near the shoreline, pausing to hover over an area about the size of a bathtub. She seemed to be guarding something there. Then she moved out. Mike watched her repeat this a few times. Then he flipped a white jig out into the area and let it sit. She approached the lure, slowly. Mike's heart skipped a few beats. Then she started blowing on the lure, something a bass will do sometimes on the bed, flaring her gills in anger, trying to get the intruder to leave. Mike figured she was a wise old bass that knew, out of instinct, that something wasn't right with the lure. Maybe she'd been stung by a hook before, a distinct possibility in this era of catch-and-release. With a couple more casts, Mike figured out the magic spot where she definitely didn't like the lure, probably on or very near the exact place she planned on depositing her eggs.

With every cast to this spot, she became more agitated. Now he knew it was time to be ready. He checked his drag, got the trolling motor out of the way, and worked out in his head exactly how he would maneuver the boat when he hooked her. Then she hit. He couldn't believe how strong she felt, how much pressure she put on his wrists when, with a jolt, she pulled his rod tip almost down into the water. Then the line went slack. She had spit out the jig after only a few seconds. He called John at work and told him he had lost the donkey—their nickname for an especially large bass. Mike was sweating profusely and had a sickening, hollow feeling in his stomach. "I just lost the donkey, and she's not coming back," he told John.

But Mike stayed put, and she did come back, an hour and a half later. He threw in the white jig again, but she paid it no mind. Then he tried a black jig, but got the same lack of response. He anchored the boat on the shore and tied on a 6-inch Castaic swimbait, a big soft rubber lure that looked exactly like a trout. It was equipped with the sturdiest and largest and nastiest hooks by far of all the lures he had in his tackle box. If he was going to hook the bass again, he would not lose her this time. He cast the lure out and it hit the water with a loud splash and dropped down onto the nest. He let it sit. He took out some sunflower seeds and chewed them. He put a Walkman on and listened to some heavy-metal tunes, like a basketball player getting pumped for a big game. The smaller males came in periodically and nudged the lure, trying to get it off the nest. An hour later, he saw the female begin to move back in, slowly. Then she quickly turned her body to a forty-five-degree angle, and hit it. She immediately ran for the shore and wrapped herself around a cable near the dock, but Mike somehow worked the line free. She took one more hard dive, then, exhausted, floated up to the surface, and he netted her. Mike heard a cheer rise from the dock. A crowd of maybe ten people had gathered and had been watching the whole thing. He hadn't noticed them until then.

He weighed the fish right away on a handheld scale called a Boga Grip. It read 25 pounds, almost 2½ pounds bigger than the world record. He yelled to a kid on the dock to run up to the ranger station to fetch the scale. He put the fish on a rope stringer. The kid couldn't find the key to open the closet where the scale was kept. It took him twenty minutes. All this time, the fish was crapping out waste and dripping out eggs. The kid finally came back to the dock with a scale, but it wasn't a certified one. Mike hoisted the now-exhausted fish onto the scale anyway and took a picture. He noticed that the fish had a dime-sized black dot just under its gills, like a beauty mark. The scale read 22 pounds, 5 ounces. One ounce bigger than George Perry's fish. Mike frantically called Lake Wohlford, a neighboring reservoir that he knew carried a certified scale. Two hours after she had been caught, the fish was finally weighed on a proper scale. The official weight: 20 pounds, 12 ounces. Not the world record, but the first bass of more than 20 pounds since Bob Crupi's almost exactly a decade earlier. The fish was twenty-seven inches long and an impossible twenty-seven inches around, like an overinflated football. "It was a pretty stressful day, but after we got her weighed and I let her go, I felt very peaceful. I had my twenty," Mike says. "But in the end it only made me want to break the record even more."

The fish at the time was the eighth-largest bass in history. Mike made all of the papers and national magazines. He had fulfilled Bob Crupi's prophecy from two years earlier. He stood near the top of the bass world, and his ascension to the very top—over George Perry and his mythical feat—seemed even more inevitable than before. He became the darling of the *San Diego Union-Tribune*'s outdoor page. He had more big bass to his credit than any man alive—that impressive stat line of 301 bass over 10 pounds, forty-one over 15, six over 17, six over 18. And now the one 20, the bass with the black dot. He owned the San Diego area lakes and was the unquestioned king who intimidated other big-bass anglers with just his presence—actual or rumored—on the water.

That is, until Jed Dickerson came along in the late spring of 2003. Then Mike Long, in the jargon of the southern California big-bass angling fraternity, got "bitch-slapped in his own backyard."

> Obsession is the single most wasteful human activity because with an obsession you keep coming back and back and back to the same question and never get an answer.   —Norman Mailer

CHAPTER THREE
The San Diego Zoo

Jed Dickerson is a shy, mild-mannered thirty-one-year-old with bright blue-green eyes. He punctuates nearly every sentence with a slight pause, followed by either a "man" or a "you know what I mean?" and a little nervous chuckle as a chaser. When he arrives at Lake Dixon on this chilly, overcast morning, he is tired, and his eyes, bloodshot and glossy, show it. He had been called in to work at 4 a.m. to give a coworker a break at a card room. Non–Native-American casinos in California are prohibited by law from putting up their own money. Outside gaming firms, like the one Jed works for, provide the betting cash, so the folks playing blackjack or Caribbean stud are, in actuality, playing against Jed's company. The casino just provides the space, the dealers, the refreshments, and the well-oxygenated air. This means that Jed or one of his coworkers is always present at each and every table, keeping a sharp eye on the dealers and their money and cashing out or refilling the bank when necessary.

Early this morning, while Jed was sleeping peacefully beside his wife, Irma, in their two-story house in a sprawling development in Carlsbad, an old woman sat stubbornly alone at a table at Ocean's 11, a windowless, well-lighted casino room in Oceanside just off I-5. She refused to give up after four straight hours of playing. She was one of those people who made Jed's stomach turn: the folks, many of them senior citizens, who were pissing away their life's savings every night. They often ended up pleading with Jed—who they knew held all the money—for a couple of dollars to get back in the game, telling him about the car they'd just hocked, the bills they couldn't pay, the families they'd lost or destroyed. This woman, Jed feared, was just another of these hard cases. A coworker had been at the table all night and was getting too tired to watch the money. Jed came in hoping to see this old woman close out the table, either by cashing in or, more likely, by losing it all. Jed sat patiently for an hour or so. The old woman finally left the table at 5:30 a.m. after one final hand, which she lost. Jed settled with the dealer, then jumped into his gold Ford Expedition SUV and drove straight for the lake.

He's a little later than usual. The gate has already been opened, and a few cars sit in the parking lot. Still, he's one of the first in a long, quiet, sleepy line of men waiting to get their daily permits. Jim Dayberry, the ranger at the lake, takes Jed's twenty dollar bill, pauses, and looks Jed straight in the eye and says with a friendly smile, "Man, you need some professional help." Jed chuckles, putting his head down shyly as he reaches for his change, and heads for the dock to get his rental boat. It's a ritual he has performed two hundred times in the past 365 days.

A few hours later, Jed has already circled the shore of the small lake a few times, guiding the trolling motor with his foot, without taking a cast, unable to find a bass worth fishing for. The dinged-up aluminum rental boat has been gradually taking on water all morning. Jed pulls up to the shore and says hello to another Dixon regular, Dennis Ditmars, a young-looking sixty-nine-year-old who has been fishing the lake since before Jed was born. Dennis is a fly fisherman who owns a number of fly rod line–class world records for largemouth bass. He's sitting on the bank among the oak trees and scrubby chaparral, done already with the day's fishing, soaking in the morning sun that burns off the early morning fog so brilliantly nearly every day.

"You need another daytime job," Dennis says to Jed, in a laid-back, laconic drawl.

"I got problems, man," Jed says as he brings the boat closer to shore. "I'm possessed."

"I know," says Dennis. "Bitten by the bass bug."

On May 31, 2003, Jed Dickerson hooked and landed a 21-pound, 11.2-ounce largemouth bass from San Diego's Lake Dixon. It was the fourth-largest bass in recorded history, behind only George Perry's and the two Castaic Lake giants caught by Bob Crupi and Mike Arujo in the early 1990s. The bass vaulted this unlikely newcomer, who had only been bass fishing for two years and whose surfer-look and shyness belies a deep inner determination and grit, to the top of the San Diego and worldwide bass heap, up and over Mike Long. It also created a tension between two bass-fishing posses that simmers uneasily beneath the surface, ready to boil over at any moment.

Jed Dickerson grew up in the town of Escondido, a San Diego suburb that has been transformed in the last ten years from an all-white, middle-class town to one that is now predominantly Hispanic. He describes his childhood as "pretty normal." His father was in real estate, a residential house builder. There is a Jed Road in Escondido, a gift his father bestowed upon him as a boy when he built a row of houses on a new street that needed a name.

In the fourth grade, Jed met Mac Weakley and Mike Winn, the

latter of whom they called "Buddha" for his bulbous belly. The three boys immediately became best friends, and remain so to this day.

The trio did everything together when they were growing up, whether it was surfing before school or getting dropped off at Lake Dixon by Mac's mom to go trout fishing. Their bond of friendship was forged even tighter by the anguish of broken families. One morning in the eighth grade, Mac awoke to his mother at his bedside with tears streaming down her silent face. His father had suffered a heart attack. Three days later, he was dead. Buddha's parents split up that same year, and he moved away to the Sierras with his father. Then Jed's parents divorced the following year. His father decided to move across the country to Melbourne Beach, Florida, to get away from his troubles and try his hand at Florida real estate. Jed wanted out of southern California as well, and decided to move with his father, but not before asking if Mac could come along. Mac's mother agreed, and the boys went to live by the Atlantic Ocean. They entered high school in Florida, but the place never really felt right to them. At school, they were out of their element, feeling too much like the outsiders they were. They passed the beach every morning on their ride to school and, more often than not, decided that the familiar act of surfing all day would be a better way to spend their time than in the classroom. Mac moved back to California after only a few months. Jed stayed behind and went to work for his father's mortgage company after high school.

But his heart was never really in it, and after a few years he missed his friends enough to move back to California. "It was hard on all three of us to be away from each other," he says. Jed went to work for a carpet installer in Escondido, and reentered the comfortable rhythm of surfing and hanging out with Mac. At the time, Buddha was working as a first mate on a deep-sea fishing boat, spending his days on the bright blue Pacific, hauling in yellowtail and tuna and sharks for well-to-do San Diego fishermen.

After work, Mac and Jed started to frequent the Native American casinos that had popped up in the area, their first brush with the world of gambling. The lifestyle, with the possibility of big wins and losses, intrigued them both, but especially Mac, who became a regular at the low-stakes poker tables. One day a man approached Mac. He was impressed with the clean-cut young man's knowledge of and hunger for gambling, and he offered him a job as a manager in his company, BJ Gaming. Mac liked the job, liked hanging out at casinos and card rooms all day and night, liked the high-risk vibe and the big money he started to make. He was good at his job, and his boss told him to hire two lieutenants if he needed. Mac called Buddha and Jed. A few weeks later, the trio was back together again, just like old times. Jed settled down and married a pretty Mexican woman named Irma, and they moved into a housing development in Carlsbad. He adopted her daughter from a previous marriage as his own, and later he and Irma had a son together. Mac and Buddha bought a big bachelor house on the beach in Carlsbad with all the money they were making. The trio hung out together every day, on the job and afterward, recapturing some part of their childhood their parents had ripped from them. They even started to fish together again at Lake Dixon, mainly for trout.

At the beginning of 2001, Jed, Mac, and Buddha started to notice a duo on the lake: one tall, intense redhead and another man, shorter and slighter, but no less focused. The two men were not fishing for trout, not just sitting in their boats lackadaisically with their lines out in the water, shooting the bull. They were on to something, working their boats slowly along the shore, staring into the water with unflappable concentration, as if the lake's bottom was lined with gold. The duo was, of course, Mike Long and John Kerr, as Jed would find out later from the ranger at the dock. Mike Long, the famous bass angler, was fishing Dixon, and fishing it hard. This piqued the interest of the three friends. Then they heard about the $8 million being offered by the Big Bass Record Club.

Mac and Buddha, ever the entrepreneurs, caught on first to the fact that something much more valuable swam in their home waters than the trout they had so passively fished for over the years. The bass in the lake, which they had seen hanging out on the cables near the docks, the same bass that occasionally devoured one of their hooked trout as they were reeling them in, those fish were worth much, much more than their weight in gold. Imagine, one fish worth $8 million. In their home lake, nonetheless. The one they knew every nook and cranny of. The lake was small, but full of the potential for a world record. They viewed the enterprise like gambling, but they believed the odds to be better than any parlor game, stacked in their favor. They told their boss at BJ Gaming about the fish, about the preposterous $8 million bounty on its head. He liked the idea so much—the thrill and the risk and the favorable odds—that he gave them extra time off and even offered to back them financially. No thanks on the financial backing, they said, but we'll take the days off. They could strike it big with $8 million, work for themselves for the rest of their lives. Mac and Buddha made a pact: If one of them caught the fish, both would share in the spoils. They put away their trout gear, bought the stout rods needed for big fish, and became bass fishermen.

They brought Jed into the fold a month later, teaching him what they had learned about bass fishing and increasing their odds. Their methods were somewhat primitive in the beginning. More often than not, they used plastic worms or live shiners as bait and had no real idea how to approach a big spawning female bass on a bed. Because they lived together and were still enjoying the bachelor lifestyle, Mac and Buddha always fished together, with Buddha mostly manning the trolling motor as Mac fished. They had their method down: They were always among the first ones at the gate every morning, and when those gates opened, they would rush in and park the car. Mac would run to the permit line, and Buddha would bring the gear down to the rental boat. Every day, they were the first boat on the water, so proficient in their methods that other anglers soon started accusing them of paying off the rangers to guarantee they got the first boat. Jed fished alone, arriving at the same time as Mac and Buddha, but lagging behind their two-pronged assault, renting his own boat. But the friends stayed in touch on the water through hand signals from across the lake or with their cell phones. They attacked this new type of fishing with passion. They studied Mike Long and John Kerr on the water, constantly learning and picking up tidbits of information. They occasionally approached John to pepper him with questions: They asked him what kind of lures he fished, what pound test he used for his line, why in certain circumstances the hook would bend and pull out of a big bass's mouth. John was always friendly. "I learned a lot from John Kerr," says Jed. Mike, on the other hand, was unapproachable, tall and aloof.

There was no real reason, at first, anyway, for Mike to even pay these newcomers any mind. They didn't even seem like serious bass fishermen, at least by looks. Mike and John fished on fancy, tricked-out Ranger bass boats on those lakes that allowed private boats (Lake Dixon is rental-only). They had sponsors who gave them serious discounts on premium rods, reels, lures, and clothes. They looked more like the professional anglers you see on TV.

Jed, Mac, and Buddha could not have been more different. They had no sponsors, outside of the implicit endorsement of their boss. None of the three owned a bass boat, so they fished only at lakes that offered rental boats, the twelve-foot aluminums with leaky hulls, outfitted with balky batteries and creaky trolling motors. Mac, thirty-one, who is wiry and young-looking, with short hair and fair skin, and Buddha, also thirty-one and still shaped like his namesake, wear jeans and T-shirts when fishing. Mac's favorite shirt is a gray number that says LOST on the front. ("I wear it playing poker sometimes," he says. "People get a kick out of it.") Instead of a Ford or Chevy, Mac arrives at the lake in a silver Mercedes SUV. Mac and Buddha also sport five dollar wide-brimmed straw hats they picked up at Longs Drugs, making them appear, as they cruise the shore on the far end of the lake, like Vietnamese women working a rice paddy. Jed looks like the typical surfer dude. He wears light-brown, wide-wale corduroy pants—extra big in the legs, like a hip-hop musician—a white T-shirt over a black long-sleeved one that covers his expanding gut, and his lucky bright blue L.A. Dodgers baseball cap. His head is shaved bald ("My kids liked doing that," he says sheepishly), and he has a tuft of thick, brownish-red hair protruding a few inches from his lower lip that Mac and Buddha call his "chin nuts." Hardly the good ol' boys we'd imagine.

The three of them eventually started to bring their own batteries and trolling motors—not trusting the rental gear—to the lake, along with homemade anchors and long-handled nets. And that's it. They are bare-bones by necessity, having to truck all of their gear down to the dock every day.

But what they lacked in gear, they made up for with grit. In that first year, the trio spent an astounding two hundred days on the water. "We never thought there would be some guys who would come along and go at it that hard," says Mike Long. Perhaps because he mostly fished by himself, Jed went at it the hardest. In the spring of 2001, he caught a bass of over 10 pounds—the magic weight that demarcates a serious bass—and he was hooked. "It's hard to explain," he says. "Once you see the biggest bass, you just can't stop. If I see a big fish one day, I'll lie in bed thinking about it, hoping it will be there in the morning."

He started keeping a journal of his days on the water, on a wall calendar, with certain promising days circled in dark black ink. His journal wasn't as scientific as Mike's, but it told him what he needed to know. He adjusted his work schedule, asking for the 5 p.m.–2 a.m. shift, so he could maximize his time at the lake. He was exhausted all the time, catching only catnaps at home and during breaks at work. "I can't tell you how many times I've pulled a drifter on the way home from the lake," Jed says, referring to falling asleep at the wheel of his car. But he remained focused on his goal. And the sleep deprivation, as it is for some poets, is a narcotic, really, for all of these guys. It's as if the time on the water is time in another world, a different reality brought on by the buzz of chasing this ghost. The lifestyle is certainly not always healthy physically, mentally, or socially.

Over the past few years, Jed has gained weight, developing a gut for the first time in his life, as a result of his no-time-to-sit-down diet of fast food and candy bars. Though generally a happy person, Jed's emotional highs and lows these days are most often related to a big catch or a disheartening miss on the lake. But as far as relationships go, Jed is on solid ground. Jed's wife, Irma, might not understand what it is about chasing the world record that's so important. She might not even care to know. But she understands that it means a lot to him. "There are many days when I wake up and ask Irma why I am even doing this. But if it's a day I have circled on my calendar, she boots me out of bed. She says she doesn't want me around the house complaining all day that I'm not on the water," Jed says. "I really couldn't do this without her support."

A moment occurred in 2001 that became a defining one for Jed. A moment after which he decided he was going for it, no holds barred, when, as he says, "The true fire got lit under my ass." Jed is a polite and gentle man who says hello to everyone he sees, who is very slow to anger, who generally gives everyone he meets the benefit of the doubt three times over. Which is why he is so reluctant to talk about the episode that happened on Lake Dixon that year that somehow bored so deeply into him, past that polite outer layer and into his inner reservoir of determination.

One day that spring, Jed was on Lake Dixon and noticed that Mike Long and John Kerr were also there, on the other side of the lake. A photographer was at work in Mike's boat, laden with camera gear, occasionally snapping a photo of Mike or John in mid-cast. Mike was already famous by then as a big-bass angler, already the anointed one, though he wouldn't catch his 20-pounder until a few weeks later. It wasn't that unusual to see him being photographed for one magazine or another.

Jed was using live shiners for bait that day, not the best method for catching the biggest bass, he would later discover. But he was still learning the art and science of big-bass angling at that point. Still, he had managed to hook and land an 11-pound bass that day, not a fish that would make the record books, but a respectable one nonetheless and his biggest to date. As he was putting the bass on the stringer, he noticed Mike and John motoring over to his side of the lake. They idled up to Jed. It was the first time Jed and Mike had formally met, despite all of those shared days on the small lake. Mike and John had a strange request: Could they borrow Jed's fish? They promised Jed they would take good care of it and either bring it back to him or release it alive. Jed said sure, they could have the fish and just let it go when they were finished with whatever they wanted with it. He was just happy to have finally met Mike, flattered that he, in particular, was asking for the fish. In return, Mike gave Jed a Mission Fish swimbait, a dynamite bed-fishing lure made by the eccentric Mickey Ellis. The Mission Fish was the latest "hot" lure for big-bass anglers, one that Jed had heard of but never seen. It retailed for thirty-five dollars. It was a nice present, but more than that it represented to Jed a treasured piece of big-bass insight that he had so craved. Mike and John took the fish and cruised back to the photographer, Dusan Smetana. Jed left the lake elated that day.

But a few months later that sweet high went sour. There on the cover of *Sports Afield*, one of the big-three national "hook-and-bullet" magazines, was John Kerr, proudly holding up and grinning into the maw of an 11-pound bass. It was Jed's fish. It didn't feel right to Jed. "From that day on, I was like, 'That's it,' " he says. "I mean, I don't want to start a controversy, but that's how the fire got lit, that's how it started." Neither John nor Mike would know that they had created their own monster who would challenge their superiority in the world-record chase. "We just wanted to use the fish as a tool for the photo shoot," says John. "But it was [Jed's] biggest bass at the time. Looking back, I guess we didn't give him enough credit."

Later that spring, Mike Long caught the 20-pound, 12-ounce fish on Dixon. Neither Jed nor Mac nor Buddha was on the lake that day, but they heard the stories from the locals, read all about it in the papers. No one had to tell them how to respond. Like a male bass protecting his soon-to-spawn female, they were agitated and ready to take on all challenges—real or imagined. The lure was dangled, the hook remained to be set.

Though world-record chasers operate in a vacuum compared to their more famous first cousins—the big boys of the Bassmaster Tour and the television personalities—they can't do what they do without a little help. They need tools to ply their trade. A stiff graphite rod, with a butt as thick as a broom handle to provide the leverage needed to haul in a bulky, angry mass of female bass. Clear monofilament or fluorocarbon line strong enough to withstand 20 pounds of thrashing, struggling weight, but thin enough not to spook a fish in crystal clear water. And a dependable reel, one with a smooth drag system and a well-calibrated spool that doesn't backlash easily. But the rod, reel, and line are just delivery and retrieval systems. The star of the show is, of course, the lure—the object that the fish finds appetizing or irritating or fascinating enough to strike and get hooked. That strike of the lure is the fundamental moment in fishing, the electric thrill of contact when the potential becomes actual, when fish meets man, when the water world and the air world collide. Carl Jung even went so far as to say that landing a fish was a symbol for bringing the contents of unconsciousness into consciousness.

The development and use of lures marked a seminal moment in the history of mankind. Prior to their use, man would harvest fish by overpowering them physically, by grabbing and wrestling them out of the water, throwing a net into a silvery school to haul them in, or stalking and spearing a fish like they would a land mammal.

But somewhere along the line, one of our hairy ancestors figured out that a flashy bit of some precious metal or some feathers attached to a hook could also catch fish. Instead of using brute strength, man used his brain to entice a fish by outwitting it. There's a moment in the New Testament when Jesus, proving himself to be a man/God way ahead of his time, hit on this idea. Seeing Simon and Andrew casting nets for fish in the Sea of Galilee, Jesus says, "Follow me, and I will make you fishers of men." He goes on to recruit the disciples James and John in the same manner. Cast aside your nets, he says, the best way to fish is to lure them in.

Over the ages, lures have taken on all shapes and sizes and

utility. As we evolved as a species, so did our lures. These days, a good lure must somehow appeal not only to the fish, but also to the fisherman himself. Some lures are carefully carved to look exactly like the favorite food of the desired fish. Others are just meant to be attractors, flashy concoctions that are struck by the fish out of instinct or irritation. And then there are those that don't look like anything on God's green earth, but work anyway.

Big companies, like Berkley and Strike King, mass-produce plastic worms, crankbaits, buzzbaits, spinners, and poppers by the hundreds of thousands for the average bass fisherman. The aisles of sporting-goods departments in every Wal-Mart in the country are lined with their products, with names like Power Worms, Tube Lizards, Wild Thangs, Zara Spooks, and Hula Poppers. And tackle stores and roadside bait shops sell crawdads, shiners, and night-crawlers for those who prefer live bait. These lures and bait are inexpensive (maybe a dozen for fifteen dollars) and, for most part, they do the job.

But big-bass anglers, particularly those who are after the record, tend to see the world a bit differently. They are not satisfied with the 2-pound bass that the average weekend warrior brags to his coworkers about catching. Thus, they believe they need something different—special lures that attract only the largest, wiliest bass in the world. And for those, they turn to men like Mickey Ellis and Jerry Rago.

Allan Cole is widely regarded as the first man to make a commercially available swimbait lure: the AC Plug. A swimbait, broadly speaking, is a 6- to 12-inch lure with a soft plastic or wooden body and a clear plastic lip under its jaw that makes it dive under the water and wiggle properly. These lures are firmly in the "realistic" category, shaped and painted to look exactly like rainbow trout, the preferred food of giant bass in California. The baits are heavy (up to one pound), and thus tiring to cast all day, but they are a marvel to watch in the water. When retrieved, they look exactly like a rainbow trout appetizingly swimming near the water's surface, just waiting to be bass lunch. Allan made his first AC Plug in 1989, and the wooden hard bait quickly became the preferred lure of southern California big-bass anglers. In the early 1990s, Ken Huddleston introduced his Castaic Swimbait, shaped like an AC Plug, but made from soft plastic, which some said made it look even more realistic. His lure was a favorite through the mid-1990s. But when Ken parted with the Castaic Soft Bait Company in 2001, he left behind a professional vacuum that has since been ably filled by Mickey Ellis and Jerry Rago.

Mickey Ellis became a lure maker because, he says, like the disciples Simon and Andrew, God told him to do so. He even named his company 3:16 Lure Co. after the famous verse in the Gospel according to John you used to see plastered on a white posterboard and held up by a spectator at seemingly every major televised sporting event. Mickey can reel off the verse on cue: "For God so loved the world, that he gave his only begotten Son, that whosoever believeth in him should not perish but have everlasting life."

Mickey's company is located in a garage among a maze of low-slung white buildings in an industrial park just off I-5 outside of Mission Viejo, an hour and change north of San Diego. His space is surrounded by little mom-and-pop cabinetmakers, mechanics, and cement companies. His garage is busy with the tools of his trade: sanders, carving chisels, resins, and paint. The voice of a man named Pastor Chuck preaches from on high, his Christian radio broadcast thundering down from the speakers overhead. Hundreds of clear plastic bags and boxes of his lures litter the floor of Mickey's office, where he sits behind a metal desk. He is thirty-five years old, and maybe 5'11" with big shoulders and a broad chest. His hands are meaty and dirty and flecked with little red scars, and he's missing a fingertip on his left one. He has scruffy brown stubble on his cheeks and intense blue bloodshot eyes. He wears a dark blue sweatshirt, shorts, and Vans skateboarding sneakers.

When I walk in, Mickey is admiring his latest creation, which he had just put on sale on eBay that morning. It's a swimbait, but it's different from anything the world has ever seen. It's his first foray into hard plastics, after a few years working with soft plastics. It weighs three-quarters of a pound and is almost 11 inches long. There are two metal door hinges in the body of the lure, and a hard plastic tail also flexes on a hinge. The lure is painstakingly hand painted down to the tiniest of details, each one—like a snowflake—slightly different from the next, "depending on how much coffee I drank that morning," he says. The lure has a vivid pink stripe on its sides, just like a rainbow trout, with little dots on its flanks and its brown back. It has glued-on eyes, which look wet and animate. It even has nostrils. The pectoral, dorsal, and anal fins are all perfectly shaped. A glass rattle inside draws the attention of the bass as the angler reels it in. The lure looks like a piece of folk art, like something you might pick up at a flea market in Connecticut. But it's meant to be fished, and fished hard. The two treble hooks attached to the base of the lure are menacing and are hooks usually used for tarpon, which can grow to 200 pounds. He calls the lure the Armageddon, after the biblical story. "In Revelations, all earthly kings gather to make war against God, the final war," he says, holding up the lure. "This is actually a weapon of war. This is a wrecking ball. They hit this thing and they're done, dude." Mickey sells his soft plastic swimbaits for anywhere between twelve and thirty-five dollars a pop, prices considered very expensive in the lure world. The Armageddon goes on sale today for $316. "I stirred up a ruckus from day one with this lure," he says. "But it's worth it. This thing swims and looks exactly, spot-on, like a trout. I caught four fish on it my first time out. This is a phenomenon. It's handmade, dude. It's not made in China; it's made right here in southern California."

Mickey Ellis is the sort of Christian that makes a pastor's job tough but worthwhile, the member of the flock who strayed far, far away, but seems to be slowly, warily circling back. A reclamation project. By every measure, Mickey had a very rough childhood. When he was three, his father was killed by a drunk driver. His mother never fully recovered, and went into a spiral of drug and alcohol abuse. She remarried, to an uptight Marine who didn't like Mickey. "Then it was my mom and the Marine against me and I rebelled since I was six," he says. He did his first stint in juvenile detention at age eleven. His stepfather believed in being a man, in providing for oneself, and made Mickey get his first job at a doughnut shop when he was sixteen. But Mickey was soon cutting high school, and like so many men I had met on my travels, he turned to fishing as a means of calming a restless soul. But even fishing couldn't save him then. "You don't know angry. I was so angry you could see red fire," he says, his eyes growing animated. "And that still pops up. Sometimes I get caught off guard. If there's one thing I'm really good at, it's just knocking people out. I've never had a fight that's lasted more than two or three punches, and I've never had a guy that I hit who could stand up. And I don't like fighting, dude, don't like anything about it."

When he was eighteen, his anger finally got the best of him, and he was sentenced to four years in jail. He went in for drug charges and assault and battery. "I sold some cocaine to some undercover cops, then beat the crap out of them," Mickey says. He was paroled when he was twenty-one, but says politics, not good behavior, got him out early. His time in jail changed him, but not for the better. "You don't want to be a white boy in the pen, let me tell you," he says. "Jail has its own set of rules, apart from regular society. You're either a bitch or a man." Mickey decided to be the latter. He went in a skinny 180 pounds. When he left, he weighed 245 pounds and had eighteen-inch biceps.

He worked a dozen different jobs after jail, mostly in the construction business learning new trades, but became quickly bored once he mastered them, and moved on. He went to welding school, then got hired as a prototype fabricator in the booming southern California semiconductor business. He learned from that job that there was nothing in the world he couldn't make, but he eventually got bored with that, too. To stave off the ennui, he started racing motorbikes. He crashed a lot, and with no money he was forced to fix his bikes on his own. He eventually opened his own collision-repair shop, which led to a job custom-painting Harleys for $3,000 a bike. He kept bodybuilding at the time and had "hair down to my butt," he says. "I was thumping skulls. You're staring right into the eyes of a thug. If I hit you, you could pick up the phone right now and I'd go straight back to jail."

In his late twenties, he hit rock bottom. "I deserved to die. I deserved to be lit up. Without a doubt, I've done more bad things than you can imagine," he says. He pauses for a moment when I ask him if he's ever killed a man. "No, no," he says, without a smile. "But picture it like this: Take a very big guy and piss him off as bad as you can and then let him out in society."

He was living with his girlfriend, Kristy, at the time. She got tired of his motorbikes and dicey friends, and kicked him out of the house. But before he left, she handed him a Bible with his name monogrammed on the back. He just put the Bible on the back of his toilet seat in the apartment he rented on Lake Mission Viejo, and went back to his bikes. He was as lost as ever, in what he calls "a black abyss."

But one day in a drunken fury, he picked up the Bible and decided to read it from cover to cover. "Six months later, I shut the thing and said, with fire on my breath, there's no way that it isn't true. Man can't think like that, dude. I read it as a very angry person, then gave my life to Christ."

For a week straight, he went soul-searching, fishing on Lake Mission Viejo, asking God what he should do with his life, knowing that he had the guts to do anything He asked of him. It hit him one evening on the water. "I honestly believe He asked me to make lures," he says. "I was like, 'What?' I had never made a lure in my life."

He started to attend Saddleback Church, a southern Baptist church in Lake Forest run by Pastor Rick Warren, famous for his book *The Purpose-Driven Life*. He went to premarital counseling with Kristy and eventually married her, and together they had a son. And, with a vengeance, he started making plastic swimbaits in the kitchen sink of his one-bedroom condo.

A few months later he took five hundred Mission Fish swimbaits to the Fred Hall Fishing Tackle and Boat Show and sold them all at twenty dollars a pop. He quit his day job. "I thought I was going to be a millionaire," he says. But four months later, he was broke and had to take another welding job to get by. Fishermen, it seemed, weren't comfortable spending that much money for a lure they knew very little about.

Another stumbling block came a year later when Kristy divorced him against his will. "I despise and hate that it happened," he says. "But that's what happens when you marry a super hot chick with an attitude. Let's put it this way. If she walked in here right now, you'd lose your breath." He points to a picture of a pretty blonde on the wall behind him. "And that's her before the three-thousand-dollar boobies."

He still had his two-year-old son, whom he saw on weekends and vacations; his hundred-pound pit bull, Pebbles, who eats neighborhood cats; and his unwavering faith, which has helped him through it all. He decided to push on with the 3:16 Lure Company. "It was a calling. I was supposed to make a difference," he says. "That's where God comes in. You take all that nasty bile and turn that effort in a different direction, and you have just unleashed one dedicated, serious animal." Everything he created was handmade. He would take a block of wood that would serve as the mold for a new lure, and he would write "3:16" on it and let it sit until it drove him so crazy that he would begin to carve the mold. "I could see it in my head," he says. "I believe that's part of what God's doing through me. God has a piece of it. I'm not a genius." He went all out and rented the space in the industrial park, working from 5 a.m. until 9 p.m., sometimes eating only one meal a day.

Mike Long, who calls him "Picasso," fished Mickey's lures and helped him get a big order from Japan. Mickey invented new swimbaits, the Rising Son, the K-9, the Sidewinder, the Top Dawg (which says, mysteriously, on the back of the package STILL THUG'N). There were baby shad, baby bass, baby bluegill, lures that sank fast, that stayed on top, that wiggled a certain way. "Any problem you got, dude, I have the solution," he says.

Mickey has built the business now to the point where it sustains itself. Still, he's not getting rich, by any means. He says the company generates maybe $50,000 a year, with little profit, just enough to get by in the high-cost-of-living world that is southern California. In many ways, the lure makers are like the world-record chasers, operating on the fringe of a multibillion-dollar industry, doing what they do because it's a calling, an obsession that they can't live without. They are hoping and working toward that day when one of their creations makes the difference, perhaps even catches the world record. "I'm not in this business to make money," Mickey says. He points out that Jed Dickerson used a Mission Fish to catch the fourth-largest bass of all time in 2003 and that Hank Parker has been on television using his swimbaits to catch big bass. But he has very little to show, monetarily, for either of those exposures.

And he has competition in the form of Jerry Rago, a short, black-haired forty-five-year-old with a graying goatee, from Bishop, California. He and Mickey are engaged in a head-to-head weapons race with their swimbaits, but they have a healthy respect for each other that at times spills over into fierce loyalty. Mickey says Jerry is "the most giving, loving, honest, down-to-earth guy there is. He's brilliant, he's just got a gift. And he's a great fisherman." He affectionately calls Jerry a "knee-high Nazi." Jerry says Mickey is "crazy and sometimes obnoxious," but a man who knows how to make a lure. "He has his following, and I have mine," says Jerry. "If I didn't make baits, I'd be knocking the crap out of the fish with his."

Jerry is most famous for the Rago Rat, a lure shaped like a rodent with a rubber worm for a tail that gyrates tantalizingly across the water's surface. He developed it in 1996, and it remains so popular that he can't keep them in stock. Mickey says it's the most phenomenal topwater lure there is. But lately, Jerry has been concentrating on his own soft and hard plastic swimbaits, which rival Mickey's in their artistry and utility. The soft plastics go for thirty dollars apiece. The hard baits sell for eighty.

Three years ago, Jerry quit his job in construction to make lures full-time. He says he works twelve to fourteen hours a day. "If I'm not sleeping, I'm working," he says. He makes about the same amount of money he made while working construction, but the lure-making takes less of a toll on his body. Jerry, just like Mike Long, is a god in Japan. One time, two Japanese men called from Los Angeles. They had been scouring the tackle stores there, trying to find his lures, but had come up empty. They got in touch with Jerry, made the six-hour drive to Bishop, and stayed in a motel for two days while Jerry made them swimbaits, for which they paid almost $10,000. Jerry has backorders that would take him years to fill, and the biggest stumbling block to further riches is the same as Mickey's: His lures take an enormous amount of time to make. "Everyone says if you invent a lure, you'll be a millionaire," he says. "But not if you make them by hand."

The process starts in the workshop in Jerry's house. There's a table saw with a belt disc and a band saw, carving tools on the tables, and buckets of rubber and resins tucked in the corners of the room. He starts by carving a wood model with knives and a sander, then carves the fins individually, gluing them to the body of the lure. He suspends the model in a white shelving box made of plywood and pours in a molding compound to finish the mold. Then he heats up soft plastic to four hundred degrees Fahrenheit and pours it into the mold, the clear plastic first, then one with the pink tint of the stripe on a rainbow trout, then a brown one for the back. Glitter is mixed throughout the brew. Then he glues on the eyes. He says on a good day he can make fifty soft plastic baits, and maybe ten hard baits, which take longer to dry. He recently hired some help to ramp up production.

Jerry and Mickey are friends, and they even fish together occasionally. The two share an almost tribal loyalty to each other. When a vendor in Japan tried to bilk Jerry out of some money, Mickey stopped using the guy as well, despite the hit he took to his bottom line. And Mickey won't give Mike Long his new Armageddon swimbait because he thinks Mike hasn't done a good enough job of promoting Jerry's lures. "If Mickey doesn't send Mike Long an Armageddon, he's got brain damage," says Jerry. But there's no doubt the two men are in competition, constantly trying to one-up each other. "I saw the Armageddon," Jerry says about Mickey's new swimbait, "and I said, 'Aw, man, I have to go back to the drawing board.' I threw away my mold and started all over again. I'll have an answer soon." He's working on a lipless trout swimbait that he says is "absolutely anatomically correct."

Both Mickey and Jerry do their best to get their lures into the hands of those most likely to catch the biggest bass and, hopefully, the biggest of them all. But they realize, as the world-record chasers do, that this is a game of chance where the odds are stacked against them, that any lure, or live bait for that matter, in the right circumstances could be the one. "You could give Mike Long a turd that I stuck eyes on, and he'd catch big fish," says Mickey. "It doesn't matter what Mike Long fishes as long as Mike Long is fishing it." But anglers like Jed Dickerson, Mickey says, are a different story. Those not as experienced as Mike need Mickey's lures. Thus he and Jerry keep striving for something that is utterly unattainable: the one magic bullet, the perfect lure that will catch a fish on every cast. "This job is never-ending," says Mickey, with deep satisfaction, finally doing something he will never tire of. And Jerry is still thinking up new schemes. "I have some evil stuff I'm working on, man," he says. One concept is a lure that is attached by one line and two rods. Two anglers would stand on opposite shores and reel the lure in back and forth to each other. "No boat to spook the fish and no loud splash of the lure," he says, grinning. "Tell Mickey about that one."

Mickey and Jerry have unique perspectives on the chase to catch the world-record bass. They are, in some ways, participants, with the fruits of their labor used by many of the biggest names in the chase, people like Mike and Jed, and the Alabaman, Porter Hall. But they are also, like the rest of us, spectators who marvel at the strangeness of the whole scene, the intensity and the madness. Both agree that Mike Long is the best pure big-bass angler out there. "Mike has a gift from God," says Mickey. "He's got a lot of power. He's a champion." Jerry offers a reason why: "He's been doing this for thirty years, spending time on the water, making mental notes." They differ a bit on Jed Dickerson, the Johnny-come-lately to the San Diego scene. "He's a one-fish wonder," says Jerry. Mickey has another take, perhaps predictably since Jed made his name with one of his lures. "Jed's just awesome, man," he says. "I mean, I'm not a fag, but he's just sweet. He's a nice, solid guy. A thinker."

Mickey and Jerry introduced me to a strange game played by the southern California big-bass angling community. In 2000, Jerry and another lure maker named Greg Vella started what, in effect, was a bass-angling mafia. Periodically, a newcomer would show up at a lake in southern California and catch a few big bass, say, over 15 pounds. If that newcomer started making noise, either to the locals or the press, the bass mafia would spring into action, ordering what amounts to a big-bass "hit" that was designed not to take out the angler, but to shut him up and put him in his rightful place. For example, in 2000, a few guys went fishing on Lake Casitas, near Ojai, and caught a couple of big bass on some new lures. They talked a big game at the dock and even brought along their own writer who plastered their names all over the newspaper and bass-fishing Web sites. No one had ever heard of the guys before, and they definitely were not showing the proper respect to the area's regulars. So Greg Vella called Jerry Rago and ordered the hit. He sent Jerry enough money to cover his expenses and Jerry went down to Casitas and stayed for a few days, catching a number of bass that were much bigger than the ones the new guys had landed. Jerry caused a stir at the docks. The poor fellows never knew what hit them and were never heard from again. And oftentimes, if a tournament was held on a certain lake, Greg and Jerry would go and fish at the same time. On one memorable occasion, the winning duo of the tourney hauled in a few bass that totaled 18 pounds. Jerry and Greg showed up at the dock a few minutes later with mess of bass that weighed 30 pounds. It was what the Greg and Jerry called "getting bitch-slapped in your own backyard." They even had jackets made up with the acronym "BSIYOB." Over the years, they made six or so of these "hits," but like mafiosi gone legit, they no longer do it. Mike Long was one of the original members of the group, and Mickey was "made" late in the game.

When I asked Jerry if there was any rivalry between Mike and Jed and their respective posses, he said that in 2003, Mike was worried about Jed and his friends because of the amount of time they were putting in at Dixon. "But in no way do I compare Mike and John to those guys," he says. Mickey was more blunt: "Anything over fifteen pounds that comes out of the San Diego area gets Mike's blood going, as it would any champion," he says. Jed, Mac, and Buddha, it seemed, had formed their own big-bass mafia family and had turned the tables on Mike. "Jed went right in there, man," says Mickey. "Mike's just pissed because *he* got bitch-slapped in his own backyard."

In January 2003, at the beginning of the spawning season, Jed, Mac, and Buddha went at Lake Dixon full-bore. They were there nearly every day, Mac and Buddha still getting on the water first to beat the unruly crowds that had begun to swarm the lake, and rent out all the boats, and run across each other's bows, and generally wreak havoc, thanks to Mike Long's giant fish and the standing $8 million prize. The lake, at only seventy-five surface acres, couldn't handle too much pressure, but as long as Mac and Buddha got the first crack at the likely spots every day, they knew they had a shot. Jed, the married man who had to get his own permit and lug his own trolling motor, battery, anchor, net, and rods down to the dock by himself, was always a little late getting on the lake. And his fishing suffered because of it. He rarely saw a good fish, because others usually beat him to the best spots. And when he finally did find a big fish worth working, it always seemed to swim away and not come back. He had a rough winter and spring, catching nothing over 8 pounds.

Mac and Buddha, on the other hand, were doing well. Their hustle was paying off. They continued using their method, Buddha manning the motor and Mac fishing. Mac was catching many big fish and was starting to make a name for himself.

In late May, the crowds began to disperse a bit. The spawn was winding down. No real huge bass had come out of Dixon, perhaps a result of the increased pressure on the lake. But in May, Mac and Buddha noticed a man fishing intently in one spot all day. Toward evening, they went over to get a look at the fish that the man was working. It was a giant. They marked the spot and the man. He was wearing a bright red shirt.

The next morning, Mac and Buddha got on the lake even earlier than usual, but there was a car in front of them. When the gate opened, they parked their car and noticed the man they had seen the day before, racing to the permit line. He was wearing the same red shirt. They knew he was headed for the same spot to try to find that fish. Mac and Buddha sprang into action and made it onto the water ahead of him. The man in the red shirt was right behind them in his boat, but he watched helplessly as Mac and Buddha got to his spot first. The man motored by and asked breathlessly, "Do you see it?" Without looking at him, Buddha said, "Yeah."

"Fuck," the man replied, and steamed off to another spot.

A few hours later, the man in the red shirt came by again his patience and politeness gone, and set up his boat by Mac and Buddha. Just as the man was about to cast to the fish, Mac hooked it. As he was bringing the giant in, the man said, "Shit, that's the world record."

It wasn't, but Mac had landed a 17-pound, 8-ounce bass, a big fish in anyone's book. And it was just a harbinger of things to come. A few weeks after that, he caught a 19-pound, 8-ounce bass, which tied him for the twelfth-largest bass of all time. He caught it with a Mission Fish, made by Mickey Ellis. "It's not that difficult to catch these fish," says Mac. "It's not rocket science. You spot them, then harass them." His catch only made the trio fish even harder, even more certain that one of them would break the world record.

A few days later, Mac and Buddha saw another giant bass. Jed happened to be fishing at Lake Poway that day, another excellent big-bass lake near San Diego. He was having another poor outing, just another bad day in what was turning out to be an *annus horribilis*. He called Mac and Buddha from his cell phone. "I could tell from their voices that they were on to something," Jed says. "They said something like 'Ahh, there are a couple around.'" Jed left Poway immediately and drove to Dixon. He arrived at around 2 p.m. As soon as he left the dock, he saw two big fish that were the bright-green watermelon-rind color that means they're ready to spawn and be caught. He anchored up on one of them and worked it for a while, but she swam away. He went to the second fish and had the same result. As it got darker, he went over to where Mac and Buddha had been, over the giant fish. He sat there until dark and saw her once. Then he had to leave.

That night at the casino, Jed begged Mac and Buddha for a shot at the fish. They gave Jed a hard time, ribbing him and telling him that they would get there first and catch it. At the dock the next morning, Jed asked again if he could try for the fish. He reminded Mac that he already had a 19-pounder, that he himself was having a horrible year, and anyway, they all thought the fish was a tad smaller than Mac's. Mac and Buddha left the dock first and yelled to Jed that they were going after the fish. "Jed called us dicks," says Mac. "I turned to Buddha who said, 'Let's give him a shot.'" So they did.

Jed went to the fish and waited patiently. It was a cloudy day, with just a touch of wind, so he could barely see her. But he knew she was there. After a while, he decided to make some casts while letting the wind gently push his boat by her. After an hour of drifting and casting, he felt the bass nail his Mission Fish. She moved first toward the shoreline weeds, then shot out to the deep water. He started reeling her in, then screamed across the lake for Mac and Buddha. But before they could get there, he had netted the fish. He went to the dock. Mac put her on the Boga Grip. It read "22 pounds." A call was placed to Fish and Game to certify the fish.

Calls went out to other places as well. John Kerr received one at work. He told his boss that he had to go see this fish. His boss said no. John told him he would quit if he didn't let him go. His boss finally relented. John called Mike Long on the way.

Meanwhile, Jed had put the fish on a stringer, alive, and tied it to the dock. There was mayhem at the scene, with crowds elbowing in to see the fish, and fishermen docking their boats and asking for the fish to be held up so they could get a photo. Jed had thousands of thoughts going through his head. He allowed himself to dream just for a moment. He couldn't believe how long it was taking the Fish and Game folks to show up.

A few minutes later, John Kerr walked down the dock and, with a big genuine smile, reached out his hand and congratulated Jed, telling him how fortunate he felt to actually see a fish like this. Then Mike Long showed up at the dock, and what was becoming a strange and fantastic day became even more so. Mike, with his commanding height, voice, and reputation, took control of the situation, lifting the fish out of the water, taking numerous photographs and a scale sample. Mac and Buddha would say later it was as if he had caught the fish himself. He told Jed to put it on a longer stringer. Jed complied, but the fish soon wrapped itself around the dock piling. As they stood over her and tried to figure out how to get the rope untangled, Buddha stripped down to his underwear and jumped into the water, swam under the dock, and undid the rope, surfacing with a big gasp and a reddened face.

Then Mike announced to Mac, whom he had not met until that day, and within earshot of others at the dock, that he had found Mac's 19-pounder floating dead on the lake a couple of days earlier. Mac, who'd been on the lake every day and had heard nothing of the sort, interpreted it as a subtle dig, meant to imply that he had not released his fish properly.

Finally, the Fish and Game rangers showed up. They officially weighed Jed's fish. It was 21 pounds, 11.2 ounces, not the world record, but the fourth-largest bass of all time, and one that made Jed an instant celebrity in the big-bass world. He appeared in all of the major fishing magazines and newspapers across the country, as well as the ESPN Web site, holding his big fish, and wearing his lucky L.A. Dodgers hat. On his calendar for 2003, May 31 is circled, and within the circle is printed these understated words: I CAUGHT A 21-POUND BASS.

In the ranger's office later that afternoon, after Jed had let the fish go, Mac found himself standing next to Mike Long. He was still smarting over Mike's proclamation to all who could hear that his 19-pounder was dead. He turned to Mike, and in a voice loud enough for all within hearing distance, said, "Does this mean *we* can now fish lakes when they're closed too?" Mike didn't reply.

A few days later, Mike was interviewed by a local newspaperman. He claimed that after reviewing the pictures and the scale samples, Jed's fish was actually the same fish that he had caught two years earlier. The clincher: It had the same black dot below its jaw. This statement got big play in the papers and in *Field & Stream* magazine. Later Mike claimed that a few trout-fishing friends had found the fish that both he and Jed had caught floating dead and gave it to him. "I took it home in two plastic bags," Mike says. "The thing absolutely reeked." He says he sent it to a taxidermist to have it mounted.

The rumor that this was the same fish that Mike Long had landed two years earlier had a global effect in the big-bass world: It single-handedly shut down the Big Bass Record Club. When AIG, which had taken over as the insurer of the club, heard about the fish, it got nervous, as doling out eight million dollars to some angler suddenly seemed almost inevitable. So in 2003, when AIG called Owens and told him that the BBRC's premium had just been tripled, the BBRC was forced to fold its tents that December.

To Mac and Buddha, Mike's "same-fish" claim seemed like yet another dis, and perhaps a ploy to keep the hordes off the ever-more-populated water of Lake Dixon. If the fish was still alive, someone might catch it again, and this time it might be the actual record. But if it was dead, the blood trail was gone. Jim Dayberry, the Lake Dixon ranger, says no one he knew saw or heard about the dead fish, adding, "And that strikes me as odd." To Mac and Buddha, Mike's whole story is pure hogwash. "Mike just got his name in there and stole some of Jed's glory. There are lots of bass that have a black dot. To say it was the same fish is ridiculous," says Mac. "To say he found both fish floating dead is even more ridiculous. I'm a math guy, and what are the odds of finding these fish again?" Buddha puts it another way, finishing Mac's thought as he so often does. "It seems like ever since we've been catching big fish, the guy's had a hard-on for us," he says. "It's just jealousy. We just rained on his parade."

Perhaps the differences between these two sets of grade-school buddies were never more apparent than during that stretch in the spring of 2003. Mike and John were men who had pursued big bass for most of their lives. They had painstakingly studied the craft, knew all of the water and the right people. They were media stars, on the covers of national magazines, worshiped by the Japanese. They—and Mike in particular—were used to being in control, were perfectionists. They *were* the big-bass game in San Diego. They were the establishment, and Mike its anointed king.

Then along comes a new trio, fresh on the scene, seeking to supplant them. They studied the craft, taking a crash course in big-bass angling. They worked hard, almost as hard as humanly possible. They watched Mike and John, mimicked their methods, copied their equipment. They were somewhat brash, as newcomers often are, especially when they felt slighted by their heroes. They were gamblers. They didn't dress or act or talk like typical fishermen. They didn't handle themselves in a manner that Mike was accustomed to. And they were good: With a few fish, they demystified Mike's aura of invincibility and the inevitability that he would break the record.

———

A year later, the dust still hasn't settled on the rivalry. Mike, with little prodding, still seems to be able to conjure some of the hurt. He believes he is still the odds-on favorite to break the world record and is ever confident in his abilities. He says that Jed has entered some of the same tournaments that he and John have participated in, tournaments that require the skill of sight-fishing for bedding fish. He says that Jed has "gotten his butt kicked. He jumped in quick, but now he's going through the school of hard knocks."

When asked to reflect on what happened in 2003, Mike says,

"It was kind of like I had a big-bass train going, and a couple of guys came along and highjacked it." He pauses. "It didn't piss me off. They fear me and John when we get on the water. There's a kind of fear in their eyes. We let them have Dixon." Mike says he's moved on to other, less-pressured lakes. "I should get a shot at another one on an unnamed lake that people don't talk about. It's just a matter of time." Still, the posses bump into one another when Mike fishes Dixon. In the late spring of 2004, they had a near confrontation when Mac repeatedly ran his boat in close to Mike's as he tried to fish over a big bass. No love is lost between those two in particular.

As for Mac and Buddha, they only fished Dixon a few times in the spring of 2004. Increased responsibilities at work have led to less time off, and the fishing was spotty that year in general. And with the BBRC shutting down at the end of 2003, and no $8 million on the table, they have less motivation to stay in the game. Mac has taken to playing high-stakes, no-limit Texas Hold 'Em games in Los Angeles, against the likes of Jack Black, Leonardo DiCaprio, and Lou Diamond Phillips. "I am one of the best poker players in the world," Mac says without modesty. Buddha tags along when Mac goes to play, watching movies in the hotel room or trying to score dates at the bar. Mac says he and Buddha know of a fish in Dixon that is definitely the world record, but that the fish won't show itself until later in the season. He says they'll be back on the water then. They've nicknamed her "Cash."

Only Jed Dickerson keeps coming back to Dixon, day after day, with Irma kicking him out of bed on the mornings he has circled on his calendar, to chase his ghost. Everyone on the lake seems to know who he is. On the last day I fished with him, we headed for the dock after a full day on the water. Jed was dropping me off, but he was headed back out to try for a fish he'd seen earlier. A teenager, perhaps a young world-record chaser in the making, saw Jed and yelled across the water, "Hey, are you the famous one?" Jed bowed his head and chuckled and said, "I guess so."

But it's not the fame that drives Jed to come to Lake Dixon almost every morning. "Big bass are just such a rare thing," he says. "I come up here for a month, two months, three months without catching one. But when you do it's so worth it. Guys who I know who are big into surfing, they catch a big wave, but those waves just go by. Once you catch a giant bass you actually have something." Then he laughs, nervously, as if he's given too much about himself away.

America is rather like life. You can usually find in it what you look for . . . It will probably be interesting, and it is sure to be large.

—E. M. Forster

CHAPTER FOUR
America's Fish

In 1773, an intrepid naturalist from Pennsylvania named William Bartram began a four-year exploration of the previously uncharted, humid, mosquito-infested tangle of woods and water of the American southeast. Bartram, who would posthumously become known as "the grandfather of American ornithology," wrote about his travels in a book that, due to a near-paralyzing bout with writer's block, wasn't published until 1791. In one chapter he described learning from some friendly Indians how to "jigbob" for fish in what is now known as the St. John's River in Florida, using a hook wrapped in deer hair and bird feathers. He reported that the fish he caught provided excellent sport, weighed "fifteen, twenty and thirty pounds" and were "delicious food."

Experts claim Bartram's account makes the first reference to largemouth bass in English literature. The only problem was that he called them "trout."

In 1802, a package arrived at the Paris, France, office of the Comte de Lacépède, sent to him by a research assistant in Charleston, South Carolina. Lacépède was a composer of operas, a well-known physicist, and a personal friend of Thomas Jefferson's. He would later go on to become a prominent French politician. But he was perhaps most famous for his comprehensive book *Histoire Naturelle des Poissons*, which identified all of the known species of fish in the world at that time. The package from America contained sketches of a largemouth bass, a New World fish, as yet unidentified, at least in the scientific sense. So Lacépède gave the fish a name based on what he saw. He called it *Micropterus salmoides*. *Micropterus* means "small-fin" in Greek. Largemouth bass actually have fairly large fins, but apparently the specimen collected for Lacépède was deformed, missing part of its dorsal fin. Such are the vagaries of naming a species based on one example. The second part of the name, *salmoides*, means "like salmon or trout," something he tacked on in deference to the name that South Carolinians had given to the fish. They called them green trout, a colloquialism that can still be heard in some of the more rural sections of the South.

That the largemouth bass would be called a trout by both laymen and scientists at the turn of the nineteenth century is not that surprising. When Europeans first settled the American continent, they brought with them the customs, appellations, and cultural biases of their home countries. The most popular freshwater fishes in Europe, and especially the British Isles, were the "salmonids"— trout and Atlantic salmon—revered both for their noble fighting ability and superiority as table fare. The salmonids were celebrated in literature. Izaak Walton's 1653 book, *The Compleat Angler*— reputed to still be the third-most-frequently reprinted book in the English language after the Bible and the works of William Shakespeare—waxes poetic on many types of fish, but is particularly doting on the trout and salmon, with the latter being referred to as "the king." At the time, all other freshwater fish in England were called, somewhat degradingly, "coarse fish," a name that's still used to this day.

Even when bass became known as "bass" (derived from the Old

English *baers*, which means "prickly," probably in reference to its hard, pointy dorsal fin that occasionally stabs the careless angler), they were denigrated in the literature of the upper classes. In the March 1831 issue of *American Turf Register and Sporting Magazine*, the editor, John Stuart Skinner, took this hyperbolic shot at bass and their habitat (if not the entire South itself), comparing it to "the monarch," his name for the brook trout:

> There is no comparison, none at all, between sitting with your rod in a shallop, in one of the low, marshy lagoons of the south, surrounded by huge alligators sunning themselves lazily upon blackened logs that float upon the turbid water, whose sluggish surface is not unfrequently rippled by the darting of the deadly moccasin hissing past you—and treading the bank of some beautiful, rippling brook in New England; gurgling and leaping in its living course to the ocean, with its cool, retreat for its watery tenant "under the shade of melancholy boughs," or amid the still water of an eddying pool.

Implicit in this account are some thinly veiled prejudices. The good: the industrial, forward-thinking North and the sleek, beautiful fish of the wealthy, angled primarily for sport with wispy fly rods. The bad: the agrarian, backward South, and its graceless and brutish fish of the lower classes, caught only to satisfy the basest hunger.

Fifty years after Skinner's scathing essay, James A. Henshall wrote *Book of Black Bass*, which was the first of its kind to give bass the same serious treatment as a game fish that trout had been afforded since the seventeenth century. But his efforts fell on deaf ears, at least for the fashionable fishing society, which continued to ignore the bass in favor of the trout. Theodore Roosevelt, true to his iconoclastic nature, was thought to be perhaps the only aristocrat who wanted anything to do with bass. His mental and physical disposition—pugnacious, aggressive, and full-bodied—certainly matched that of his supposed favorite finned quarry. There is some evidence that when he was governor of New York, he had a hand in stocking the lakes of his beloved Adirondack Mountains with largemouth bass and their cousins, the smallmouth, and fished for both species occasionally. But even he gave them short shrift in print: "Every hunter of the mountains and northern woods knows the many kinds of spotted trout; for the black bass he cares less," he wrote in 1893 in *The Wilderness Hunter*.

To the literate upper classes, bass were thought to be inferior quarry to trout, sought after only by uncouth southerners who lacked access to trout streams (and presumably, proper manners). Even by 1937, when Wallace W. Gallaher wrote *Black Bass Lore*, a book that celebrated the virtues of the fish, bass fishermen were still considered to be backwoods rubes hiding in their outhouses. Gallaher seemed to realize this, almost plaintively dedicating his book to "The Great Unorganized Brotherhood of Black Bass Fishermen." Trout- and fly-fishing snobs have kept this bias alive to this day. Navel-gazing literary books like *A River Runs Through It* by Norman Maclean and *Fly Fishing Through the Midlife Crisis* by Howell Raines became a movie and bestseller, respectively. There are no similar tomes about bass fishing.

But the poor misnamed and unappreciated *Micropterus salmoides* would have the last laugh.

The largemouth bass is actually not even technically a bass. It's just a big sunfish, part of the *Centrarchidae* family whose roots go back almost thirty million years. But the largemouth bass as we know it is relatively young in the evolutionary sense, coming into being around three million years ago, just as the Pliocene became the Pleistocene. The changing of epochs was a traumatic time for the earth and her creatures. The tropical climate had begun to cool with the coming of the last ice age. Tectonic shifts created an isthmus that hooked North and South America together, and the peninsula of Florida fully emerged from the depths of the Atlantic Ocean. Many species, like the saber-toothed cat and the mastodon, didn't make it through this stressful period and became extinct. But the bass held on, merely the first example of its hardy, adaptable nature. It was later in the Pleistocene that a bipedal friend of the bass would show up, one that would help spread it all over North America and the world. That friend was known as *Homo sapiens*.

Largemouth bass are indigenous only to North America. By the time the Europeans began to settle the New World, the species ranged from Florida north to Ontario and west to the Mississippi watershed. The Florida-strain bass was found only in what is now its eponymous state and perhaps southern Georgia. Every other largemouth bass in America was a northern strain, or a natural integrate of the two.

Those same Europeans would have a big hand in unwittingly pushing out their beloved salmon and trout and putting out the welcome mat for bass, because as it turned out, they liked to dam up rivers. Between the time of European settlement and 1900, there were 2,661 dams built across the United States, just a harbinger of things to come. In 1920 the Federal Power Act paved the way for engineers to use rivers as sources of power. Then came the Depression, and with it the dual need for the government to generate cheaper power and create thousands of new jobs for its destitute citizenry. From the New Deal sprang three separate dam-building entities. The Bureau of Reclamation was responsible for power generation in the west. The U.S. Army Corps of Engineers was in charge of controlling floods in the Mississippi River watershed. And agencies like the Tennessee Valley Authority did a little of both for the southeast. And the nation went on a dam-building spree like never before seen in history. Today, according to the Association of State Dam Safety Officials, more than 100,000 dams are located in the United States, making it the most "dammed" nation in the world (interpret that however you like), with a storage capacity of one billion acre-feet. Put another way, that amount would cover the entire state of Texas in six feet of water.

The result was a wide-scale shrinking of native habitat for riverine fish that need cold running water, like salmon and trout, and the creation of bigger, warmer, often muddy, still-water reservoirs, perfect habitat for you-know-who. The federal government quickly stocked these man-made lakes with bass to mollify fishermen who complained that the dams would destroy their fishing. Overnight, those griping former trout anglers became bass fishermen.

And in the mid-1940s, the Soil Conservation Service (now known as the Natural Resources Conservation Service) began to encourage farmers across the country to build ponds on their property. The idea was that these smaller bodies of water would save soil, helping to avoid another Dust Bowl era, the eight years of drought that began in 1931 and ran many farmers out of business. As an incentive, the federal government offered to stock the new ponds with fish from national hatcheries. Their favorite fish to stock? You guessed it: the resilient largemouth bass. Between 1936 and 1985, there were some three million farm ponds built across the country. Another million or so have been added since.

Largemouth bass now reside in every state in the Union, save Alaska.

After World War II, the sport of fishing in the United States boomed. Some of that had to do with money, as in people having more of it. Between 1949 and 1969, the median family income in the United States doubled just as the post-Industrial Age was affording Americans with more leisure time. From 1955 to 1970, freshwater fishing expenditures doubled to $10.3 billion, and a lot of that scratch was spent on new fishing equipment that was coming onto the market. Scientists at DuPont invented a polymer they called nylon in 1939 and shortly thereafter began marketing a new, pliable fishing line that made the precise "cast and retrieve" method of angling—as opposed to the act of trolling lures behind a boat—available to anglers, especially those fishing from the shore. With the 1945 introduction of the Zebco reel—which had a revolving spool that sharply reduced backlashes—the Zero Hour Bomb Company in Tulsa, Oklahoma, officially washed its hands of the war business and went full-throttle into the new frontier of fishing equipment. Companies like Shakespeare introduced fiberglass (and later graphite) rods in the mid-1940s, which were lighter and cheaper than their bamboo and steel forebears. A young man named Carl Kiekhaefer started a boat motor company in Fond du Lac, Wisconsin, he named Mercury after the fleet-footed messenger of the Roman gods, introducing the two-cycle, 10-horsepower Lightning in 1947. And in 1968, Forrest L. Wood and his wife, Nina, started building watercraft that had durable, lightweight fiberglass hulls. His Ranger boats remain the preferred mode of transportation for most bass anglers to this day.

With these new innovations, fishing was suddenly made simpler and more affordable to a populace with plenty of time to fish. As a result, the number of freshwater anglers in the United States tripled from 1946 to 1970, to 31 million. And the vast majority of those fishermen were after largemouth bass.

However, that "great unorganized brotherhood of bass

fishermen" from Gallaher's time remained just that, a disparate group with no unifying force or voice. That is, until a tall and lanky insurance salesman from Alabama hit the scene.

———————

Ray Scott has always been a natural salesman. According to his biography, *Bass Boss*, when he was a teenager growing up in Montgomery, Alabama, he was put in charge of fund-raising for his YMCA football team. He did such a good job at getting the local merchants to pony up dough that he got to choose his own position on the team. He, of course, decided to play quarterback, which relegated a boy with a dynamite arm named Bart Starr to the tackle position.

According to Scott, his epiphany, which to him had all the power and portent of Saul's conversion on the road to Damascus, took place in March of 1967 in a Ramada Inn in Jackson, Mississippi. Scott was an insurance salesman at the time and was in town on a little fishing holiday. But heavy rains had washed out his day on the lake, so he lay on his bed in the hotel room and turned on the television to a basketball game. As he watched the men in short, tight pants dribble up and down the court, it dawned on him that almost every sport you could ever imagine was televised. That is, except for one, which happened to be his favorite: largemouth bass fishing. Scott knew that there were minitournaments held on bass lakes across the country, which were called "derbies" at the time. But they were small affairs, disconnected and known only to hard-core locals. According to the story, Scott shot straight up and thought, "Why can't bass fishing be on TV too?"

Three months later, Ray Scott held a tournament on Arkansas's Beaver Lake with first-place prize money of $2,000. By 1968, Scott had quit the insurance business and founded the Bass Anglers Sportsman Society, known by its acronym, BASS. As part of the new organization, Scott created a magazine that functioned as a clearinghouse for all things bass, written by BASS members who shared fishing tips and their own fish tales. Today, the first issue of *Bassmaster* is described on the BASS Web site as "a grammatical monstrosity that dealt a heavy blow to the English language." Nevertheless, it finally got those millions of bass anglers out of their outhouses, providing them with the unified voice that Gallaher had so yearned for. Scott tirelessly promoted the new organization, crisscrossing the country like a presidential candidate, pressing flesh, raising sponsorship money, recruiting more members and telling everyone he saw, "I can inspire people! I can make them dance!"

BASS grew from an initial 2,000 members to 54,000 by 1972. Scott became famous for his performances at the tournament weigh-ins, for the loud, folksy style in which he introduced competing anglers and their "big 'uns" as he drawled into a microphone under his signature white cowboy hat. That year he also enacted a new rule for the tourneys, brought on by the reaction of local fishermen who were appalled by the huge stringers of dead bass and believed that the tournaments were fishing out their home lakes. Scott, ever mindful of public opinion, decided to award bonus points to anglers who released their fish alive after the weigh-ins in a campaign he called "Don't Kill What You Catch." The anglers responded by constructing aerated livewells on their boats to hold the fish until they could be released. Catch-and-release is now commonplace for all types of anglers all over the nation. Ray Scott, it turns out, was the founder of a modern conservation movement as well.

Scott sold BASS in 1986 to Helen Sevier and a group of private investors for $15 million. Afterward, he took a bit of time off, fishing his private pond in Pintlala, Alabama, with the likes of George Bush the elder and Chuck Yeager. He also hunted deer from an easy chair in an air-conditioned tree stand that had a television and a refrigerator. Scott, now seventy-one, remains the most prominent figure in the bass-fishing world, almost single-handedly responsible for the sport's phenomenal growth. "I just pricked the potential," he says, ever the zealous bass evangelist. "I lit the fire."

That fire spread rapidly. In 1971, a young tournament fisherman and part-time guide named Johnny Morris asked his father for eight feet of retail space in his liquor store to sell fishing equipment. Three years later, he sent out a catalogue to a few friends for a store he called Bass Pro Shops. "I was really just pursuing my interests from a fisherman's perspective," says Morris. "There was really a lack of availability of products. Most bass fishermen couldn't get their hands on good lures and equipment. There was this huge pent-up demand." His company now annually delivers thirty-six million catalogues worldwide, and is worth over $1 billion. The flagship store, in Springfield, Missouri, has 300,000 square feet of retail space and features a four-story waterfall, streams, and a log cabin with a working water wheel. With four million visitors a year, it is Missouri's top tourist attraction. Bass Pro Shops now has superstores in nine cities—like Detroit, Dallas, Charlotte, and Houston—with a few more on the way. "I'm pretty amazed by it all," Morris says with a chuckle.

Then in the early 1990s, a man named Irwin Jacobs picked up on the bass craze that seemed to be sweeping the nation. The former owner of the Minnesota Vikings and a well-known Wall Street takeover artist, Jacobs owned Genmar Boats, the largest recreational boat company in the world, which boasted top brands like Ranger and AquaSport. He was selling enough of them to make a fortune, but he saw another opportunity with the success of BASS. He believed there was room for another tour, but decided that he needed the backing of the biggest sponsor of them all to make it competitive. For one full year, Jacobs called the office of Lee Scott (no relation to Ray), the president of Wal-Mart, at 6:20 on the dot every morning, begging him to hear out his pitch. Lee Scott eventually gave in. "It was either that or join a witness-protection program," Scott told the *Wall Street Journal*. It was the retailing giant's first foray into sports sponsorship. "It proved that Wal-Mart is the smartest company in the world," crows Jacobs. In 1996, the Wal-Mart FLW Tour was launched, named after Forrest L. Wood, the man who founded Ranger boats.

Combined, the Bassmaster and FLW tours have 85,000 pro and amateur contestants and award $35 million annually in purse money. The tours have minted twelve millionaires and enabled another five hundred or so anglers to make a healthy living fishing for bass full-time. They've even spawned two bass-fishing fantasy leagues on the Web and a half-dozen wildly popular bass-fishing video games.

Though fishing tournaments have their roots in early twentieth-century Europe, where anglers competed in "matches" for coarse fish, the bass tours are a wholly American spectacle. Tournament anglers use outrageous technology, like boats that approach speeds of seventy-five miles an hour, global positioning systems that precisely chart their honey holes, and high-tech sonar that plumbs the depths for schools of bass. The prize money for the winner of the Bassmaster Classic, bass fishing's equivalent of the Super Bowl, is $200,000. The FLW Tour Championship doles out $500,000 to its winner. And advertisers and sponsors like CITGO, Kelloggs, Chevrolet, Pepsi, and Visa have eagerly jumped in, with their product names now adorning patches that cover every stitch of an angler's shirt. The tournament weigh-ins are now held in huge arenas and feature all of the noise and pyrotechnics of a World Wrestling Entertainment SmackDown event.

The tours have created media stars, men like Roland Martin and Bill Dance, who host their own television shows. ESPN, which bought BASS and its membership of 547,000 in 2001 for

$40 million, has eight bass-fishing shows, and the Outdoor Life Network has fifteen. One of the star anglers, Rick Clunn, upon receiving the Outstanding Achievement Award in 2002 for his glorious Bassmaster career, said in his acceptance speech: "Please don't try to make professional fishermen into heroes. Instead, just consider us examples that illustrate the American dream and the potential that exists for everyone who lives in this great country." Indeed.

Bass fishing as an American sport is said to be where NASCAR was ten years ago, just on the verge of getting even bigger, commanding more attention in the nation's sports pages and on SportsCenter. Some have even begun to refer to the entire industry as "BASSCAR." One sign of the growing popularity is the fact that the tournaments have even infiltrated the once-reluctant North, home to the trout, taking place on Lake Michigan in Chicago and Lake Champlain in Vermont.

The popularity of the tours helps explain the huge numbers of recreational participants in the United States. According to the Sporting Goods Manufacturing Association, there are now forty-four million freshwater fishermen in the United States. The U.S. Fish and Wildlife Service says that 11.3 million people in the United States are hard-core bassers who fish at least fifteen days a year, and spend $5.5 billion annually. The entire bass-fishing industry is now worth an estimated $12 billion, roughly the Gross Domestic Product of the country of Panama. And that figure doesn't even take into consideration the growing international scene, where legions of anglers in Mexico, Japan, Europe, and South Africa are just getting hooked on the sport.

But the rise of the tournaments is only one side of the story. Bass fishing is such a big sport mainly because of the fish itself. Their ubiquity certainly has something to do with their popularity. Bass are the Everyman's fish, and fishing for them is a true democratic pursuit.

Largemouth bass have other alluring characteristics. They make for good game on a rod, fighting hard for a short time before exhausting themselves quickly. They are fiercely adaptable, able to live in reservoirs, lakes, ponds, rivers, drainage ditches, and even large mud puddles. They can survive in water of up to ninety degrees Fahrenheit, making them a perfect postmillennial, global-warming fish, multiplying on earth as coldwater species like salmon decline. And the relentless assault of human development hasn't seemed to slow them down. In fact, they seem to thrive on it. All of those golf courses built in the last decade? Most of them have things called water hazards, which could easily go by another name: bass ponds. (That's why bassers Tiger Woods and Davis Love III bring fishing rods with them on the PGA Tour.) Largemouth bass are the top predator in nearly every place they are found. They are slovenly consumers of just about anything that comes across their nose, feeding out of hunger or reflex, using their outsized mouths to greedily swallow their prey whole as opposed to biting it. If they could breathe air, they would shop in malls, live in the suburbs, order out every night, and sit in front of the TV. Bass are, in short, a purely American fish.

Like the soccer moms of the early 1990s, bass dads have become their own unique demographic, with their own particular shared tastes and values. Through their participation and love of the sport of bass fishing, they are finally connected, through television, the Internet, tournaments, magazines, and word-of-mouth, in a massive, tight-knit community that neither Wallace Gallaher nor Ray Scott, in their wildest dreams, could have ever imagined. *Bassmaster* magazine has a readership of 4.2 million. There are approximately two million bass fishing–related Web sites, like *www.ultimatebass .com, www.bassfishin.com,* and *www.bassdozer.com,* most of which have chat rooms and message boards where anglers share angling techniques, reports, and stories about the big ones that did and didn't get away.

And there is one question that every one of these anglers seems to circle back to at one time or another, something that gets to the heart of the atavistic ego of the sport of fishing itself, something that every angler wants to know on a micro scale every time he gets back to the dock and engages in the one-upmanship of displaying his catch after a day spent fishing. It's a question that in and of itself is so quintessentially American: "So who the hell caught the biggest bass ever?"

The answer: a poor farm boy from Georgia named George Washington Perry.

What were history if he did not exaggerate it? How comes it that history never has to wait for facts, but for a man to write it? The ages may go on forgetting the facts never so long, he can remember two for every one forgotten. The musty records of history, like the catacombs, contain the perishable remains, but only in the breast of genius are embalmed the souls of heroes.

—Henry David Thoreau, *Thomas Carlyle and His Works*

CHAPTER FIVE
The Record Holder

In April of 2004, I went down to Augusta, Georgia, the week after the Masters golf tournament had been played there. The town was still in the throes of spring, ablaze in blooming dogwoods and azaleas. It was bigger than I expected, busy with traffic and shopping malls, with a municipal airport (the same one that Tiger Woods and Phil Mickelson use as their private runway during Masters week) in the thick of it all. On a quiet backstreet on the sleepier side of town, I met Bill and Beatrice Baab in the two-story house that they've lived in since the 1960s. The house is a testament to their insatiable curiosity for things old and unusual. Every room is packed to the ceiling with various knickknacks: antique soda, liquor, and ink bottles that they've rummaged out of the dumps of rural Georgia towns; wild, multicolored jugs and kiln-fired pottery picked up at roadside flea markets; dusty books that range from dime-store westerns to rare first editions; and—stacked like a copse of bamboo shoots in the corner of the pantry—fishing rods of various lengths and utility. Their dog, a Yorkie named Princess Augusta Tickletummy, has free rein over the back part of the house, flitting in and out of the crowded rooms like a ubiquitous clerk in a cluttered hardware store.

Bill and Bea met in 1965 after she moved down to Augusta from Massachusetts to become a physical therapist. They have been married for thirty-eight years and have a type of gentle, understated marital equilibrium and bond that's based, in large part, on their shared love of history and inveterate collecting. Bea, who has a sweet round face that's frequently lit up with a big smile, is sixty-nine and still retains strong traces of her New England accent, despite having lived the past forty-five years in the Deep South. She told me I should move my "cahh" from the street and "pahk" it in the driveway. Bill is also sixty-nine years old, 6'6" and trim, with a slight stoop to his shoulders. On and off since 1958, he has been an outdoor editor of the *Augusta Chronicle*, a newspaper with a circulation of 100,000. Now in semiretirement, he still edits the fishing page once a week. He never went to college, instead teaching himself to write by indulging in a lifelong love and habit of reading.

In 1984, the State of Georgia decided to erect a monument commemorating the poor farm boy who caught the world-record largemouth bass fifty-two years earlier from Montgomery Lake near the town of Helena. State officials asked Bill, as a leading fishing newspaper editor, to be the master of ceremonies at its dedication. Bill, who had met George Perry in 1959 and carried a lifelong interest in his fish, jumped at the chance. He contacted the surviving members of the Perry family, including George's widow, who were all present for the dedication. The ceremony took place on the side of Rural Route 112 in Georgia's Telfair County. Doing research for that monument led Bill into the most abiding passion of his history-hunting and collecting life: the tale of George Wash-

The man who initiated the chase, George Perry, in 1934 with a mount of his *Field & Stream* contest-winning 13-pound, 14-ounce bass—nearly 9 pounds less than the record setter he caught two years earlier. (Bill Baab Collection)

J.J. Hall's grocery store in Helena, Georgia, where George Perry first showed off his world-record bass in 1932. (Bill Baab Collection)

George Perry's family with a fiberglass replica of his world-record fish in 1984. From left: his daughters, Celina Brown and Barbara Williams; his widow, Pauline Perry; and his sister, Rubye Latham. (Bill Baab Collection)

Bill Baab, the world's leading authority on the story of George Perry, and its fiercest protector, in his study in Augusta, Georgia. Baab is holding a replica of the Creek Chub Wiggle Fish, the lure used to catch the world-record largemouth bass.

LAPD motorcycle cop Bob Crupi and his 22-pound, ½-ounce bass, the second-largest of all time, in 1991. (Bill Baab Collection)

Bob Crupi sits alone on Castaic Lake in southern California in July, 2003, the site where he caught two fish over 21 pounds twelve years earlier.

A bumper sticker sold in the gift shop of the Texas Freshwater Fisheries Center in Athens, Texas.

Mike Long, perhaps the most accomplished big-bass angler alive, holding a 14-pound bass on Lake Jennings, outside of San Diego.

John Kerr, the silent half of the "Long-Kerr" duo, displays a 15-pound bass on Lake Jennings.

Jed Dickerson, who landed the fourth-largest bass of all time
in 2003, manning a rental boat on San Diego County's Lake Poway.

Mac Weakley, gambler and possessor of the thirteenth-largest
bass ever recorded, on a boat on Lake Dixon, a small drinking-water
reservoir near San Diego that harbors enormous bass.

Mike Winn, aka "Buddha," the third member of the Dickerson-Weakley-
Winn trio, working the motor on Lake Dixon.

Boutique lure-maker Jerry Rago displays two of his swimbait creations on Lake Jennings.

Mickey Ellis, owner of 3:16 Lure Company and the mad genius of bass lure-making, holding two of his soft plastic swimbaits in his workshop near Mission Viejo, California.

Mickey Ellis's $316 hard plastic swimbait, dubbed the Armageddon.

Fisheries biologist David Campbell in the Lunker Bunker at the Texas Freshwater Fisheries Center in Athens, Texas, showing off a cylinder in which he hopes to hatch the world-record bass.

Allen Forshage, the director of the Texas Freshwater Fisheries Center in Athens, Texas, and the lead architect of the Lone Star State's plan to breed the next world-record bass.

Porter Hall's shack on his seven-acre pond in Mississippi in which he is attempting to grow the world-record bass.

Philip M. Jay, perhaps the most infamous big-bass fisherman in the world, holding what he claims was a 24-pound, 1-ounce bass. This fish would have bettered Perry's record by almost 2 pounds. Jay's fish was never certified.

Samuel Yera, daydreamer and perhaps the best bass fisherman in Cuba, on the forbidden island's Lake Hanabanilla, rumored to be the hideout of the world-record bass.

ington Perry and his world-record bass. He has become, in the process, the world's undisputed leading authority on the subject.

On the afternoon I arrived, we all went up to the second floor of the house, which consists of one large room that the Baabs have converted into a sprawling office space, with two computers on desks at opposite sides of the floor. This room, too, is full of books and bottles. Various plaques hang on the walls, commemorating the writing awards that Bill has won over the years, and, sitting on a table is an old Royal typewriter that he occasionally still uses. While Bea played solitaire on her computer and Princess Augusta Tickletummy barked for attention, Bill reached under his desk and pulled out two large cardboard boxes packed full of his twenty years of accumulated research on George Washington Perry. They contained articles that he had written for various magazines and his newspaper, along with every other story about Perry that he could get his hands on. Black-and-white photographs of Perry, spanning every era of his life from his childhood until just before his death, spilled out of the overstuffed file folders. There were also lures. He had a replica of the one that landed the world-record bass, the Creek Chub Wiggle Fish, that actually came from George Perry's tacklebox. He also had a real 1932 Wiggle Fish. He had letters that Perry himself had written to the Creek Chub Company in Garrett, Indiana. We spent the afternoon talking about Perry and his record, with Bea occasionally chiming in from across the room, finishing one of Bill's sentences.

Bill sat behind his desk in gray slacks and a short-sleeved oxford shirt, frequently touching his head with his hands and closing his eyes before answering a question, as if he was actually picturing in his mind the stories he was sharing with me. After a few hours, as the late-afternoon light on his gentle face faded through the window behind his desk, Bill said it was time to have his daily, pre-dinner Jack Daniel's and ginger ale, something he has "to relapse . . . I mean *relax*." We needed to eat soon so we could get some rest. Tomorrow we would be leaving at the crack of dawn to make the three-and-a-half-hour drive down to Telfair County to see the lake from which the world-record bass came 72 years ago.

On the morning of June 2, 1932, George Washington Perry awoke to the sound of a thunderclap. His mother, Laura; sister, Rubye; brother, Jim; and Jim's wife and child slept on, their gentle breaths mingling with the raindrops that pattered soothingly on the aluminum roof of the one-story house, the former quarters of a nineteenth-century sharecropper. Heavy, waterlogged clouds darkened the sky. A perfect day to sleep in. But George willed his sore shoulders and legs out of bed. He pulled on jeans, then tiptoed around the maze of beds into the kitchen and gently closed the door behind him. George liked being the first one awake. He was the man of the house now.

He boiled a pot of coffee on the woodstove, careful to remove the kettle just before the steam whistled through the hole in the spout. His mother had left some hard-boiled eggs on the table, which he peeled carefully and dipped into a glass saucer of salt. This had been his morning ritual throughout the spring: rising before the sun, wolfing down some breakfast, then heading out to the barn to saddle up the old ornery plow mule. For three straight months, George had labored behind the slow but reliable mule, standing on the metal plow or walking alongside, tilling the sandy brown-black soil, his shoulders aching in the hot and humid air. It had been a slow process, the plowing, then the seeding of row upon row of corn and cotton. But the planting was almost done now. The others pitched in after they awoke. He couldn't do it all by himself. But he was always the first out in the morning and the last in the house in the evening. He wanted to set an example, to prove something.

It was the first spring without his father, George Sr., who had finally succumbed to cancer in December, just after the harvest. His decline had been brutal and ugly. The cancer from his father's lungs had spread all over his body, horribly disfiguring his once-handsome face, and he had spent his last days turning and tossing in the sweaty cotton sheets of his bed, his moans sometimes turning into shrieks of utter agony. George's mother and sister attended to him night and day, but could do little other than wipe his brow with cool, damp towels, whisper gently into his ear, and give him an aspirin in the hopes that he could keep it down. George worked harder and longer in the fields those days, seeking refuge from the horror in the house. Cancer was no way for a man to go, George decided. The cruel withering away of sound body and mind, the loss of all dignity, and the suffering—both his father's and his family's—was almost too much to bear. When I go, George always said, God willing, it will be quick. The first thing George had done after his father was buried in the Georgia earth was rid the house of all cigarettes and ashtrays. No one in his family would ever smoke in his presence again.

George sipped his black coffee and stared out of the rain-streaked window onto the plowed fields that flattened the horizon for a quarter-mile to the hardwood forest. There would be no planting today. The rain had turned the rows of soil into a thick dark-brown soup. He looked at the barn, where the old mule poked out his black nose and shaggy light-brown mane, ready for another slow, hard, hot day in the fields. "Nothing for you today, you lazy old brute," George said softly, "not in this gully-washer. Go back to sleep." George penciled a note to his mother and left it on the table. He took one more gulp of coffee and walked out into the summer rainshower without a jacket, down the rocky driveway. The twenty-year old—still very much a boy, tall, with a slim build and bright blue intelligent eyes just like his father's—was off to his friend Jack Page's house. They were going fishing.

Fishing, for men like George Perry and Jack Page in 1932, was not in a strict sense a recreational activity. These men still had to put food on the table every day. To be sure, a day on the water was better than any of the backbreaking ones in the field. But this day, dawning as it did with the serious push of rain, had an ominous feel to it. "We were crazy to go out anywhere in that weather," George said later. But they drove on anyway in Jack's 1930 Ford Model A truck, splashing through brown mud puddles on Rural Route 112 on the twenty-mile ride through the green-breasted late-spring beauty of Telfair County. They were headed to Montgomery Lake, an oxbow of the Ocmulgee River, where George and Jack had left a handmade 14-foot boat, built with maybe fifty cents' worth of cast-off wooden barn boards.

The ominous mood may have transcended the weather. The world in 1932 was in the throes of its own dark storm that would last for almost a decade longer. The day before, on June 1, the stock market had reached what would be the market bottom of the Great Depression, and millions of Americans had lost all hope of ever recouping their life's savings. An ambitious and charismatic young politician named Adolf Hitler was only eight months away from his appointment as the chancellor of the German Reichstag. About the only man in America fishing for pleasure was President Herbert Hoover, who, oppressed by the demands of Washington, D.C., frequently left the capital to fish for trout on the Rapidan River in Virginia. He would pay dearly for his nonchalance, with the sound beating he took from Franklin Delano Roosevelt in the 1932 election and in the cold assessment of history. Some good news was peppered among the grim headlines:

Just two weeks earlier, Amelia Earhart had become the first woman to fly solo across the Atlantic. And Babe Ruth was swatting the New York Yankees to the World Series, his last.

It's likely that George and Jack knew very little of the recent headlines. They would have had no reason to keep up with current affairs. While the Depression destroyed the lives of many, it had little, if any, effect on subsistence farmers in the backwoods of Georgia. As George put it, "We lived three creeks farther back in the woods than anybody else." The nearest place with a name was Jacksonville, Georgia, and there wasn't much there but a lonely crossing of two rural roads. Helena was the only real town for miles. There the locals congregated at J.J. Hall's store to chew over current events. But there was rarely any reason for George and Jack to go there. Well, almost never a reason.

George Perry was remarkable for reasons that go well beyond what he accomplished that day in June of 1932. He was in many ways the embodiment of the triumph of the Depression generation, a generation that fashioned good, full lives from the depths of despair. George, like many Americans then and now, was faced with Job-like obstacles in his life, which he always seemed to overcome through self-will. He was no Horatio Alger hero, but he did become successful beyond the wildest dreams of a farm boy from rural Georgia. Rising from the dry dirt of extreme poverty, he taught himself how to be successful, carving out his rightful place among the great American middle class of the 1950s and '60s. In the process, he passed on to his children the tools, and perhaps more importantly, the belief that they too could succeed. His life is arguably a truer representation of the American dream than any story of Horatio Alger's ever will be.

As the man of the house, George struggled to keep his farm

afloat, but three years after that rainy day in 1932, he lost that battle when the bank foreclosed on his property—a common occur-
rence in the days before World War II. George moved to Pearson,
Georgia, where he worked as a mail guard at a railroad station. He
quickly realized that there was not much upward mobility in that
job, so he moved again, this time to Brunswick, Georgia, a coastal
industrial town halfway between the major seaports of Savannah
and Jacksonville, Florida. By this time, George had taken a wife
and started his own family. According to Jim Paulk, who grew up
in Brunswick and knew the Perry family, George worked for a
while at Brunswick Pulp & Paper Company, but left after a short
stint to work for the town's fastest-growing industry: boat manufacturing, which boomed before and during the war in both the
commercial and military markets. George took a job at the ship-
yard, putting to use his good hands that had built and rebuilt
everything on the farm. He was not drafted, the government be-
lieving his skills were best utilized on the home front, manufacturing the Liberty ships that delivered everything from toilet paper to
warplanes to Europe and the Far East. Ten years later, he started
his own Chris-Craft boat dealership and raised his family, which
by this time included his wife, two boys, and two girls. But a
tragedy, the second in George's life, was just around the corner.

George's eldest son, Emory, was a tall and handsome seventeen
years old, a popular boy fawned over by the girls at Brunswick
High School. In some ways, Emory was to be George's finest
achievement. He would graduate that year, 1958, the first in the
family to do so, something George was immensely proud of, as his
own formal education had ended after the eighth grade. Emory,
like his father, was also infatuated with all things mechanical, especially planes and automobiles, and was thrilled when his father
brought home the family's second car, a rebuilt 1949 Ford sedan.

Emory had just received his driver's license, and he drove around town in that sedan for hours on end.

One muggy summer evening, a classmate challenged Emory to a drag race on a lonely back road, a thrilling high-risk activity made popular by movie-idol James Dean in *Rebel Without a Cause*, which had premiered three years earlier. Emory didn't back down. He liked to drive fast, to take these machines to their limits, and he was, by all accounts, good behind the wheel. The two boys lined up their cars, someone gave the sign, and they took off. According to accounts by witnesses, the other boy's car veered into Emory's on a corner, knocking him off the road. His car flipped once, and Emory was thrown from the driver's seat. With a second flip, the car landed on top of him, killing him instantly. George was called to the scene. The accident almost killed him, too.

George had not only lost his father at a young age, but was deprived of seeing his eldest son grow to be a man. But he reacted to this tragedy like he had to all the others he had faced: with determination and action. George decided to honor his eldest son by getting into aviation, one of his son's abiding interests. He set himself to learning the trade at the airport in Jacksonville, Florida, then eventually opened up a repair shop at the Brunswick Airpark. In the process, this man with only an eighth-grade education taught himself to fly, practicing touch-and-go's on the long, flat, hard beaches of the islands near Brunswick—St. Simons, Jekyll, and Cumberland (which would be the site of John F. Kennedy Jr.'s wedding almost forty years later). Soon thereafter, George became the owner of the airpark and ran his own charter business, flying shipbuilding tycoons to Jacksonville, politicians to Atlanta, and steel barons to Birmingham, usually in the company of his mutt dog, Blockhead, whom he called "Block."

It became one of the happiest times in his life. And George was not above having fun. A couple of times a year, he and his pilot buddies would take out their planes and stage faux dogfights over the marshes of Glynn County in the World War II style. They would "flat-hat," running the planes so close to the marsh that you could hear the tires hitting the grasses as they chased and tailed each other, registering mock "kills." George and Block, in their J-3 Piper Cub, were the unquestioned aces of the airpark. Neighbors used to watch the planes buzz over the marshes from the safe havens of their homes.

George was nearing his sixties. He had developed a paunch by then, but his easy, blue-eyed grin remained unchanged. He was a man of seemingly incongruous traits—happy, with a great sense of humor, but also stubborn and rebellious when it came to authority. His personality could be summed up by the sign he had on a windowsill behind the desk in his office at the airpark. It said, simply and playfully, STUPIDVISER.

George loved and was loved by children, all of whom he called "frogskins," and took a special interest in teaching kids to repair and handle boats and planes. His son George L. Perry, who goes by the name "Dazy" (a truncated form of the nickname his father gave him—"Lazy Dazy"—because he slept so much as an infant) took a special interest in flying. On his father's lap, he did touch-and-go landings on the surrounding islands, and made his first unassisted landing at age twelve. In the 1960s the two of them flew to Alaska—stopping every few hours to refuel—to go hunting.

Dazy, now sixty, got his license at sixteen, and became a Delta pilot at twenty. On his business card, underneath the Delta Airlines logo and his name, are two words: "Numero Uno." Dazy was, until he retired in 2003, Delta Airlines' number-one pilot, flying the most prestigious plane, the 777, across the Atlantic to Europe. He says he owes it all to the patient teachings of his father.

George was also loved by adults, who prized his honesty and humor and became fiercely loyal to him. One friend, George J. Gray, described Perry in his eulogy as "having a twinkle in his eye that said, 'Let's get serious, but not too dern serious.' "

But George hated authority, especially when it interfered with his business. The Federal Aviation Authority in particular became his sworn enemy. One year, the FAA enacted a new rule that said any plane over 1,200 pounds would have to give them a cut of any charter money. George thought it unfair that they get a piece of something he worked so hard to obtain. When he won the bid to fly the Jacksonville Suns minor league baseball team to their away games, he decided to actually lease the plane to the team, thereby circumventing the FAA rules. One year he also salvaged a Navy plane that had been rusting for years on a beach in the Bahamas. When he got it back to Brunswick, someone claimed he stole it. The FAA investigated. Perry won every legal battle he had with the FAA, but the larger war with them continued throughout his life.

George never lost sight of the hardships of his upbringing, even in the late 1960s, when the interest in his world-record fish began to grow. A handful of sportswriters across the country began to track him down, showing up at his doorstep, trying to get an interview. His legend was growing in stature every day as bass fishing began its ascent into the national consciousness, and as sportswriters and bass fisherman started to wonder who this farmer was who had caught the record almost forty years ago. George never really liked talking about himself, so he generally shied away from interviews. But a few got through. Vic Dunaway wrote the first major article about George in 1969 in *Sports Afield*, but left many questions unanswered, questions that would unlock many of the secrets and myths of George's huge bass. In 1973 Ray Scott sent a writer named Terry Drace to Brunswick to do an interview with George for *Bassmaster* magazine. Scott gave Drace one command that he believed would answer the biggest question of all. He instructed him to set up a polygraph test and ask George to verify his bass.

When George and Jack reached Montgomery Lake, the water was already high and turning the color of coffee with cream. The rain still fell hard. At times, all fisherman knew, rain could actually improve the fishing, particularly when it had just started and the lake had begun to rise. The commotion on the surface sometimes stirred the fish, and the rising water washed in food from the banks, like insects and terrestrial animals. It had been raining all night and day, though, and the lake was on the verge of a blowout. But they had driven all the way there, so they carried on.

George sat in the middle of the boat and manned the oars. Jack gave it a push off the bank and jumped into the bow. George slowly paddled the boat near the shore, careful to keep the oars quiet. Thick-trunked cypress trees, dripping with spongy Spanish moss, stood in the shallows. Their intertwined roots, called cypress knees, poked out of the water and provided excellent cover for largemouth bass. Jack took a few casts toward the cypress trunks. The lure they were using that day was a Wiggle Fish, number 2401, the latest creation from the Creek Chub Company in Garrett, Indiana. Though somewhat primitive by today's standards, the lure was still remarkable for its lifelike features. The 2401 was designed to imitate a perch—a forage fish for big bass—with shiny, black epoxy eyes, and olive bars on the side of the body. The body of the lure was jointed in the middle to give it the wiggling motion of a baitfish. The metal lip protruding under the lure's chin kept it straight as it swam just under the surface. It cost eighty-five cents, in those days a king's ransom, and was their only lure.

The boys saw nothing promising in the early going, and the day had begun to have a sinking, fishless feeling. At this point, they were primarily focused on not losing the Wiggle Fish in the thicket of cypress knees. The only thing worse than not catching any fish would be to lose their only lure. Earlier that year, the two men had been out in the boat and George had hooked a jack, or chain pickerel, a toothy, submarine-shaped predator of the shallows. The fish had taken the lure hard and run for the bottom. The line had popped, snapping the rod straight. Their only lure was gone. As they glumly paddled back to shore, they heard a splash in the water behind them. The pickerel had come to the surface and spit the lure, which bobbed unattached on the surface. They paddled back out and retrieved it.

Fishless after an hour, Jack handed the rod to George. George took a few casts. Then, out of the corner of his eye, he spotted a rippling in the water. He threw a cast toward it. George's only recorded play-by-play of what happened next appeared in Dunaway's 1969 *Sports Afield* story:

> I don't remember many of the details but all at once the water splashed everywhere. I do remember striking, then raring back and trying to reel. But nothing budged. I thought for sure I had lost the fish—that he'd dived and hung me up. I had no idea how big the fish was, but that didn't matter. What had me worried was losing the lure.

George goes on to describe the rest of the fight as a "quick tussle." The fish came to the boat quite quickly, as truly enormous fish, paradoxically, are sometimes wont to do. With both arms

George scooped the fish into the boat. It was the biggest fish either man had ever seen. But the fact that it was a potential world record never crossed either man's mind. "The first thing I thought of was how nice a chunk of meat to take home," George told Dunaway.

But they didn't go home at first. They paddled back to shore, secured the boat, and put the fish under a burlap sack in the back of the truck. They drove on Rural Route 149 to Helena, a town with a post office, county jail, a church, a schoolhouse, and J.J. Hall's store.

George and Jack pulled up to J.J. Hall's twenty minutes later, intending to do what most fisherman want to do when they catch a big fish: show it off. They brought it into the store where Jesse Hall, the proprietor, stood behind the long front counter inside. He also happened to be a public notary. He took out a measuring tape. The fish was 32.5 inches long and 28.5 inches around. Then they took it to the post office across the street and weighed it on a government-certified scale. It read "22 pounds, 4 ounces." No one there knew it was the world record, but they sent in the details to *Field & Stream* magazine, which was running a big-bass contest that year.

George showed off the fish to a few others who wandered into J.J. Hall's, then he and Jack drove home. His family wasn't quite as impressed as the men at the store, but George didn't mind. He had accomplished what he had set out to do: provide his family with food. "I never thought about mounting it or taking a picture," he said. He cleaned the fish, using a sharp hunting knife to slice open the belly. Hundreds of amber-colored eggs came out. He carefully cut from the back down to the tail on both sides, creating two extremely large fillets. His mother, Laura, fried up one side for dinner that night and served it along with corn bread and some onions and tomatoes from the garden. It fed the family of six. They had the other side for dinner the next night. They reported that the bass tasted a little "fishy."

George Perry's fish would be the last officially recorded large-mouth bass over 18 pounds that was caught primarily for food.

George won the *Field & Stream* contest. The prize was seventy-five dollars' worth of gear—a Browning automatic shotgun, some shells, and some clothes—quite a haul in those days. In 1934, he would win the contest again with a 13-pound, 14-ounce bass caught on the Altahama River near Brunswick. That same year, the magazine would formally recognize his 1932 fish as the world-record black bass, surpassing Fritz Friebel's 20-pound, 2-ounce fish caught in Florida's Big Fish Lake in 1923. George was offi-cially the best big-bass fisherman in the world, but he thought lit-tle of it at the time and was amused at the attention he would eventually garner in the late 1960s and early '70s. "Daddy never thought the record was any big deal," says his eldest daughter, Bar-bara, who lives near Savannah. "He never felt comfortable with the attention."

The story of George Washington Perry and his world-record largemouth bass has been told and retold many times, in newspapers and magazines and television shows and on lakeshores across the United States and even overseas. It's easy to see why writers and fishermen take so much joy in recounting it. The circumstances— a poor farm boy, a handmade boat, a rainy washout, and the biggest bass ever recorded—make it all almost seem like a fable or some great frontier myth, like the tale of Paul Bunyan. Like any story told over and over, it takes on different iterations with al-most every retelling. One of the reasons for this is that there has never been a credible eyewitness account. No one knows who Jack Page was or what happened to him after that day, only that his name is mentioned as George's fishing partner. One theory is that the two men had a falling out over George's winnings and notoriety, which, of course, Jack had played a large part in securing. But those who knew George say he was always kind and humble and that it was very unlikely that he wouldn't have shared some of the booty with his best fishing buddy, Jack Page, who has disappeared into history like the early morning mist over a Georgia swamp.

And there are only two written stories, Dunaway's and Drace's, that actually used George Perry as a primary source. Perry himself rarely talked about the world-record fish, even with his own children. "I kept meaning to ask my father about that day he caught the fish and I never did," says son Dazy. "Then, boom, he was gone. I could kick my own ass."

Some have always doubted the story's veracity. They make the fair argument that by today's exacting standards, George's fish would have never passed muster. Too many variables are left unaccounted for. There was no mount of the fish, no existing photograph, no physical remains. The measurements seem all wrong, too long for a largemouth bass, and they vary in many accounts. Naysayers point to the fact that Perry lived in an unscientific time, that he easily could have faked the measurements and sent them in. They point out the fact that only one largemouth bass of over 17 pounds (an 18-pound, 1-ounce fish) has come out of the state of Georgia since. One prominent bass expert, Doug Hannon, a writer and angler known as the Bass Professor, has repeatedly cast doubts on George's fish. Hannon suggested in an article he wrote for *In-Fisherman* in 1983 that George's air-freight business allowed him access to Florida and some commercially netted fish, which have been reported to be that big. He told *Southern Outdoors* in 1996 that "the Perry fish was never documented to my satisfaction. There are no photos of the fish. There were striped bass in the river system that feeds Montgomery Lake, and I suspect the fish was a striper rather than a largemouth." Striped bass can reach weights of up to 70 pounds. Hannon is hardly alone in his skepticism. Bob Crupi is only one of a number of big-bass fishermen who thinks the story is merely a legend.

And this is where Bill Baab steps in. The more he researched the story of George Perry, he says, the more he became convinced that it was absolutely true. "One of the reasons I got into it was that I kept running into myths. Some people were claiming that they saw Perry that day with the fish even though they say they saw him in a county that's two hundred miles away," he says. "The further I got in, the more I became sort of a self-appointed guardian." That job included refuting claims that he saw printed in various publications, including a long rebuttal he wrote to *In-Fisherman* after Hannon published his story. In that letter, he made the convincing point that when George Perry caught his fish, he was twenty years old, twenty-five years away from opening his air-freight business and becoming an aviator, thus in no position to fly down to Florida and pick up a fish. About the naysayers, Bill says, "It's baloney. *Field & Stream* would never have verified the fish. They didn't just send seventy-five dollars' worth of gear to just anyone. And anyway, these folks, George and the rest, were country boys and fishermen. They knew what a largemouth bass was." As for the record, Bill says he has no doubt that it's true, but of course, without seeing it himself, "you still have to take it on faith."

Bill explained this to me as we began the three-and-a-half-hour drive from his house in Augusta to Telfair County. Bill and I sat in the front of his cramped Nissan Sentra, while Bea crocheted in the back with Princess Augusta Tickletummy perched in her lap. We took the back roads, since there really aren't any other types in this part of the state. Bill drove sixty miles per hour the whole way. "If you stay at sixty, the cops don't pay you any mind," he says. "If you go sixty-five, they'll give you a look. At seventy, they'll pull you over." Bea says Bill drives slowly because he's always watching the roadside and will frequently stop the car to help a turtle across the road or chase butterflies. Outside of the window passed the poor beauty of the country South: the pecan trees and budding azaleas and the Spanish moss that hung in branches like tinsel on a Christmas tree.

We arrived in the town of Helena and went to the Chamber of Commerce so I could get some information. Bill introduced himself to the woman there, and everyone he met that day, telling the story of George Perry—a story he knows by heart. He let everyone know that I was writing something about the man. Bill has spent a lot of time making sure that Telfair County gives out information on Perry, erecting more monuments that describe what had happened here so long ago, keeping the story alive.

We went to the main drag, still only a two-lane road. The town appears, with the exception of a handful of fast-food restaurants, like it was in 1932. On a row of abandoned storefronts and windows taped up with cardboard boxes is a small white façade with the words FOWLER'S STORE above it. It is the old J.J. Hall's store where Perry weighed his fish. We followed that road for a while. Many of the front yards we passed had placards with the Ten Commandments written on them. We pulled over to visit Charlie Grimsley, an eighty-year-old man sporting a row of silver front teeth and wearing bright red suspenders over his barreled chest. Charlie used to work at the sewage plant in town. When he retired, he took scrap metal, turned it into sculptures, and put the art in his front yard.

We saw an old cannon that had a mailbox on the end of its barrel, two roosters with red heads made from pitchforks, a metal wire stick-figure man swinging a golf club. And up above everything else, on a revolving wheel, was a man in a boat with a fishing rod. A metal wire attached the fishing rod to a giant bass made out of metal scraps. As the wheel turned, the man reared back on the rod, pulling the wire tight on the fish. "I had a friend in McRae who said I should build a big fish being caught, being that Telfair County is home to the world-record bass and all," Charlie says. He made it from scratch in 1997, and will turn it on for any curious motorist who stops by. He creates all of his art in his shop, a roughly twenty-by-six-foot half of a metal cylinder which was fashioned out of an old sewage treatment tank. After we said good-bye and drove away, we passed a green roadside sign that proclaimed this area GEORGIA'S TECHNOLOGY CORRIDOR. Since I saw no signs of technology startups—or anything else for that matter—on the side of the road, I assumed the sign was in reference to Charlie.

After lunch, Bill, Bea, Princess Augusta Tickletummy, and I drove a stretch of country road down to Montgomery Lake, located in the Horse Creek Wildlife Management Area. We turned off the pavement and traveled a few miles down a dirt logging road. When the going got too rough for the Sentra, we hopped in with Mike Geihsler, a Department of Natural Resources fisheries biologist, who had a truck. We parked and walked the last hundred yards.

At one time eons ago, the Ocmulgee River actually flowed through what is now Montgomery Lake, creating what's known as an oxbow. Since the river channel is still gradually shifting away and constantly creating a new channel, Montgomery Lake has fallen on hard times, often deprived of fresh water. The day I saw it, it looked like a small fetid mud puddle. Mike says that with heavy rains, it can fill up again, but that happens pretty rarely. Very few people ever come back here to fish, he says. Around the lake, along with the chiggers and mosquitoes, hundreds of pretty white and yellow honeysuckle flowers were in full bloom, and the cypress trees with their knees poking out of the water were still there, along with a plaque that was erected on the bank that very few people see these days. Bill brought down a rod with his Creek Chub Wiggle Fish replica and posed for a picture by the plaque. I asked him if he was going to take a cast with his lure. "No way," he said. "I don't want to lose it in those cypress trees."

On the drive back to Augusta, Bill told me about how he had met George Perry once, back in 1959, when the Brunswick Chamber of Commerce had hosted a writer's conference. The idea was for the state's outdoor writers to get to know the area's hunting and fishing opportunities in the hopes that they would give it some column inches. Bill says that the writers spent the day fishing some local water and then retired to Bennie's Red Barn for a barbeque dinner with some local dignitaries. He remembers that there was nothing unusual about the dinner, just men eating and talking about fishing. Right after dinner, they moved to the porch for drinks. Then the local host walked up and, over the din of men's chatter, announced that he'd like to introduce someone. A man with hair graying at his temples, a slight paunch, and smiling blue eyes stood beside him. "Boys, this is George Perry," the host said. Bill and the other writers were dumbstruck. They all knew of course who he was, but couldn't believe that he'd been dining among them and they hadn't realized it. "He stood there and answered a few questions with a pleasant, bemused smile," recalls Bill. "He was there for about thirty minutes." They didn't know it at the time, but Bill and the other writers had the biggest fish in their grasp, only to let him off the hook. "We asked him some questions, but not the right questions," Bill says. Those questions unasked included things like who Jack Page was, if there were any other eyewitnesses, what type of rod and reel he was using. "No one knew that we wouldn't be able to talk to him again."

The record, Bill says, has become so important because it's lasted so long. Breaking it, he says, "is probably the dream of every angler on this continent and others." George Perry's record is important to him, too, as the guardian of its legacy. Though he said he would be pleased to see a new record, as long as it was done legitimately, I hoped, for Bill's sake, for the work and stewardship and part of his soul that he's put in for the last twenty years, for his general break-your-heart gentleness, that George Perry would hold on to the record for the rest of his lifetime.

The morning of January 23, 1974, was cool and misty on the coast of Georgia. George had spent the last two days doing a routine inspection on an eight-year-old Cessna for a wealthy dentist in Birmingham, who in return offered to fix George's front right tooth, which was chipped at a forty-five-degree angle. The dentist wanted the plane back that day. George jumped into the pilot's seat. He lifted the plane smoothly off the runway in Brunswick, flying one last time into the "emerald twilight, over the glooms of live oaks" that ringed the poet Sidney Lanier's "wide sea-marshes of Glynn." The flight to Birmingham was four hundred air miles, one that George had done maybe fifty times in his life. He could fly the route without any instruments, just by following the landmarks of the sleepy towns below, but never did. As he neared Birmingham, at 11:30 a.m., he requested landing instructions from the Birmingham airport. The tower operator reported that there was a storm ahead, but that the transponder would lead him in. George flew on, a child of the Depression made good, an American success story for so many more important reasons than the fish he had caught almost forty-two years earlier.

His interview with Terry Drace for *Bassmaster* magazine would be published a month later, in February, the most comprehensive story written about him to date, reporting that he was "alive and well." The story would answer some questions about his fish, but raise a few more. Drace, the writer, had not followed Ray Scott's orders. He didn't ask George about taking a polygraph test. Ray Scott would fire Drace shortly thereafter. George had always smiled about the fuss people made over his fish. It was, after all, just a damn fish.

Then the plane bounced violently to the right. What the hell was that? he must have wondered. The tower, relying on the relatively new technology of the transponder, had vectored him into a squall. Outside, the gray day suddenly turned black and blue. George could no longer see the towns below. The plane was jolted again, this time so hard he couldn't hold the controls. There was a blinding flash of lightning. "I'm having trouble descending," was George's last transmission to the tower. Then they lost him on the radar. There was a deafening thunderclap. And George Perry's plane slammed into the north slope of Shades Mountain on the outskirts of Birmingham.

I was a religion major in college, and one of the things I studied is a school of thought in theology that interprets certain parts of the Bible—especially in the Old Testament—not as literal stories, but as myth-histories, or in academic speak, stories that are "profoundly true." That is, there might not have been an evil talking snake in a garden, or a parting of an entire sea, or a tower that reached up into the heavens, but the details in those cases aren't the point. Instead, these stories are meant to impart some knowledge: of the divine, of some explanation for His will and design, and of some lessons for man.

The George Perry story is, in many ways, the Genesis chapter of the world-record bass chase. I started to think that maybe the George Perry story—true or not—could be interpreted the same way. Maybe it's a lesson from the bass gods that the world record is meant to come from the masses, given to someone of their choosing, perhaps again a poor farmer whose main purpose for fishing is food. Perhaps the lesson, too, is that lusting after the record for the record's sake is a perversion, a false god. A modern-day bass theologian might say that the sport has become idolatrous, full of heathens, and that record chasers should be instead working on their boats, on the lookout for a big flood.

If indeed the George Perry story is meant to be a myth-history, a story that functions as a canonical lesson with a moral that's meant to be heeded by the masses, there are some folks out there who just aren't listening.

I dearly love the state of Texas, but I consider that a harmless perversion on my part, and discuss it only with consenting adults.

—Molly Ivins

CHAPTER SIX
Bigger IS Better

After the grisly University of Texas sniper attacks in 1966, Pete Hamill wrote in the *Boston Globe* that, "There is a growing feeling that perhaps Texas *is* really another country, a place where the skies, the disasters, the diamonds, the politicians, the women, the fortunes, the football players and the murders are all bigger than anywhere else." If the aspirations of Allen Forshage and David Campbell ever become a reality, one could tack on to Hamill's list the sentiment I saw on a bumper sticker on FM (that's farm-to-market in Texas parlance) 2495 in Henderson County: TEXAS: WHERE EVERYTHING IS BIG, ESPECIALLY OUR "BASS."

It's impossible to come to grips with Texas without first tackling the state's well-perpetuated myths and clichés about itself. All the unavoidable talk of courage and loyalty and largesse have the strange effect of simultaneously sealing off the state from the rest of the Union and, in some odd way, making it somehow more quintessentially American—a microcosm of the nation's hubris and soul. And perhaps the state's most hallowed story, which has become almost canonical in its retelling, is the last stand at the Alamo. Maybe you remember from your eighth-grade history book that back in March of 1836, 180 Texian (they included an *i* back then) soldiers barricaded themselves in the Alamo of San Antonio, a fort that was originally built as a Franciscan mission in the eighteenth century. The freedom fighters, led by William B. Travis and Jim Bowie, and joined by the frontiersman Davy Crockett, were surrounded by a Mexican army that numbered in the thousands and was led by General Antonio López de Santa Anna. But the Texians refused to lay down their arms in the face of overwhelming odds. In trying to literally hold down the fort in the ensuing siege of the Alamo, every one of the Texian defenders died, but not before killing twice the number of Mexicans in the process. Their heroism (if you're from Texas) or vainglory and thickheadedness (if you're not) inspired the well-known phrase that became the rallying point for the entire Texian army, which marched on to a quick and decisive victory against the Mexicans less than two months later. From 1836 until 1846, the state of Texas was its own republic, engendering a proud, individualistic streak that is part of the DNA of every one of its natives to this day. It's even infected its fisheries biologists.

In May of 2004, I traveled to Athens, Texas, to meet with Allen Forshage and David Campbell, two lifelong servants of the Texas Parks and Wildlife Department (TPWD). Every place I had gone so far in my journeys, I had met people who had configured their lives around some aspect of the world-record largemouth bass— some wanted to catch it, others wanted to furnish the lures that would do the job, and still another was solely interested in some-how protecting its legacy. I found out quickly that Allen and David—and by extension, the state of Texas—were no different in this regard. But their obsession had manifested itself in a differ-ent way. Neither Allen nor David desired to be the person who catches the next world record. After all, that would seem unfair, almost like a Lottery Association employee winning the Powerball jackpot. Neither man made lures, or even fished all that much because of their busy work schedules. And the story of George Perry's fish was interesting and all, but mainly because it set a target for them to aim for. No, what Allen and David wanted was simply to make their beloved state the place that the record bass called home.

To do this, these two men have taken the quest to perhaps the height of its extravagance. Under Allen and David's leadership, the state of Texas is attempting to *grow* the world-record bass.

The reason, at least the one they feed to the press, is that a new world-record bass from Texas would result in a public-relations bonanza for the state's fishery program, attracting a whole new gaggle of sunburned anglers—from both in and out of state—to join the 815,000 Texans who already fish for bass. Presumably, those new anglers would also bring along their wallets wherever they fished, adding at least another billion dollars to the reported $1.2 billion in direct taxable revenues that bass angling generates in Texas annually.

But in truth, it's about more than money for Allen and David, and for Texas in general. In the past twenty years, the ego of their cocksure state has been badly wounded. The largemouth bass is the state's most important fish, culturally and economically, and Texas has always thought of itself as "the bass capital of the world." For years, anglers have visited its hundreds of lakes, each of which promised a kick-ass time fishing for big badass bass. But beginning in the early 1980s, the harsh reality is that Texas had become nothing more than a bass-fishing backwater. The state watched helplessly from the sidelines as California produced twenty-one of the top twenty-five largemouths ever recorded, even as it struggled to place one in the top 100.

Rankling Texas officials even more was the fact that California fisheries biologists seemed so laissez-faire about their good fortune. After all, it was on a lark, a suggestion from a homesick baseball player, that California decided to stock its reservoirs with the bigger Florida-strain bass in the first place. And when those bass started gobbling up all of the state's other stocked fish—the rainbow trout—and California became the best big-bass fishery on the planet and the clear front-runner in the race to produce the world record, the reaction from the Golden State's fisheries managers was, "Wow, that's cool." Then they stepped out of the way.

But Texas was not ready to relinquish its self-billed title—not without a fight, anyway. So the state determined that their bass had to get bigger. When the fisheries biologists looked at all of the options, they realized they could never compete with California when it came to forage fish needed to grow giant bass—Texas had no trout-stocking program. So with Allen as the project's Dr. Frankenstein, Texas decided it would breed and grow the world-record bass in the laboratories, holding tanks, and raceways of the place they called the "Lunker Bunker," located in the vast basement of the $18 million Texas Freshwater Fisheries Center in Athens, which was built specifically for that purpose.

Perhaps predictably, California has reacted with the dismissiveness that one might show a recalcitrant child. "Texas is notorious for this kind of crap," says Jim Brown, who was the de facto leader of California's big-bass efforts until 2003, when he retired as the director of the San Diego city lakes. "Trying to grow this fish in a hatchery demonstrates a tremendous amount of self-absorption on the part of the people doing it. They're obviously under a lot of pressure and they want attention for big bass. It's really a funny thing."

But that kind of talk only serves as more motivation for Texas to proceed with a program that might seem a bit over the top in most places, but not here. "This is Texas, man," says Allen, with typical resident panache. "We always want the best of everything."

Allen Forshage, fifty-five, bears more than a passing resemblance to a few well-known TV bass-fishing personalities. He is slightly plump and his sun-bleached blond hair frames a round and freckled face that seems amiable when it's lit up by one of his frequent smiles. But it also often acts as a barometer. When he gets defensive or adamantly wants to make a point, his face quickly turns crimson, signaling a distinct change in the weather.

Allen has been fascinated by fish all his life. One summer during college he found his calling while working as a member of a bass gill-netting survey crew for the TPWD, gathering measurements that were used to help the state manage its most important fish. He has never worked anywhere else. Over the course of his thirty-three-year career that has culminated in his being named director of the Texas Freshwater Fisheries Center, no one has had more influence on the state's bass-fishing program. But for Allen, one major mission remains to be completed in his lifelong work.

When Allen joined the TPWD in the early 1970s, Texas, like other southern states, was in the throes of a reservoir-building boom, with more than four hundred impoundments constructed in just a twenty-year span. The new federally funded, man-made lakes were built with power generation and drinking water in mind, but they also offered a fresh opportunity for the TPWD and anglers alike. When each new reservoir was completed, the TPWD would stock it with largemouth bass. When those bass matured, anglers showed up in droves, harvesting almost everything they caught until the lake was fished out. Then the entire process would repeat itself on the next new reservoir. These were what Allen called the "boom–bust" years. The consumption without regard to preservation was done with the same obliviousness that the early settlers of the prairie had when they planted the same crop in the same field season after season until the soil was ruined. The solution? Just move on to the next field and do the same thing over again.

But those early farmers eventually ran out of land and had to learn new techniques, like crop rotations, to keep their soil productive. Similarly, in the 1980s, as the reservoir boom subsided, Allen and the state's other fisheries biologists realized that they would soon be running out of new water. They needed to manage their fishery in a new manner, and decided to abandon the harvest fishery and encourage catch-and-release. "We had to get people to realize that you didn't have to kill these animals to enjoy them," says Allen. Thanks to Ray Scott and BASS, releasing caught bass alive was slowly gaining acceptance across the country. But, thinking big, the Texas fishery brass decided they needed something special to jumpstart the new strategy.

In 1986, the TPWD entered into negotiations with Lone Star, a beer company, to start the Lone Star Lunker Program. The idea was to have anglers donate any largemouth bass of 13 pounds or heavier to the state in exchange for a replica of the fish, provided by Lone Star. The program had three end goals: The first was to get anglers in Texas excited about bass fishing. According to Allen, any hubbub about big bass accomplishes this trick. Second, in only accepting live bass, the state would promote its new catch-and-release philosophy. And third, the state of Texas would improve the quality of its bass fishing by using the 13-plus-pounders as brood stock in its hatcheries. This last goal, with its implicit goal of creating bigger bass, would help soothe what had become a raw nerve for the state, one that was aggravated with every report of a big bass coming from California. More importantly, it would lay the foundation for Allen's more ambitious long-term plans.

But the program would have gone belly up had it not been for a serendipitous boost from a big bass named Ethel.

By late 1986, the TPWD's negotiations with Lone Star were well under way. But on the day before Thanksgiving, Allen received a call from a man named Mark Stevenson, who had been fishing on Lake Fork Reservoir in Alba, some eighty-five miles east of Dallas. He had landed a bass that weighed 17 pounds, 6 ounces, eclipsing the state record by almost 4 pounds. Allen immediately thought that the fish offered an opportunity that he couldn't pass up, a way to kick off the Lone Star Lunker Program in grand style with a state-record fish that would surely garner national attention. The problem was that the program was not supposed to start until the following month. The ink had barely dried on the set of official rules and regulations, and no release forms existed for an angler to sign. And an even bigger risk surfaced. "I was thinking, 'What if we picked up this fish and it died?' " Allen says. Because the program had not officially begun, if the fish didn't make it, Allen and the TPWD—and not Lone Star—would have been stuck with the $300 bill for the promised replica of the fish. And since a state agency could not legally award a prize, that money would have most likely come from Allen's pocket. But more worrisome was the potential for the public-relations disaster that would surely ensue if the fish croaked in the hands of the TPWD's new program—a distinct possibility. "Here we were, wanting to promote the idea of *not* killing these fish," Allen says. "We were pretty nervous."

Allen spent a frantic two hours on the phone with Lone Star representatives, who eventually agreed to foot the bill for the replica. Then he decided that the reward of having this new state-record fish to kick off the program outweighed the risk of it dying. So he and his lieutenant, David Campbell, jumped in the car to make the fifty-mile trek to Lake Fork. Aware of the significance of this fish, they invited Steve Knight, an outdoor writer for the *Tyler* (Texas) *Morning Telegraph*, to accompany them and record the historic journey. On the way, they threw together a release form, as David says, "right quick."

They picked up the bass and brought her back to the fish hatchery, which at the time was located in Tyler, thirty miles from its present site in Athens. The fish arrived alive, but just barely. David already had travel plans for Thanksgiving, so the initial nursing duties were left to Allen. Though he lived twenty minutes from Tyler, he drove to the hatchery every two hours for the next three days to worry over the bass and make sure she wasn't floating belly up. "That poor fish," Allen says. "She had a fungus on her mouth from being lipped so much. You could actually see the fingerprints on her."

After Thanksgiving break, David took over the care of the fish, hand-feeding her, treating the fungus, and monitoring her every move. And through their combined efforts, the bass survived. The angler, Mark Stevenson, decided to name the fish Ethel, after his adored ex-mother-in-law. The bass became an instant celebrity. The story ran in most major national newspapers. Dan Rather, a Texan, featured Ethel on his nightly news broadcast. And the locals fell for her hard. David remembers reporting to work after church a week after she arrived, and being forced to drive up the side of the road to get to the hatchery gates. Some forty cars were lined up for a chance to see Ethel, who was eventually donated to Bass Pro Shops, where she was displayed in a 140,000-gallon viewing tank in the company's Springfield, Missouri, store.

When Ethel died a few years later, Allen and David received a call from a Bass Pro Shops representative who wanted to know if they could attend her funeral. They were too busy to make the eight-and-a-half-hour drive to Springfield, but 1,500 mourners did show up for the event, which was written up in the *Wall Street Journal*. But Allen and David remain eternally grateful for that fish. "Ethel made the program," says Allen.

Almost exactly ten years after Ethel's arrival, on November 19, 1996, then-Governor George W. Bush stood in front of 23,000 square feet of sprawling, interlinked, beige brick buildings topped with shiny green tin roofs in what had once been a pasture in Athens, Texas. Man-made ponds and streams meandered among the structures that housed 300,000 gallons of aquaria and featured more than fifty species of fish and reptiles. In the photo, the boyish-looking governor, without a trace of gray in his hair, is grinning ear-to-ear as he grasps a two-foot-long pair of scissors in the shape of a paddlefish, having just cut the red ribbon that officially opened the Texas Freshwater Fisheries Center. That the center was built in Athens was an enormous point of pride for George W. Bush, who has a vacation home on Rainbow Lake in Athens and is also an avid bass fisherman. In his remarks to the press, he mentioned another source of pride: The $18-million center had been built without one penny of state money. The town of Athens had won the right to have the center with a $4-million bid, hoping to capitalize on the expected tourism revenues. Anheuser-Busch chipped in another $1.5 million and took over the fish donation responsibilities from Lone Star in what is now called the Budweiser ShareLunker Program. And the remaining $12.5 million came in the form of a Sport Fish Restoration grant, courtesy of the federal government.

Ostensibly, the center was built as a tourist attraction. Visitors paid $5.50 to walk the grounds and learn about fish and flora, watch hundreds of catfish, bass, and bream swim lazily around a 25,000-gallon viewing tank in a 150-seat theater, and fish for easy-to-catch trout in the center's two-acre casting pond. So far, it's been pretty successful on that count, averaging 60,000 annual visitors. But the museum within provides a better idea of what the center is really about. There, in a prominent, well-lit display, is a replica of George Perry's fish, photos of the man himself, and plaques that recount the story of his historic fish (everything but the replica is courtesy of Bill Baab, of course). And above the display, in bold blue lettering, the text reads, simply QUEST FOR THE WORLD RECORD.

In 1998, the hatchery side of the center was completed. Outside, forty-five rearing ponds occupied 107 acres. And inside, twenty blue circular holding tanks, two 5,000-gallon viewing tanks, six eighty-foot spawning raceways, eighteen troughs, and two laboratory rooms were built within what is known as the "Lunker Bunker." With the ponds, hatchery, and technology in place, Allen and his fellow biologists finally owned up to what they had been planning for the past dozen years, and what the true intent was behind the construction of the $18-million center. That year Allen officially announced to the world that Texas's brood stock bass program had become a selective breeding one instead. From that point on, all the 13-plus-pound ShareLunker bass that anglers turned over to the state would be used with one objective in mind: to grow the biggest largemouth bass in the world. In case there was still any confusion, Allen named the program "Operation World Record."

David Campbell describes himself as the "Hey you" guy at the Texas Freshwater Fisheries Center, as in "Hey you, go do this." David is sixty years old, and has worked as a fisheries biologist for the state since 1965. He is lanky like a cowboy, with thinning brown hair, wide-rimmed glasses, and a white, brushy mustache. He speaks in a Texas low-country accent, a curious mix of a southern drawl and a Midwestern clip. He wears the same outfit to work every day: a short-sleeved brown oxford shirt with the fisheries center's emblem over the left breast and standard-issue green wildlife biologist pants, from which a set of a dozen keys dangles from a belt loop to his mid-thigh.

David never goes anywhere without his pager and cell phone. His is the voice at the receiving end of the ShareLunker hotline, and he is a one-man retrieval-and-delivery system who is always on call to pick up a Texas bass of 13 pounds or larger. When he goes to sleep at night in his house on the center's grounds, he puts his pager and cell phone on his bedside table and keeps his shoes, pants, shirt, and a little gym bag "with all the necessities" nearby, ready to be mobilized at a moment's notice. If Allen Forshage is the mad genius behind the plan to grow the world-record bass, David is the little engine that makes the plan go.

The official ShareLunker program runs from October 1 to April 30 of every year, but David, in his fervor for his job, will pick up a big bass in any month on the calendar. Of the 367 bass that have been entered into the program, he has personally retrieved 352. Because of Anheuser-Busch's money and Ethel's fame, the program has been well publicized in the state, so that most marina managers and dock attendants at the state's 425 bass lakes have the ShareLunker number handy should any angler come to shore with a bass that meets the requirements.

When a call comes in, David drops whatever he's doing and hops into the Lunker Truck, a white Ford Super Duty F-250 with green Texas Parks and Wildlife Department seals on both doors. The truck, part of the Anheuser-Busch booty, is specifically outfitted for David's missions. In the truck bed sits a 95-gallon tank—hooked up to a 12-volt aerator—which he fills halfway with water from the center and tops off with water from the bass's home lake. He does this so the bass will gradually become acclimatized to the environs of the center. On the inside of the cab, within easy reach, there's a switch for the aerator (under the dashboard) and a gauge that monitors the temperature and oxygen levels in the tanks in the back (on the dashboard). The passenger's seat is littered with detailed maps of the state's main and back roads. And on the jumpseat, right behind the driver's seat, David keeps a tackle box that contains everything a bass EMT would ever need to keep his patient alive: syringes, latex gloves, tags, a measuring tape, forceps, hydrogen peroxide, antibiotics, and cotton swabs. "The aspirin is for me," David says. Tucked in with the tackle box is a certified scale and a digital camera. The whole interior of the truck has a ripe, fishy aroma.

Sometimes the job requires extraordinary effort on David's part. In the fall of 2000, he received a phone call just after noon from an angler named John Lindsey, Jr. John had been trout fishing below a dam on the Canadian River on the Texas panhandle when he hooked and landed a huge bass. "When he called and told me where he was, I said, 'Aw, that's five hundred miles away,' " says David. "But there was no hesitation." He jumped in the Lunker Truck at 1 p.m. and then drove the 1,000-mile round trip, stopping only for a forty-minute nap on the side of the road. He was back in Athens at seven the next morning with a live, albeit weary, 14-pound, 2-ounce bass that was nicknamed Rosie.

When asked how he has maintained the energy and stamina to do this for almost twenty years, David shrugs. "There's just an adrenaline rush when the beeper or cell phone goes off and I know someone has a fish," he says. "It's just something I gotta do. I understand how important these fish are to us and the angler. And that provides me with all the drive I need." David says he sometimes arrives at two or three in the morning and finds the angler asleep in his or her truck. "But when they wake up, they get excited and start talking about the fish and how it was caught," he says. "I've never met an angler who's just caught a 13-pound-plus bass who's angry about a thing. And that makes me happy."

When David arrives to pick up a fish, first he must get the angler to sign the Budweiser ShareLunker agreement sheet, a more professional version of the one he and Allen hastily threw together for Ethel. The angler provides a phone number and address and signs a form that releases the TPWD from any liability should the fish die. The angler has the option of getting the fish back after one year or letting the state keep her for as long as it likes. By participating in the program, the angler receives a free replica of the fish; a Budweiser ShareLunker cap, shirt, and jacket; and a complimentary pass to the fisheries center in Athens. The angler with the largest ShareLunker at the end of the year gets a free lifetime Texas fishing license, worth $600.

With the fish in his possession, David quickly notes any injuries or distinguishing marks. Then he puts her in the tank and starts home, minding the temperature and oxygen gauge on the dashboard with the attentiveness of a young father watching a baby monitor. David rarely loses a fish in transit. The critical part is what comes next.

With the same sort of controlled mayhem of an ambulance pulling into a hospital, David speeds the Lunker Truck up to the doors of the hatchery at the fisheries center. Everything from this point on is a precisely choreographed Texas two-step, since these are the crucial moments when the bass is in the greatest peril, when her injuries must be diagnosed and dealt with in a matter of minutes. The first order of business is to transport and sedate the fish. David fills an ice chest with twenty-five gallons of water. Before putting the bass in, he adds equal amounts of MS222 (tricaine methansulfate, a fish tranquilizer) and baking soda, which regulates the pH level, to make a 75-parts-per-million solution. He stirs the additives until they dissolve and places the fish in the ice chest, which functions as a gurney. Then he carries the bass through a set of swinging doors into the Lunker Bunker, underneath a big sign that says: WELCOME TO THE BASS CAPITAL OF THE WORLD.

Once inside, David waits for the solution to do its thing. The MS222 acts like Valium, and after only a few minutes the bass will roll over in a drug-induced trance. When that happens, David is able to give the fish the first real checkup since picking her up. Because the ShareLunker bass are often handled a great deal before they reach the center, they occasionally arrive in bad shape. Human hands can cause funguses anywhere on the fish, like they did on Ethel. Sometimes the fish has sustained abrasions or hook scars from the battle with the angler. And the air bladder of the fish is often overinflated if she was wrenched from deep water when caught. David will administer antibiotics to any fish with open wounds or a fungus, or puncture the air bladder with a needle if need be.

When the fish has been fully stabilized and treated, David takes its weight and length measurements. Then he places a hand-held scanner between the pelvic fins, looking for a Passive Integrated Transponder (PIT) tag, a microchip the size of a small grain of rice that's also used for identification in the cattle industry. If he finds one—a rarity—it means that the fish is a ShareLunker veteran who has done a tour of duty in the Lunker Bunker only to be released and caught and brought back in again. Only two fish have made it back in seventeen years. If there is no PIT tag, David uses a syringe to insert one just behind the pelvic fin, through the muscle tissue. He pulls a scale sample from behind the right pectoral and dorsal fins, and another one from behind the left pectoral fin. The scales are placed in an envelope that's printed with an assigned Lunker number, the date, the angler's name, and the reservoir from which the bass came.

The last step is also the most recently added one. A biologist clips a sample of the bass's tail fin, which is then sent to a lab in

San Marcos for genetic analysis. It's part of an aggressive new program that Allen has initiated that will study the DNA "fingerprint" of big bass—a process called marker-assisted selection—with the aim of isolating the magic genetic markers that made her so big. Fast-growing fish will be compared to slow-growing fish, lunkers to non-lunkers, for genetic marks consistently found in the exceptional fish but absent from the ordinary. "The techniques have the potential to accelerate the benefits of the selective breeding program that's already in place," says Allen. But one wonders if this could also be the first slippery step on the slope to bioengineering, to the creation of a Frankenfish, like those farmed Atlantic salmon that grow in their pens at a faster rate than their wild cousins, thanks to gene splicing? "No way," Allen says firmly. "We're not going there."

After all the work on the fish is completed, she is placed, alone, in a 500-gallon blue circular holding tank that's labeled with her number and the name of the angler, and covered with wire so she can't jump out. Hanging from the tank is a clipboard with a sheet that tracks all ailments and treatments, just like the one found at the foot of a hospital bed. The entire process from Lunker Truck to Lunker Tank takes ten minutes. Generally speaking, a bass needs twenty-one days to recover from the MS222, and only after that time will the staff begin to feed her. A ShareLunker will either stay in the Lunker Bunker for one spawning attempt and then be returned to her home lake or angler, or she will be kept there for the rest of her life.

When I visited the center in May of 2004, ten bass finned sluggishly in the tanks, recovering from their journeys to the Lunker Bunker. They joined the five other ShareLunkers on the grounds. The heaviest resident in the Lunker Bunker was a 17-pounder that had been in the center for two years. Perhaps because of her size and good health—and thus, potential—she had earned the privilege of living in a special 5,000-gallon tank, with a big glass window on one side, where she swam in long, loping circles as her eventual meals—a handful of koi carp, sunfish, and trout— nervously tried to stay out of her way.

In the spring, if a female bass is deemed fit and healthy enough, she'll get to play her part in Operation World Record. The female is moved from her tank and placed in a sixteen-foot-long partition of an eighty-foot-long raceway. There she meets her mate, a male of three years or older, whose lineage in the program most likely traces back to 1987 as an offspring of one of the original Lone Star Lunkers. It's important that the male bass has some size and strength to contend with his new mate-to-be, because these big girls are dangerous. "If the males aren't big enough, the females will eat them when we put them together to spawn," says Allen. "I've seen it happen."

The idea is pretty simple: take a big female and a big male and hope that the couple will produce even bigger offspring. In an effort to find the perfect genetic combination, the biologists at the center have begun to experiment with backcrossing siblings, and David has procured big female bass from the San Diego reservoirs, Castaic Lake, and even from Cuba. "What we're doing is no different from what the cattle industry does to get better beef or milk, or what they do to breed a horse to win the Kentucky Derby," Allen says.

If all goes according to plan, the duo will spawn, producing up to 50,000 fertilized eggs that come to rest on a square eighteen-inch by eighteen-inch Astroturf spawning mat. David will take up the mat and carefully strip the amber-colored eggs into a clear glass cylinder, where they will hatch. When those fry are a few days old—at maybe 8 millimeters long—they are placed outdoors in a rearing pond that is protected by netting to keep them from becoming bird food. The ponds are fertilized with cottonseed meal, which causes a plankton bloom that will feed the fry. As the bass grow, they are moved into a series of larger rearing ponds. The entire forty-five-pond complex is surrounded by a six-foot-high chain-link fence that's topped with three intertwined strands of barbwire to keep out intruders. And just to be sure, David's house is perched on a knoll overlooking the rearing area. The "Hey you" guy also does duty as the security guard.

Mating wild animals in captivity is never an easy trick, and big bass are no exception. The spawning success rate for Operation World Record females is only 20 percent. Though an occasional fish will complete five or six spawns, most ShareLunkers will never release eggs. "These fish are old, and they've been under a tremendous amount of stress," Allen says. "They've been caught, photographed, and handled. Sometimes it's a miracle they live at all." The center only produces 40,000–100,000 ShareLunker offspring a year. But it is those prized fish, of course, that Allen and David pin the success of the program on, hoping against the odds that one of those baby bass will one day grow up to be the world record.

When the fry mature into 35-millimeter fingerlings after a month, half of them are stocked in lakes across the state. The other half stay behind to fatten up on minnows and koi carp at the center. In 2003, some 800,000 ShareLunker progeny from various spawning years went to forty reservoirs, a relatively small percentage of the 3.5 million total bass annually stocked by the TPWD. Three years ago, Allen started stocking some of the fingerlings in "contract" lakes—that is, private water—to see if they would grow faster or bigger in water with little or no fishing pressure. The TPWD signs a deal with a private landowner to stock the ShareLunker offspring in his lake or pond and reserves the right to electroshock and study these fish at any time, while as part of the deal, allowing the landowner to cull the smaller bass. The benefit to the landowners is that once the study is done, they'll have some bass in their lake with the some of the best pedigrees available. It's far too early to tell if the contract-lake program will have any success.

As for Operation World Record as a whole, the jury is still out as well. On one hand, the publicity the program has generated has been invaluable, and the private donations that are the lifeblood of the program have continued to pour in. Anheuser-Busch has endowed the program with another $500,000 and chips in an annual $25,000 for good measure. Other major donors include Bass Pro Shops, Coca-Cola, Exxon Mobil, the National Rifle Association, and the Texas billionaire Perry R. Bass (no relation to the fish). The program has even inspired imitators, like the state of Louisiana, which has embarked on a similar, though vastly scaled-down project. But Allen doesn't view that state as a threat because he says the catch-and-release mentality has no shot of taking hold there. As he told *Sports Afield* magazine in 2001, "You know what they call juvenile Florida bass in Louisiana? Breakfast."

But in terms of growing the biggest bass of all time, Operation World Record is still a work in progress. Though the mean weight of those bass classified by the state as "lunkers" did grow from 9 pounds in the 1970s to almost 12 pounds in the 1990s, Allen is the first to admit that the increase in weight is due mostly to the introduction of Florida-strain bass some thirty years ago. Another troubling statistic is that almost 60 percent of the fish entered into the program since 1986 have come from one place: Lake Fork, a relatively young reservoir constructed in 1980 that entered its prime a decade later, producing the current state record, a fish of 18 pounds, 3 ounces, in 1992.

And Allen and David have weathered some bleak years. In 2001, only five fish entered the program, primarily due to the Largemouth Bass Virus, which attacks the swim bladder of the fish, causing it to lose buoyancy control and eventually die. The virus devastated Texas lakes for two years and seemed to have a particularly destructive effect on the older, larger fish. No one could figure out what caused it, and no known cure or preventative measure exists. But to the relief of the state, in 2003 the virus disappeared as quickly and mysteriously as it showed up. The most disturbing thing to Allen, though, is the fact that no fish in recent years has come close to the state record set back in 1992. But that, he insists, is just a function of time.

And this is where we circle back to Texas and the power of her myths and forward-looking optimism. What we have here are two men, stubbornly fighting a battle that seems all but impossible to win. And in this way, Operation World Record has become Allen and David's own Alamo, something they are willing to stand by until the end. And clearly California is the large, cocky enemy army that doesn't realize yet that it will be overmatched when all is said and done.

The odds of the two men emerging victorious in the race to produce the world-record bass, at least while they are still in charge, are daunting at best, something to which Allen and David pretty much admit. "I hope to see the new world record, but this is a long-term project, and I'm running out of time," says Allen. Operation World Record could take another fifteen to twenty years or more to work, if it ever does, meaning both Allen and David will most likely be fishing for pleasure in retirement. Still, Allen sounds satisfied with his lifelong work. "I've spent my whole career doing this, and have never once gotten up out of bed and dreaded going to work," he says. And like his forebears at the Alamo, he sees any loss now as merely temporary and remains confident that in the end, Texas will win the larger war.

Near the end of my visit to the Texas Freshwater Fisheries Center, Allen, David, and I sat in a conference room that was separated from the Lunker Bunker by a white wall. David sat next to me, fiddling with a pen in his hand, looking antsy to get back on the road to get another fish. Across the table, Allen leaned back in his chair and tugged on his belt buckle. We talked about the motivations for the program. The word *California* hung in the air. Allen stared straight ahead at me, his face beginning to flush. "There's no question in my mind that we can beat them," he said. I asked him if anyone had expressed any concerns that attempting to grow the world record in a lab was somehow unnatural or unethical. He said the only critics of the program were those who didn't like the fact that a beer company was sponsoring it.

"Look," he said, leaning toward me from across the table. "The idea is simple: We want to break the record, and our desire to do so is greater than anyone else's." Then he brushed aside any doubts about what the state was doing, with a dash of Texian pride. "I believe in this program very strongly, and we won't give up. This is the most important fish we've got, and we're going to beat them all one day."

His phrasing sounded eerily familiar. On February 24, 1836, mere days before he would die in the fall of the Alamo, William B. Travis wrote a letter that was carried by courier from the Alamo through enemy lines. It was addressed to "The People of Texas and All Americans in the World." In the letter, Travis wrote: "I shall never surrender or retreat . . . I am determined to sustain myself as long as possible & die like a soldier who never forgets what is due to his own honor & that of his country."

The country that Travis was referring to was, of course, Texas.

What is possessed is devalued by what is coveted. —John Updike

CHAPTER SEVEN
Trying to Grow the World Record, Part II

An unforgiving sun beats down on the water and the heavy air feels like hot breath on the skin. Huge, billowing, cotton-white clouds inch ever closer across the broad Southern sky. Following them, though, are even bigger clouds, these dark and bruised and grumbling with distant thunder. Oblivious to the weather's portents, Porter Hall, a short, stout man with thick graying hair, wary blue eyes, and a Tom Selleck mustache, is guiding his boat around the edges of his seven-acre pond, one of two smack-dab in the middle of the kudzu-infested, sandy-soiled coastal plain of Mississippi. Porter is wearing his fishing outfit—a gray shirt and dirty blue jeans—and sucking on a Winston Light, his twenty-fifth on a day that's not yet half over. He is crackling with energy, fiddling with the handle of the boat's motor, jerking the light blue hat off his head, and pushing a sweaty hand through his hair. He swivels his body around to check on the orange bobber that's trolling behind the boat. Then he takes a deep, audible, head-clearing breath. Restlessly, he waits.

He knows she's not in there yet, the object of his abiding passion since he was a teenager, the mythical bass that swims circles in anglers' heads, sometimes driving them mad. To some folks in California, she's named "Sowbelly," and others have dubbed her "Cash"; he just calls her "a big muthafucka." Not one of the bass in his pond is even close yet, he realizes, but this is merely a scouting mission. He wants to see how far they've come along. The fishing also provides an excuse to get out of the two-room shack that's perched at the western end of the pond, the place he spends a few months out of every year, alone except for the company of a babbling television that's on twenty-four hours a day.

He desperately wishes that all of this was unnecessary—his ponds, his solitude. He wishes that he still lived with his family and could be a proper husband and father. But they've left him and live in their own home now, in Gainesville, Florida. He keeps an apartment there so he can be near his only child and his ex-wife of just over a year, so he can keep alive any hopes that they will all be united again.

Porter Hall also wishes he was still out there, in California, in the thick of it all. Southern California, near San Diego. That would be one place to go. Or somewhere new, off the radar screen of the big-bass guys and the media, a place he could jealously guard as his own. When he daydreams, he's always back in California, because he knows that's where the world record is coming from, if it's coming from anywhere.

That is . . . unless the record holds off for a few more years. Five, six, seven years at a minimum. But ten or twelve would be better. Most people think his project doesn't stand a chance in hell of working, and even he has the occasional dark cloud of doubt that casts a chilling shadow over him. Sometimes he feels nervous, like he's wasting his time, spinning his wheels in this dark Mississippi mud and not being out in California, that he's just distracting himself with an income-and-time-consuming fantasy. But you never know, he tells himself whenever the feels the anxiety of being stuck here and not out there. That "big muthafucka" may not even presently exist. At any given moment in time, there may not even be a world-record bass swimming around *anywhere on the planet.* Oddly, that thought makes him feel better, helps him maintain focus on his own grand plan, one that, at its essence, is really about the measure of time. He just needs time to keep feeding these girls in his Mississippi ponds, to allow them to grow. He needs time to keep perfecting their habitat. But most of all, he needs time to wait.

So as he continues to dream his California dreams, he's making the best of what he's got with his two ponds in this rural nook of a generally rural state, his only option for now; for both his life and his obsession. He can't let go of his family, even though they are no longer one unit together under one roof. But he can't let go of his dream to catch the world-record bass, either.

These two opposing urges are at war within him. The friction they cause has led him to this point in his life, and it defines his very being.

Throughout my travels, many "civilians" who weren't directly involved in the world-record bass chase asked me this question: "Why doesn't someone just grow the damn fish?" They didn't have in mind what the state of Texas was doing, selectively breeding big bass and turning those progeny out into the world to grow on their own. No, they meant why not put a bass in your backyard pond and feed the thing until it almost pops, then catch it on a rod and reel. It's a fair question in this world where tomatoes have been grown to the size of watermelons (world record: 7 pounds, 12 ounces), watermelons have reached the size of an NFL linebackers (world record: 255 pounds), and the largest human ever, one Robert Earl Hughes, weighed in at 1,067 pounds and was buried in a coffin the size of a piano case.

So why not grow a largemouth bass?

Because it's not that easy. In order for a largemouth bass to even *approach* record size, a number of stars must perfectly align. The fish, first of all, must have the right genes. In this case, only female Florida-strain bass need apply. Their cousins, the Northern largemouth, generally top out at a mere 12 pounds or so. After genes, the next most important thing is a proper growing environment in a generally warm climate. (In North America, that means below the 35th parallel.) Ideally, the incubator would be a brand-new lake or one that's been born again by being drained and refilled, so that the initial stocking—or "class"—of bass won't have any competition when it comes to feeding. (Something tells me no one ever got in the way of Robert Earl Hughes in the all-you-can-eat buffet line.) And on the subject of food, there should be plenty of it, in the form of literally thousands of pounds of forage fish, like golden shiners, bream or, preferably, rainbow trout. Then that first class of bass should be allowed to grow and prosper to the ripe old age of eleven to thirteen years. California has been blessed with all the necessary ingredients, but so far it's proven an impossible task for an individual, or even another state, like Texas, to replicate those conditions.

Countless folks have tried anyway, in various farm ponds across the country. Bill Baab remembers encountering a fee-fishing pond on a Georgia back road with a sign that read FUTURE HOME OF THE WORLDS RECORD BASS. And Glenn Lau, a bass filmmaker and former guide, made a small splash with his effort in the mid-1980s. After building a 10,000-gallon tank in Silver Springs, Florida, Glenn told the Associated Press that he planned to grow a 30-pound bass, going so far as to start a company he called World Record Bass, Inc.

After four mainly fruitless years, Glenn says he finally produced a bass of 18 pounds with a strict diet of thousands of shiners and crawdads. But some kids snuck into his hatchery one night and snagged the bass with large treble hooks. The bass was so heavy that they couldn't lift it out of the tank, but they ripped open her belly in the attempt. Glenn stitched her up, but she never recovered, and he gave up on the project shortly thereafter. Other bass, like the ones in the tanks at the Texas Freshwater Fisheries Center and at Bass Pro Shops, have put on substantial weight, but no homegrown fish has ever really come close to threatening the record.

But the feat just seems so doable that entrepreneurial anglers persist, despite the odds and the prohibitive cost. Especially those desperate enough to continue their pursuit of the world record who have nowhere else to turn, like Porter Hall.

In May of 2004, I flew down to Jackson, Mississippi, to meet Porter. We had spoken on the phone a number of times, and I was looking forward to meeting the man whose name seemed to pop up everywhere I had traveled, usually with a question that went something like: "Isn't that the crazy guy down in Mississippi?" Similarly, he appeared to be fluent in almost every aspect of the chase. As I found out, there was a reason for that. Porter Hall is the Forrest Gump of the world-record bass chase, making a memorable appearance in nearly every one of its theaters. He is from the South, born and raised in the city in which George Perry died in a plane wreck. He was at Castaic Lake in California during its big-bass boom in the early 1990s and was one of the few people Bob Crupi felt comfortable enough around to share time with on the water. He's met Mike Long and spent a week presciently scoping out the reservoirs near San Diego before leaving California in the late 1990s. He orders lures from Mickey Ellis. He's had a taste of the controversy that seems to shadow any bass of noteworthy size. He has snuck down to Cuba, seeking the off-limits bass there that have grown heavy with angling mystique. And now he's following the path of the state of Texas—though on a micro level and with less of a genetics bent. Porter Hall is attempting to grow the world-record bass on his property in Mississippi, a plot of land he bought in 2001 for that sole purpose.

As I would find out, Porter's latest endeavor was just the next chapter in an ongoing monomaniacal narrative, one that's full of all the hope and resolve and heartbreak that comes with trying to keep a childhood dream alive.

Porter met me in the baggage-claim area of the Jackson International Airport. He was wearing jeans and a red knit Tommy Hilfiger shirt, looking very much like a middle-aged suburban father in his weekend street clothes. I jumped into his Ford F-150 truck, and maneuvered my legs around a white scooping bucket that was full of tiny brown pellets of fish food. We started the eighty-five-mile journey south, where we would take I-55, then turn off to follow the back roads that wended through the green countryside, the trailer homes, and the cotton fields. We were headed to Jayess, a town consisting of two convenience stores on opposite sides of a crossroads some forty miles north of the Louisiana border. There, Porter had ninety acres of land, a fishing shack, and two ponds from which he hoped to make history.

On the drive down, between drags on his Winston Lights, Porter filled me in on his background. He grew up in Mountain Brook, a tony suburb of Birmingham, Alabama, where large red-brick colonial and Georgian houses gaze down from the hills that rise above the city that was once known as "the Pittsburgh of the South" before the steel industry fell into decline. (Mountain Brook happens to be a place I know a thing or two about. I lived there for a number of years, and my mother still resides within the Birmingham city limits.) The main drag of Mountain Brook is its own version of Rodeo Drive, where pretty wives with designer bags strapped to their tanned shoulders stroll unhurriedly among the various antique, bridal, and jewelry stores. Denizens of the suburb are known as "Brookies," a term at once derisive to those who don't live there and endearing to those who do.

Both Porter's father and grandfather had been mortgage bankers in Birmingham. His grandfather, John Cox Hall, was wildly successful in his career as a founding partner of Cobbs, Allen & Hall, and had served a term as the chairman of the Mortgage Bankers Association, a national organization that reserved this prestigious leadership post for only the most successful among its membership. In 1968, Porter's grandfather and his partners sold Cobbs, Allen & Hall to the Bank of Boston, ensuring that at least a few generations of the Hall family would never suffer for money.

Though the Halls were entrenched in the debutante balls and cocktail parties that made up the Mountain Brook scene, Porter, the second-eldest of his seven brothers (which included half- and stepbrothers from various marriages), never felt comfortable in a place where wealthy children got an early start in the role-playing of their parents' society. "As a kid, I just wasn't that sociable," he says in a pronounced Heart-of-Dixie drawl. "I mean, gawd, they had fraternities in my high school."

But his father, John Cox Hall, Jr., also happened to be a serious weekend warrior–type bass fisherman, and was a student of the sport's history. In the 1960s he read a story about George Perry's record and decided that he had to own a Creek Chub Wiggle Fish, the antique lure that Perry had used to catch his bass. After trolling the local tackle shops and coming up empty, he called the Creek Chub Company in Indiana. They told him that they only sold the lure in bulk. So Porter's father bought 140 of them.

One spring when Porter was twelve, his father rented a U-Haul and loaded up the seven brothers and all of their bikes, basketballs, and fishing tackle and drove down to Lake Talquin, near

Tallahassee, Florida, for a vacation. It was on this week-long trip that Porter would catch the bug that would infect him for the rest of his life. His father knew that of all his sons, Porter was the one who was most into fishing. So one night, his father left the other boys in the hotel room to watch TV and took Porter with him to the lake to go fishing. Porter remembers that his father tied on a homemade Jitterbug—a lure that skimmed the water's surface—to his line and told him to cast into the darkness. A few minutes later, Porter felt a heavy tug on his rod. He pulled the fish in, out of the black night. It was a 10-pound bass, his largest fish and bigger than anything that even his father had ever caught. Father and son raced back to the hotel to show the other boys, but received a chilly reception. "They were jealous because I had gone fishing with my dad alone," says Porter. "But they were really jealous when they saw the fish." His brothers, in retribution, picked on him mercilessly, so much so that his father eventually had to get his bass-crazed son his own hotel room. But Porter didn't mind the ribbing. He liked the attention. "As far as getting turned on to big bass, yep, that was it," he says. "It was pure luck that I got that fish, but I just *loved* it."

And bass fishing became his avenue of escape from the Mountain Brook life that he decidedly did not want. As soon as he was old enough to drive, Porter spent part of every Christmas break, and all of his spring breaks, at Lake Jackson, also near Tallahassee. He could usually rustle up a few friends to accompany him. But after only a day or two of fishing, his friends would get restless and head over to Panama City to chase girls. Porter would stay behind and fish.

As with Bob Crupi and Mike Long, bass fishing claimed a prominent role in Porter's life early on, primarily because he was good at it. "I got a kick out of it," he says. "When I was seventeen and eighteen, I would go down there and outfish guys who were forty-five years old. It was kind of an ego pump, I guess."

Bass fishing was the only thing that really mattered to him. Every free moment he spent either doing it or thinking about it. As a result, he became a listless student in high school, neither succeeding nor failing dramatically enough to attract notice. He wasn't too keen on attending college, but was urged on by his family, particularly his grandfather. He graduated from high school in 1973 and chose Florida State University, even receiving a partial scholarship for his pole-vaulting skills (his highest vault was a respectable fourteen feet). But he really had no intention of going through with his education at that point. All he wanted to do was fish for bass. Looking back, everyone should have known what he was up to. After all, FSU was only a twenty-minute drive from his preferred institution of higher learning: Lake Jackson.

Porter started going to the lake before freshman orientation, and didn't stop when the fall semester started. He participated in only a few preliminary workouts with the FSU track-and-field team. And just four weeks in, he dropped out of college and went to live in a tent in the Ocala National Forest, which was dotted with dozens of prime bass lakes.

For Porter, this marked the official break from what had once seemed to be his destiny. Both his father and his grandfather wanted very much for him to become a mortgage banker like them or, at the very least, something respectable like a doctor or a lawyer. Instead, Porter decided to discard the comforts and confinements of that type of life and chose one of relative discomfort, but of real meaning—at least to him. Part of his choice stemmed from a desire for control. "I wanted to succeed or fail based on my own decisions," he says. And bass fishing offered that opportunity on a daily basis.

Somewhat ironically, his choice was made possible by the money he would eventually inherit from his grandfather, something that seems to be a source of embarrassment for him. He doesn't like to talk about it and doesn't want to seem like the guy who "can fish all the time because he has money," he says. But it's a central part of his story and the choice he made to live the life he's lived, even as the last of the stash, in true Southern aristocratic fashion, has begun to slowly trickle away.

Porter fished with abandon for nine straight months, living in his tent, as far away as he could possibly be—if not geographically, then at least mentally—from the life of a mortgage banker. He teamed up with John McClanahan, an itinerant bass bum who shared the same burning, all-consuming passion for the fish that Porter had. The duo started a guiding service called Trophy Bass Unlimited, utilizing the knowledge that they had accrued by trial and error during their respective years on the water. They specialized in big bass, and because they lived in tents, they were mobile, able to choose from as many as a dozen bass lakes on a given day. But the tent life began to wear on him. "In that area there were a lot of thunderstorms," he says. "They would come through and blow down the tent and absolutely soak my clothes and everything else. Since that nine-month stretch, I have not been camping one fucking time." Porter bought an Airstream trailer and moved to the outskirts of the park. And to the delight of his family, he got engaged to a woman with whom he had gone to high school in Mountain Brook.

But in 1975, Porter began to notice a pretty, petite brunette teenager who lived in a trailer park down the street from where he had parked his Airstream. He courted Cindy Powell cautiously at first. She liked him, liked his graciousness, but she thought that he did seem a little obsessed with bass. "He was pretty much already a really serious bass fisherman then," Cindy says. "Where I grew up, no one at that age was serious about anything." But she also liked that part of his makeup, his commitment and determination. Porter broke off his engagement to the Mountain Brook woman, and a year and a half after they first met, he asked Cindy to marry him. He was twenty-one. She was seventeen. They moved into a trailer home. Porter eased up on the guiding, and he and Cindy opened up a bait business, selling golden shiners to local tackle shops. They also sold worms that they cultivated on a worm farm near Ocala. "It was just a way for us to be able to afford to fish and be around fishing," Porter says.

Porter undoubtedly was the first "Brookie" in history to become a worm farmer, something his grandfather in particular was not too happy about. The old man, Porter knew, had doggedly held on to his own aspirations for his grandson. He offered to foot the college tuition bill for both him and his new wife. It was yet another choice Porter had to make in what would become a recurring battle within him between family and bass fishing, one that would come to a bigger head later on in his life. Porter finally relented, giving in to what he had known had been his family's wish all along. And after seven years of bait-selling and bass fishing, he and Cindy moved to Gainesville where they enrolled at the University of Florida in 1984. Cindy majored in journalism. Porter studied resource conservation. Porter didn't really mind being back in college because, as it turns out, he hadn't really kicked his obsession. "Old habits are stubborn and jealous," Dorothea Brande once wrote. "I mean, yeah, I was studying and everything," Porter says. "But I went to school in a place where there was a lot of good fishing."

Porter and I arrived at his shack in the early afternoon on my first day in Mississippi. We hopped into his aluminum-hulled boat and tooled around his seven-acre pond, which was surrounded by tall oaks and longleaf pines that soughed soothingly in the wind. Within the pond, old dead cedars poked their gray heads out of the water. Porter placed them there to mark the channel and provide cover for his bass. "They make for a good place to catch a big girl," he says. A regal pair of great blue herons stalked the shoreline, and the occasional black-backed snake S-curved its way across the top of the brown, yellow-pollen flecked water. All in all, it was a very peaceful scene, one that Porter patiently waits by every day he's here.

Porter explained to me how he arrived at choosing the property. Mississippi intrigued him for a number of reasons. It was a bearable 550-mile commute from his apartment near his child and ex-wife in Gainesville, and the land was still relatively cheap and open compared to neighboring states. A few years ago, a friend of Porter's named Larry Bankston had dug out his own pond in Mississippi with the aim of just growing some trophy bass. His fish had reached weights of up to 15 pounds. Porter believed he could take what Larry had done a step further. And he liked the direction that Mississippi had taken with its own bass-fishing program.

The state, Porter believed, was flying under the big-bass radar. In the past few years, every new reservoir Mississippi had built was stocked with pure Florida-strain bass, providing good candidates for stocking his ponds (taking a live fish from a public lake is allowed in Mississippi) and good public bass-fishing opportunities for him to pass the time. But there was one other thing that factored into his decision, one that had to do with Porter's keen sense and appreciation of the history of the world-record bass. He only looked at property in Mississippi that was roughly on the same latitude as Telfair County, Georgia, where George Perry's fish came from. If he was going to grow the world-record bass, he thought, it might as well have the appropriate geography.

In 2000, Porter started hunting around for land, but it took him a few tries to get it just right. The first property he bought looked perfect, but the soil turned out to be too sandy to hold enough water for a big pond. The second, bought a year later, turned out to have too much gravel in its soil. But after two false starts, he finally found the perfect place.

In 2001, after reselling the first two pieces of land, Porter purchased ninety acres from a farmer. A run-down hunting shack slumped on the property, and the old cotton- and cornfields had become grassy meadows. The farmer had built a seven-acre pond on the eastern end of the land. The outflow of the small pond drained into a swale—the perfect place to construct an even bigger pond. And to Porter's relief, the soil on the property contained just the right mixture of sand and gravel.

Porter renovated the shack, fixing up the eat-in kitchen with modern appliances and installing a satellite television. He screened in the porch to fend off the summer maelstrom of mosquitoes and chiggers and added a bedroom onto the back, where he keeps his easel and paintbrushes. Painting is a self-taught hobby he pursues to fill the hours he spends out there by himself. When I got there, he had just finished a painting of a lone hiker struggling to reach the top of a snowy summit that looked like Mount Everest.

Behind the shack, he's installed two hundred-gallon aerated tanks to hold the golden shiners that he uses as bait. But the tanks could also serve another purpose somewhere down the road if his dreams for this property come true. "They're big enough to hold a giant bass," he says with a sheepish grin, perhaps slightly embarrassed by the optimistic forethought he's put into what some think is the longest of longshots. "I could keep a fish alive in there for a while until the Fish and Game people showed up."

But he focused most of his attention on the ponds. With input from Larry Bankston and a fisheries biologist friend at the University of Florida named Mike Allen, he set about trying to construct what he thought would be the perfect growing grounds for the largest bass in the world.

He drained the seven-acre pond dry, killing all of the bass and forage fish within it to give the site a fresh start. He limed the pond bottom to keep the acid in the soil down so that a natural algae bloom would take place and feed the baby bass and forage fish. Then he refilled the lake and stocked a few hundred bream and chubsuckers as forage, and another hundred or so golden shiners, the three-to-six-inch baitfish that serve the dual purpose of being bass food and eating bass eggs. Porter would prefer that there be no reproduction in his pond, to allow his initial stockings to live and prosper with no competition.

But his original intent was to concentrate on the bigger pond that he was to build in the swale below the smaller one. He hired the farmer from whom he had purchased his property to use a track hoe to build a dam for a twenty-three-acre pond. The pond was to be twenty-five feet deep in the middle, much deeper than the typical Southern pond, which would give the bass a range of comfortable temperatures in which to live and grow. He brought in truckloads of gravel to create reefs that ran in bars across the pond's bottom and pushed around the earth with bulldozers to create humps like some mad golf-course designer. "I really wanted a diversity of habitat in there," Porter says. Then he watched hopefully as the pond filled up. But a year later, the water inexplicably started to drop. When it got down far enough, he saw that a sinkhole had developed on the bottom. Though he has since patched it up, he has now turned all of his energies toward the smaller pond.

In late 2002, Porter started stocking the seven-acre pond with mature bass that he had caught mainly from nearby Lake Columbia, a four-year-old reservoir containing only pure Florida-strain bass. There are now eighteen of these females swimming in the small pond, their weights at put-in ranging from 7 to 15 pounds. Then he put in an initial stocking of 150 pure Florida-strain fingerlings at fifty cents a fish. "When I dumped those little ones in there, I said 'Which one of you little fuckers is going to be the one?' " Porter recalls.

On opposite sides of the pond, Porter has installed two metal drum feeders that go off twice a day, at 8 a.m. and 6 p.m., spouting catfish food pellets that he buys from Plunkett's Feed on the outskirts of Jayess. The feed is for the shiners and bream. The reasoning is the fatter the prey, the fatter the predator. When the feeders go off, the tranquility of the lake goes with it. As the pellets hit the water, hundreds of shiners and bream congregate and pop the water in a feeding frenzy. Curious turtles swim in close and hold their heads out of the water to take in the commotion. And every once in a while, there's a loud splash, like a large stone has been tossed into the water. That's one of Porter's big girls who's come in to feed on the momentarily distracted baitfish. "That pond is so full of damn food right now," he says. "And that first group of bass I put in, they're lone wolves with a lot to eat."

But Porter's masterstroke came in 2003, and it demonstrated just how far he's willing to go with this project. He called a hatchery in Tennessee, and for $2,000, he had them deliver 1,000 pounds of rainbow trout, which he dumped into his little seven-acre pond. His bass gobbled them all up in a matter of months. "I figured, why not?" Porter says. "I'd seen it work out in California." He's planning to make the trout-stocking an annual event.

As he finished describing all of this to me, I asked a few questions that had been on my mind since I had first heard of him and about his project that others had labeled "crazy" and "impossible." Did he truly believe that he could raise the world-record bass here in these ponds? Porter let out a little chuckle, like he knew this had been coming, then said firmly, "Yes, I think it's possible." But, I wondered, as I had in Texas, was this somehow unethical? "Well, I've thought a lot about that," he said. "I guess my answer is where do you draw the line? Does the fish have to come out of its native range in the Southeast? What they're doing out there in California, feeding the bass all of those trout, that's not natural. And even the technology used now, like the fishfinder? Everyone grumbled about that, but then everyone got one. You have to adapt. The record will be the record."

In all, Porter figures he's spent $300,000 so far on the project.

That night, Porter and I went to a diner in Monticello, a town named after Thomas Jefferson's plantation home, but pronounced down here as, "Montisello." When we walked in, everyone in the place stopped what they were doing to turn and stare at us in silence. After a few awkward quiet moments, the woman behind the counter asked if we worked around here, a politely indirect question, for we weren't sporting grubby garments like the other men in the diner, who had obviously just gotten off the late shift. Porter explained that he owned a piece of property nearby, which seemed to satisfy the denizens of the diner, who turned back to their eating and talking and smoking. Porter and I ate cheeseburgers and collard greens. One of the men at a nearby table was wearing a black hat with a bright orange Confederate battle flag across the bill. He was missing a finger—the second person I had seen in Monticello who had been without a digit. Porter noticed me looking at the man and explained in a whisper that many men in this town worked on oil rigs off the coast of nearby Louisiana.

On the ride back to the shack, Porter had as many questions for me as I did for him. He was curious about what I had seen in California. He asked about his old acquaintance, Bob Crupi, and wanted to know if the gruff motorcycle cop was still after the record. He asked about the reservoirs near San Diego, about the techniques that Mike Long and the others were using to fish those waters. When I told him about the size of the bass I had seen out there, he just shook his head in disbelief. "My gawd," he said. "I wish I had grown up in San Diego." Then he suddenly slowed the truck to a complete stop and started to turn it around. He looked at me with an embarrassed grin. We had missed the turn that took us back to the shack. "Sorry. My mind was in California," he said. "And we were just on our way to Louisiana."

I was impressed by Porter's knowledge of the record-chasing scene. He knew about every big bass that had come out of California since he left in late 1998. He kept tabs on what was going on through his treasured weekly subscription to *Western Outdoor News*, which compiles a list of all of the notable bass caught in the state. What that didn't tell him, he learned from some friends he had made while he was out there, people like the lure maker Allan Cole. Almost every time he had mentioned his ponds or fishing in the South in general, he had qualified the comment with a "but it's not like California." And he made it very clear about where he really wanted to be. "I'd still be out there if I could," he said on more than one occasion. "I'd love to fish with those guys. I think about going back a lot. But that's not possible. At least for now."

After graduating from college, Porter and Cindy remained in Gainesville. He worked for the university, studying the effects that hydrilla, an exotic aquatic plant from southeast Asia, had on lakes in Florida. He guided a bit on the side. Cindy worked for the local newspaper. They had a good, full life there, with friends and family nearby.

But it was around this time that Porter felt the first hints of an itch that he knew he would eventually have to scratch. When he was younger, he believed that Florida, with its natural lakes and naturally big native fish, was the center of the bass universe. But it was becoming clear that the white heat of the big-bass world had moved west, that ironically, these natives in their own natural lakes could no longer compete with the transplants prospering in artificial environs elsewhere. During the 1980s, California was producing big bass the likes of which had never been seen before. Two fish over 20 pounds, five over 19, and dozens over 18. And all of this was happening as the average size of the bass in Florida was going down, most likely due to the large number of anglers in the state who hung every 10-pounder they caught on the wall of their study at home. This wasn't a good sign for Porter, who was just beginning to realize the depth of his obsession with big bass. "I really started to entertain the thought of moving to California then," he says. "It took me a long time to really admit to myself what I was doing, what I was working towards. Really ever since that trip when I was twelve I've liked to catch big bass. But when you catch one big one, you need to catch another that's bigger than that, then another, then another. Ultimately, I realized I wanted to catch the world record. And it was starting to become clear that the record was not coming out of Florida."

Then there came that one-year stretch beginning in March of 1990 when Bob Crupi and Mike Arujo landed three fish over 21 pounds out of California's Castaic Lake, each within a pound and change of breaking the record. For Porter, those three bass marked a seminal moment in his life. It wasn't quite like hearing that John F. Kennedy had been shot—Porter doesn't remember exactly where he was when he heard about the fish, and they were caught on different dates. But the cumulative news did have the same potency. "The fact that there were three big fish like that made it seem inevitable," he says. He suddenly *had* to get out there.

In the summer of 1991, after Bob Crupi caught the second-largest bass of all time, Porter and Cindy went out to California on what Porter billed as "a vacation." They flew to San Diego and drove the 180 miles to Castaic. Cindy realized what was going on right away. "I knew that we weren't just sightseeing," she says. They hired a guide and fished for three days. Porter got instantly fired up. "We only caught bass that weighed three or four pounds, but they just looked so different from the fish I was accustomed to in Florida. They were so *fat*." That was all he needed. The Halls flew back to Florida and packed up their belongings, then turned around and went straight back to California to find a place to rent, even though they had just bought a house in Gainesville that Cindy had spent a few months remodeling. "She'd done a lot of work to get it set up," Porter says. "I think she was disappointed." In retrospect, that disappointment was something he should have paid more attention to.

The Halls found a tract house in Valencia, about ten miles from Castaic. Porter bought a new boat, sturdy enough for Castaic's big water and waves. And they fished, together, five days a week.

It was rough going at first. Despite the time he'd spent with the guide on Castaic, Porter had no idea how to fish the deep canyon reservoir. In Florida, the lakes he'd grown up fishing in were shallow and full of grasses and cover. On Castaic, which was 270 feet at its deepest point, the fish tended to hang near dropoffs. "Nothing was the same except the casting," he says. He quickly figured out that the biggest fish on the lake were being caught on crawdads, but he didn't really know the proper way to fish them. He would drop big flat-bottomed anchors, as he would have in Florida, and the boat would sway violently in the wind and waves, jerking the bait along with it. But he caught on, at first by watching other anglers on the water. Then one day at the dock he cornered Dan Kadota, one of the Castaic regulars and Bob Crupi's sole confidant. "I asked Danny a ton of questions and he answered everything," Porter says. "He was great. He told me in detail how to set up a double anchor, what type of rope and curved anchors to buy. That was the name of the game." Still, he and Cindy didn't have immediate success, even after learning the tricks of the trade. But a few months in, Porter hooked a bass that felt heavy. He looked it over as he brought it to the boat. Judging from the length of the bass, he guessed it was a good fish, but under 10 pounds. But when he weighed it, it turned out to be 13 pounds, 12 ounces. "I couldn't believe it," he says. "In Florida, that would have been an 8-pound fish."

The scene at Castaic was unbelievable as well. In Florida, Porter had always preferred to fish smaller lakes that he would often have to himself. But on the 2,500-acre Castaic, three hundred boats a day was the norm. "People were cutting each other off at the boat ramp, running across each other's bows on the water, spying on each other with binoculars," he says. "It was crazy."

But it was all part of the adrenaline rush. "Part of it I hated," he says. "There was nothing remotely peaceful about it. But there was this incredible anticipation when you pulled off the lake every day. You wanted to see if anyone caught it. You knew it could happen any day." And Porter, as Brad Wetzler pointed out in a story for *Outside* in 1995, was a big part of the scene as "the South's last great hope," the man who could at least nominally keep the record in George Perry's backyard. "When I was out there at Castaic, there was a side of me that said if the record is going to be broken, it should be by someone who's from the Southeast."

Like everyone else, Porter knew that Bob Crupi was *the* man on the lake. But while others spied on Bob and horned in on his spots, Porter gave him a wide berth, always keeping a polite distance from him on the water, being the Southern gentleman that he is. But Bob, as a fisherman at the boat ramp told Porter one morning, viewed his refusal to try to beat him to his spots as a sign of disrespect. "Does this guy think I suck?" was the phrase the fisherman said Bob had uttered about Porter. Bob would eventually find out that Porter didn't think he sucked, but instead viewed him as some paranormal bass angler. This respect would ultimately earn Porter a few days on Bob's boat. "That was cool," Porter says. "But I never really felt like we got to be, you know, buddies or anything."

Instead, Porter's main fishing buddy continued to be Cindy. "She was really into it," Porter says. He was amazed at how she had the same stamina and determination that he had on the water, and how, every day at just ninety-eight pounds, she could pull up a twenty-pound anchor from fifty feet deep. The Halls usually took two days off a week to change lines, tune up the boat, and go grocery shopping, but mainly to recuperate. "Fishing on the lake was pretty wearing," Porter says. "There was a lot of wind and sun. People tend to think of fishing as restful, but with all the stuff you have to do before and after, and all the concentration you have to maintain on the water, an eight-hour day is really more like a twelve-hour one."

In 1993, the Halls fished Castaic with the knowledge and confidence of regulars. They went at it all year, hard. The fishing started to take a toll on Porter, who, like the Florida bass introduced to California, ballooned in the new environs, going from

160 to 220 pounds. Cindy was also gaining weight, but for a different reason. She was pregnant. A few months later, after sixteen years of marriage, the Halls had a daughter they named Trechsel. Porter had a good year on the water as well, catching big bass of up to 15 pounds.

But in 1994, something was amiss on the lake. The Northridge earthquake and the invasion of striped bass had knocked Castaic's largemouth population for a loop. The biggest fish that year on the lake was only 17 pounds, very small considering the 21- and 22-pounders that the lake had kicked out just three years prior. Restless, Porter started sniffing out other lakes. It was then that he found out about Lake Casitas, located fifty miles west of Castaic, near the upscale town of Ojai.

Porter and Cindy very quietly bought a house in Ventura that overlooked the ocean. With a new house and baby, their California dream seemed refreshed. But trouble was just around the corner. That same year, Porter came down with what was later diagnosed as Chronic Fatigue Syndrome, an affliction with no known cause or remedy that leaves its victims virtually immobilized with exhaustion. For two years, Porter stayed in bed for almost twenty hours a day, suffering from night sweats caused by a constant fever of 100.5. "It knocked my ass for a loop," he says. He willed himself out of bed to fish Casitas for two hours a day because he knew he was on to something. The big-name anglers on Castaic had not yet caught on to Casitas, only an hour away, and he was one of the only people he knew of at the lake who was employing the Castaic method—crawdads and a double anchor—on this suddenly virgin water.

Porter's hunch about Casitas would turn out to be a good one, but the secretive manner in which he fished the lake landed him in the middle of a controversy. In the winter of 1995, battling through his illness, Porter caught an 18-pound, 8-ounce bass. It was a monumental fish for him, the biggest of his long career. As it had for Bob Crupi, Porter's big fish, in many ways, justified his lifelong pursuit—to his fellow anglers, to his family back home in Alabama who had never quite understood the path he had taken in his life, to Cindy, and maybe most importantly, to himself. The bass would remain the largest one caught in the world for the next six years until Mike Long's big bass binge at the turn of the century. But it brought on its share of pain, too.

When Porter caught the fish, he was ecstatic, but in his mind he was already thinking a few steps ahead. He knew that where there was one exceptionally large fish, there were usually a few more, and his bass only made him more determined to find an even bigger one. And to do this, he reasoned that day, he had to keep Casitas to himself. He had caught the fish on a crawdad, but he didn't want anyone else to know this. "I knew that there were fifteen to twenty people on Castaic who were damn good at fishing crawdads, so I didn't want those fuckers over here," he says. "So I lied about what I caught it on."

When he took the fish back to the dock to be certified, he told everyone that he caught it on an artificial trout plug. He figured that this vital piece of information would be enough to keep the Castaic hordes from overrunning his lake, pressure he felt for sure the lake—and in his present sickened state, he himself—could not endure. The problem was there had been some other fishermen in a boat nearby who had seen him catch the fish, and they started contradicting his story at the dock right away, saying they saw him catch it on a crawdad. So Porter had to immediately modify his story a bit, saying that he had been alternating back and forth between a crawdad and the plug, but had caught the bass on the plug. "It really backfired on me and it was tough to stick to the story," he says. But he did, even telling Jim Bertken, who wrote a piece about his fish in the *Los Angeles Daily News*, that he had indeed caught it on the plug. He was so insistent that even the fishermen who had seen him catch the fish started to back off. He has stuck with the story for nearly a decade, until now. "I thought I would go to my grave with that secret," he says. It hurts him to talk about it, but he seems relieved to have finally set the record straight. "That killed me, having to keep that lie going," he says. "I've always prided myself on being a real straight-up guy."

But no one could deny the size of the fish, no matter what he caught it with. And it looked like the bass was just the beginning for Porter. "After that fish, the record seemed plausible for me, it was something more than a wild dream," he says. "I figured someone was going to catch it and it could possibly be me."

But things were going in the opposite direction at home. Cindy, who had stopped fishing with Porter even before Trechsel was born, had begun to suffer from debilitating headaches. And with a child, her homesickness for her family in Florida was growing greater every day. But she was most worried about Porter and his fishing and the effect it was having on the family. "He was living his dream," Cindy says. "He was in California, he knew all of the big-bass guys, he was catching big fish. It seemed like he was just getting ready to attain his goal. But in my view he wasn't able to pull away from it enough to raise his daughter." She told him as much. Porter stubbornly fished for another few seasons, but finally decided that his wife and child had to come first, that he needed to nurture himself and Cindy back to health and provide a good home for Trechsel. So after seven years in the Golden State, the Halls picked up and moved back to Florida.

Porter had indeed given up on his dream just as it seemed reachable. This time, his family had taken precedence over his obsession. But that fact didn't make it any easier to swallow. "It bothered me a lot," he says. "I was not happy. I didn't know if I could get inspired at all to go fishing ever again if I couldn't be in California. At that point, I felt like the chase for me was certainly over."

On my second day in Mississippi, Porter took me to the town of Columbia, where the legendary NFL running back Walter Payton was born and raised. On the outskirts of town, the state had built a sixty-five-acre reservoir, called Lake Columbia. Porter wanted me to see it because it had been the original home of most of the eighteen mature bass that he had stocked in his pond.

When we arrived, I wandered around the property a bit. Next to the lake's parking lot, there was a big open-air awning that covered six large picnic tables. An only-in-Mississippi sign under the awning read NO WATERMELON CUTTING UNDER SHED

The lake was beautiful and empty. Only one other truck sat in the parking lot when we got there, something Porter says he encounters on most public lakes he's fished in the state. I found it peculiar that a lake in the heart of Deep South bass country would be this way, but Porter pointed out that the dominant piscatorial pursuit of most Mississippians was the farmed catfish. Most of the ponds that dot the farmland across the state are occupied by the whiskered fish that is farmed commercially and has become a prized table food across the country. But this lack of attention on bass in the state was fine with Porter. He's never caught anyone trying to poach his ponds. Most of the locals, he reckons, would think they just contained catfish anyway.

As I walked back to the dock, Porter was getting everything ready. He placed a cooler full of shiners in the boat, next to the four stout graphite rods. Just as he was putting the boat in the water, I noticed that he still had a registration sticker on the side of the craft that said LAKE CASITAS, CALIFORNIA. We shoved off and ran across the lake to a spot littered with the lily pad–like Lotus plants that make for excellent bass habitat. Porter set up the rods one by one. Each of them had an orange bobber positioned maybe four feet up the line from a big gold hook. Porter put the hook point in his jeans to hold it still as he reached into the cooler, which buzzed lightly with the sound of the aerator, and scooped out a shiner with an aquarium dip net. Then he hooked the bait-fish through both lips and cast out behind the boat where the orange bobber sat until the bait either got loose or was gobbled up by a bass. It was incredibly hot out on the water, unprotected from the blazing Mississippi sun. And it was only May. It was difficult to fathom how much hotter it would be down here in August. But this was bass weather.

We spent seven sweaty hours on the lake, going through four dozen shiners. The fishing was exciting, the bobber pulsating as a bass neared the bait or violently plunging underwater if one hit. We landed maybe twenty-five bass, most of decent size, but none big enough for Porter to even think about bringing back to his pond. I noticed a few times during the day that Porter kept an eye on the other boats on the lake (we were eventually joined by two other crafts). Whenever one of them would come in close, Porter would move off his spot, far enough away so that the other fishermen couldn't see how he was fishing the water. He was still secretive about his methods, though he was on a young reservoir with virtually no chance of spitting out the record. "I think I'm the only one on this lake who uses shiners," he said. And he aimed to keep it that way.

When the Halls moved back to Florida in August 1998, they set about trying to heal from the maladies that had struck them out West. But Porter felt aimless without the focal point of the record chase and says he compensated by drinking too much and putting on even more weight; he was up to 240 pounds. After a restless year, he decided that he just couldn't let go of his dream. That's when he concocted the idea of growing the fish himself and began to look for land to do just that in Mississippi.

The family had been through a lot together, and Porter thought that familiar Florida would be the salve they needed. But he was getting hints from Cindy that just being back home was not enough. She started to talk about starting anew with a different life for herself and Trechsel. In 2002, Porter decided to get his act together to try to save the marriage, turning the same vast energies and determination he had shown in his bass fishing toward improving his appearance. "I thought I could lose the weight and keep my wife," he says. He stopped drinking, cold turkey. He walked ten miles a day, in sweaty repetitive circles around his apartment building in the hot Florida sun. He watched what he ate for the first time in his life. And in just under a year, he lost seventy-five pounds. His before-and-after photos look like two different people. But his efforts were in vain, at least as far as the marriage was concerned. In March 2003, Cindy divorced him.

The obvious question, from someone looking at this situation from a distance, is whether Porter spent too much of his time and energy chasing the world record. Had his bass obsession been the reason for the divorce? Porter, to this point in my visit, had been very open about his passion for the record, bass in general, and the not-always-positive effect it had on his life. But this question left him somewhat stumped. "I don't know," he said. "Very possibly."

Cindy was a bit more candid about the effect that his lifelong quest had on the marriage, noting that while it wasn't the sole reason for the divorce, it was a dominant one. "Anyone who has spent as much time as he has on the water, traveling to get there, educating himself about other big-bass anglers, and building his own lakes like he has would be classified, by most people, as obsessed," she says. "And this will look worse in print than it really is, but we had Trechsel when he was just about to reach his goal, and he had an inability to see beyond that. I'm not sure he ever recovered from that."

For Porter, the divorce remains a fresh wound, just over a year old, and he still doesn't understand exactly why it happened. "Divorce is a real mind-fuck. I thought a lot of crazy thoughts after it happened, like selling everything and buying a trailer and moving out to California," he says. "But there's Trechsel . . ."

Seeing his daughter, being with her as she grows up into adolescence, he says, is the only reason he says he's still here in the South growing his fish in what he calls "clearly his second-best option when it comes to the world record." But the feeling I got from Porter is that there is another reason. He and Cindy talk almost every day on the phone, with the familiarity of best friends. And he spends every moment that he's not in Mississippi in the apartment he rented in Gainesville to be near them. It was an amicable divorce, they both say, with no spitting matches or battles for money or custody of Trechsel. They both agreed that the best scenario for their daughter was to live with her mother, as long as Porter could be close by. But Porter, from both his actions and his words, makes it clear that if it had been up to him, the split with Cindy would have never occurred.

On the day of my departure, Porter and I woke up early and went for a quick fish on his seven-acre pond. The scouting mission from two days prior had yielded only a few fish, so Porter wanted to try again. It would be just the fifth time he had fished the little pond (he's never fished the twenty-three-acre one and says he won't for years), and his restraint demonstrated his refinement of a virtue all record chasers knew so well: patience. "I just need to give these girls some time to grow," he says.

Patience is something that Porter has shown he possesses in spades when it comes to chasing the world record. After all, he has held on to the dream longer than most. At forty-nine, he has essentially become the eminence grise of the world-record bass chase. Most of the hardcores had given up by his age, after having spent their youth meticulously constructing the artifices they thought could get them the grail, help them reach the sun. But like Icarus, they all eventually succumbed to the intense heat and pressure. Bob Crupi was done by his mid-forties, and Mike Long, at only thirty-eight, seemed to be on the verge of burnout. But perhaps Porter's temporary respite from the California water wars had actually turned out to be a good thing, helping him avoid the seemingly inevitable crash down to earth. "I'm in it for the long haul," he says. "Most people have a good ten years in them. But I'm plodding along."

And he still sees himself going back out to California at some point in time, maybe when Trechsel enters college. He realizes that he can't fight off the urge too much longer. He says when he goes, he'll patiently scope out the scene for a few months before diving in. "I think I'd go where no one else is really trying to catch the record, maybe somewhere around the Bakersfield area to some obscure little lake," he says. He wants to find his own private Casitas again.

But there was a question that remained unanswered for me about Porter: What was it about this whole chase thing that kept him going, kept him motivated? He sat silently for a moment before answering. "I think about it a lot, why I'm addicted to this shit. I don't know if I can adequately put it into words. But I wake up every single day and think about it," he says. "There's just something about seeing a giant bass, I don't know, it cranks me up. To me there's just something beautiful, just beautiful about a giant bass, which is weird because the ones that get really big aren't all that pretty. In fact they're obese freaks of nature. But it's the rarity of the damn thing. You're just out there for years and years and years and all of a sudden—*bang*—there's this thing you've been looking for, for so long."

But was it all worth it? "It may not be. There are times when I realize that I ain't gonna live forever," he says. "And I wonder if I've been a complete idiot, that maybe I could have done something better for society and used my time on earth in a more giving way. This has been kind of a selfish use of my life." Left unsaid is the one sacrifice that he's made that turned out not to be worth it, the one he has the hardest time owning up to.

But a more pressing problem for Porter, at least in the near term, is that the money he inherited from his grandfather is nearly gone, especially after the $300,000 he plowed into the Mississippi project. The bank isn't broken yet, "but I'm walking the fine line," he says. With his support of Cindy, and Trechsel eventually going to college, he says it's not out of the question that someday he will be forced to sell the property, perhaps sometime soon.

But he's taken a step to rectify that situation. Next year, Porter will start working part-time for the University of Florida, in the fish biology department. It's a modest job. He won't even have his own desk, and the pay is just above minimum wage. But it will be the first real job he's had in thirteen years. From 1991 on, his "job" was essentially chasing the world record. The money, though it won't be much, will come in handy. Still, it seems to be a passive attempt at straddling the fine line between what was expected of him as a child—a "normal" life—and the life that he really wants to lead.

Porter mentioned to me on a few occasions that he's scared that someone else might beat him to the punch in the world-record chase, and even more scared of the effect it would have on him. "To be honest with you, if someone broke the record, I would quit fishing altogether," he says as we make one final long loop around the pond. "That's something I've really thought about. Hell, it might be good for me. I could finally relax."

But I find it hard to believe that Porter would give up on this chase. How could he, after going this long and this far? After all, the record is not a static entity. If it were broken tomorrow, it could be broken again the day after that. And after the time and energy and money and soul that he's put into it, he really has little choice but to press on, even if the record is broken. These ponds are his million-in-one shot, a Hail Mary that he's tossed up only because he has to. They are merely the latest manifestation—though perhaps the apex so far—of an obsession that has ultimately cost him his family. This quest has defined him. As the novelist Thomas McGuane once wrote, "You reach a point at which you have to view your life through the things you've spent so much time doing. The alternative is a perilous feeling of waste."

Just as we're nearing the dock, one of the orange bobbers behind the boat is pulled under the water, deep. Porter stops the trolling motor and picks up the rod, letting the fish run with the bait and line for a bit. He leans toward the fish, like a bowler staring down the alley at the pins, something he has done thousands of times in his life with varying degrees of hope and desperation and obsessiveness. When he feels the time is just right, he engages the spool on the reel, which abruptly stops the line. Then he turns his body backward, away from the fish, and swings the rod with as much force as his 5'7", newly lighter body can produce. He looks like an eager little kid taking an overhead swat at a piñata. The motion hooks the fish well, and he reels it in quickly to diminish any potential harm. It's a small bass, maybe 4 pounds, which means it's one of the fingerlings he stocked two years ago. Still, 4 pounds in two years is an excellent rate of growth—more than twice the normal rate—and on pace for his ultimate goal. He holds his bass by the mouth and admires its ample belly for just a second before gently laying it back in the brown water and watching it swim away. "I am really happy with the way they're growing," he says as we make for shore. "Really happy."

After we pull the boat out, Porter walks onto the dock alone, a man caught for the moment between the two distinct urges of family and obsession. He sits in a chair and gazes out over his pond. He lights a cigarette and fidgets a bit, and waits.

All fishermen are born honest, but they get over it.   —Ed Zern

CHAPTER EIGHT
Bassholes

L eaha Trew, a forty-five-year-old self-employed landscape main-
tenance worker in Santa Rosa, California, and her twenty-
one-year-old son, Javad, are an infamous fishing duo who call
themselves the "Trew Crew." According to the Trews, on August 24,
2003, Leaha cast a Storm Wildeye swimbait into Spring Lake, a
seventy-four-acre reservoir in Sonoma County, hooked a bass, and
ten minutes later was holding the new world record. The Trews said
that they weighed the fish on a Boga Grip, one that was certified
by the IGFA, and that the fish was 22 pounds, 8 ounces, surpassing
Perry's record by 4 ounces.

Javad took one photo of his mother with the very big bass. It
was the last exposure in his disposable camera, he said. In the picture, which was circulated widely on the Internet and reprinted in
Field & Stream, the petite, blond Leaha, wearing jean shorts and
with a cell phone clipped to her pocket, held the fish away from
her body and toward the camera. It's an age-old technique known
to most anglers, which artificially makes a fish appear bigger by
foreshortening the human in the background. The measurements,
the photo, and the fish—before it was released—were witnessed by
a man named Charles Fleming who was picnicking at the lake that
day. Apparently, no one thought to use Leaha's phone to call the

Fish and Game Department, which could have certified the fish on the spot.

The Trews sent an application to the International Game Fish Association. Leaha's fish, for a number of months, was listed as a "pending" world record on the IGFA Web site, the first fish to hold that spot in the Internet age. Millions of fishermen knew about her catch instantly. The first reaction was shock. Then the big-bass community came out of the woodwork, wielding their whuppin' sticks. Mike Long, Jed Dickerson, and bass expert Doug Hannon told *Field & Stream* that from the photograph they could tell there was no way that her fish was the record. Mike called the bass "a sixteen- or seventeen-pounder at best." But Leaha told the *Charlotte Observer*, "I'm absolutely positive I caught the world-record bass."

The IGFA took the application very seriously, convening a special verification committee that was made up of the IGFA president, its ambassador-at-large, and BASS founder Ray Scott. The organization went through months of fact-gathering and debate, driving the big-bass guys crazy with the agonizing wait. In the end, the IGFA ultimately rejected the Trews' application. "There just wasn't enough documentation or evidence," says Mike Leech, the organization's ambassador-at-large. The IGFA was not satisfied with the sole existing photo of the pixieish Leaha thrusting the fish toward the camera. And, as it turns out, that Charles Fleming who acted as the witness was actually a friend of the Trews, according to the IGFA. "We would certainly need a disinterested witness," says Leech.

Three months after the catch, Javad told a writer named Jeff Schroeder that when Leaha caught the fish, he didn't think it was anything special. "I don't get all the [fishing] magazines or follow the tournament trails, so I didn't know if it was a world record," he said. But that seems disingenuous, given the fact that he submitted an application to the IGFA and that he owns four line-test records for bass that he earned in 2002 and early 2003 from the National Freshwater Fishing Hall of Fame, another record-keeping organization. To some locals this episode was just another example of the Trew Crew's disturbing pattern of deceitful behavior, all instigated, they say, by Javad who, in this instance, was merely using his mother to shield him from scrutiny. "Javad is nothing but a publicity hound," says one local fisherman who wished to remain anonymous. "This is nothing but a bunch of bullshit. They're in it just for the money."

Money does seem to be a motivating factor, at least for Javad. When I reached him on the phone, he refused to let me speak to Leaha, then told me that he wouldn't talk unless I paid him to do so. When I turned down his request for money, he said, "Then I'll pass," and abruptly hung up.

According to news reports, the rejection of their application hasn't slowed the Trew Crew down. They're still hard after the fish. But as a result of their sketchy application, the IGFA has formally instituted a new process that allows the use of a polygraph exam for world-record bass applicants. Ray Scott admits that a polygraph—as a deterrent and detector—is not a watertight method, but says, somewhat cryptically, "It works better than heart surgery."

As I traveled around the United States researching this book, I kept running into stories about various hoaxes, near misses of the record, and devious deeds done to fish that all had something to do with the world's biggest bass. Some were gruesome enough to make you want to join PETA. A guy in California supposedly pumped concrete through a hose into a bass's mouth. A few were just too far-fetched to believe. A kid in Georgia told me that his friend had a 40-pound bass trapped in his parents' swimming pool. And some others might have even been true. Two fishermen in Florida claimed they caught a 25-pound bass, but left it out overnight as they slept in a tent. By the morning, raccoons had eaten everything but the head. The story of Leaha and Javad Trew was merely the most recent I heard.

That these types of stories are told and retold by bass fishermen all over the world should come as no surprise. If there is one axiom in the world of big-bass fishing, it is this: Controversy follows any giant bass of note. You will remember that George Perry's standing record has its fair share of doubters. And that Bob Crupi was accused of illegally using live trout to catch his bass. And that the bass that Jed Dickerson caught was the same one that Mike Long landed two years earlier, at least according to Mike Long. And Porter Hall's 18-pound, 8-ounce bass was caught on a plug lure, right? Or was it a crawdad? The controversy surrounding any fish—legitimately caught or not—that threatens Perry's hallowed achievement perhaps provides the truest measure of how important the record is to its pursuers.

As I investigated some of the stories I had been told, it struck me that there are three reasons for these suspicions, all of which are illustrated in the tale of the Trews. One is that fishing records are relatively difficult to police. Another is that there is a bass La Cosa Nostra that seems to believe that the record should fall only to one of their own. And lastly—and this one may come as a surprise—the world is full of liars and cheaters.

For the most part, recent record-breaking sports performances have been done in a very public manner, in packed stadiums and on television, in full view of thousands—if not millions—of eyewitnesses. We watch as Barry Bonds's seventy-first home run of 2001 sails 442 feet into the right centerfield stands at Pac Bell Park, breaking baseball's single-season home-run record. Or as

Emmitt Smith stumbles and stretches for an eleven-yard gain in Texas Stadium in 2003, surpassing Walter Payton as the NFL's all-time rushing leader. And if we missed seeing it live, all we had to do is flip to SportsCenter to watch the countless replays. There it is, we say, feeling satisfied. We saw it with our own two eyes.

But bass fishing—at least outside of the tournaments—is a solitary, secretive endeavor that takes place on lakes far away from the madding crowds and the electronic eye. No rules and regulations govern how the game is played, no referees and instant replay help ensure that it's all done fairly. The IGFA does its best to make sure any new record is legitimate, but it's a daunting task and an inexact science. Fishing records are verified by a scale (one that's sometimes owned by the angler himself), a measuring tape, a few easily doctored photographs, and an eyewitness or two who just might have some stake in the outcome. Then the fish, more often than not these days, is released to die another day. The record application process functions like a referee who's been brought in two days after a game has been played to call the penalties and make sure the score is correct—all based on accounts from the players and a few photographs. But the method is the best we've got. The IGFA can't be everywhere all the time to actually witness a catch.

And for some reason, Americans, though they revere achievements, sometimes also revile the achievers. As Roger Maris tracked down Babe Ruth's legendary single-season home-run record in 1961, fans—even in his own stadium—routinely booed his every at-bat. Similarly in bass fishing, the outdoor press revels in the stories of controversy, which seem to make for juicier copy. And the big-bass boys, well, they jealously guard their opportunity to break the record, and go on the attack whenever that's threatened. The majority of the most damaging rumors and innuendo about big bass start with this crowd.

But there is another damn good reason for the rampant skepticism, especially as far as the largest of the largemouths is concerned. Like diamonds, truly giant bass are rare, precious, and overpoweringly intoxicating to those who pursue them. Anything assigned this kind of hypervalue will cause more than a few people to lie, steal, and cheat (and even kill, at least in Carl Hiaasen's 1987 novel *Double Whammy*, a hilarious send-up of bass fishing mania) to obtain them. My cousin, Latham Gaines, invented a name for the perpetrators of these devious and dishonorable deeds. He calls them "Bassholes."

Lake Miramar is a small reservoir located some fifteen miles north of San Diego. Among the big-bass crowd, it is considered to be one of the most likely candidates to produce the next world record, having pumped out numerous fish of over 18 pounds. But it is most famous—at least in bass-fishing circles—for producing two of the most bizarre stories in the annals of the world-record chase. Miramar is bass fishing's Roswell, a place where cover-ups and conspiracy theories emanate like a foul, fishy odor.

On June 23, 1972, a twenty-six-year-old angler named Dave Zimmerlee caught a 20-pound, 15-ounce bass on Miramar. The fish sent a jolt through the big-bass community. It was the second-largest bass ever recorded at the time, and the first of 20 pounds or heavier since George Perry's fish forty-one years earlier.

But just three days after Zimmerlee's historic catch, sportswriter Rolla Williams penned a piece in what was then known as the *San Diego Union* that called the entire episode into question. Under the title "Big Bass Mystery: Dead or Alive?" Williams reported that the story had "two versions to choose between." Williams had interviewed an eyewitness who accused Zimmerlee of committing a cardinal sin in the fishing world, something that only a Basshole would dream of doing: that is, picking up a dead fish, or "floater," and claiming to have caught it.

"My wife and I were trolling for trout, getting ready to leave when we passed this big fish in the water," the eyewitness, Ed Metcalf, was quoted as saying. "I didn't want a dead fish, but then I thought maybe I should carry it over to the dock and let somebody examine it. So I turned around and here comes this guy who lifts it out of the water. He didn't have a fishing rod or anything. And he goes off to the dock. You know the rest of the story."

The rest of the story is still a matter of debate. Though Metcalf said that "several fishermen at the dock saw the same thing," Zimmerlee maintains that he didn't pick up a floater, but caught the fish on a nightcrawler. But most don't believe him. "Yeah, maybe he had a nightcrawler on his hook when he reached over and picked up the dead fish," says Rick Felchlin, a ranger who has worked at Miramar since that time. And Mike Butler, a taxidermist at Lyons & O'Haver in La Mesa who did the mount for Zimmerlee says: "When that fish came in, it absolutely reeked like it had been dead for days."

Either way, Zimmerlee's fish still stands as the seventh-largest bass of all time. And his fish, as it turns out, wouldn't be the wackiest thing Mike Butler would witness during his thirty-year career as a taxidermist for Lyons & O'Haver. That would come nearly fifteen years later, from another bass that formerly called Miramar home.

Sandy DeFresco, a forty-seven-year-old fuzzy-haired woman, sold Cokes and candy bars at the concession stand at Miramar. On the morning of March 14, 1988, she caught a bass that weighed 21-pounds, 10-ounces, ranking just behind Perry's, making her the first woman to crack the list of the top twenty-five largemouths. Her story proved to be so irresistible that she was forced to hire a lawyer named Kevin Mineo to handle interview requests and negotiate tackle endorsements. Syndicated columnist Mike Royko wrote a story about her in the *Chicago Tribune*, and the president and vice president of Zetabait—the maker of the plastic worm she used to seduce the bass—flew out from Jacksonville to meet the new queen of bass fishing.

Mineo and DeFresco decided they needed a mount of the fish to show off on the various television interviews they had lined up. So they brought the fish down to Lyons & O'Haver and struck a deal with the owner, Hughie Lyons, to have the famous fish mounted for free.

Taxidermists generally use one of two types of fish mounts. The old way is known as a skin mount and, as the name implies, the actual skin of the bass is buttressed by an interior layer of plaster, then touched up with glossy paints. These types of mounts, found in old sporting lodges and yard sales across the country, don't hold up very well over the years, tending to flake and discolor or fade. The more modern method is to make a plaster mold—from either the physical body of the fish or its recorded measurements—then construct a fiberglass replica from said mold. Mineo and DeFresco, knowing that they would be subjecting this mount to some serious wear and tear while shuttling it back and forth between interviews, opted for the fiberglass method, and made the fateful decision to use the actual fish for the casting mold. And Hughie Lyons knew just the right man for the job.

As DeFresco, Mineo, and Lyons gathered around, Mike Butler began to cut the belly of the bass wide open. He wanted to get the entrails out of the fish so he could replace them with dampened sawdust, which holds up better under the pressure of the casting process. But when he reached his hand into the belly, he felt something odd. Something hard. He gave it a yank, and out popped a lead weight, the type commonly found on a diving belt. It measured three by four inches and weighed exactly 2 pounds,

8.75 ounces. "Everybody just stood there for a moment in shock," says Butler. DeFresco and Mineo appeared horrified. Finally, Hughie Lyons looked over at them both and said, "Take your fish back. We won't be mounting it," dismissing the Bassholes from his shop.

So the million-dollar question (literally, it seems) was, did De-Fresco put the weight in the fish? Butler, for one, says he doesn't think so. Most convincing to him is the fact that she and Mineo were actually present in the shop when the weight—and her claim—plopped to the floor. "Why would she have brought it to be mounted, knowing that I was going to cut the fish open?" he says. Speculation about how the weight got into the bass has been the subject of newspaper and magazine stories as recently as 2004.

The juiciest rumor going is that DeFresco and her now ex-husband (one wonders if the fish caused the split), Phil DeFresco, went fishing on Miramar one night, and she caught a huge bass. Fishing at night was legal in 1988 for Miramar employees and those who lived on the lake, but it was a practice that was frowned upon by other anglers who believed that it gave the few who could do it an unfair advantage (similar to the way that some anglers feel when Mike Long fishes closed lakes). The DeFrescos were sensitive to this criticism, and decided that in order to skirt any potential controversy, they would just bring the fish in under the light of day. When they got back to shore, they tied the fish up on a stringer line that was attached to the boat to keep it there overnight. Phil wanted to make sure the bass would remain under the water and out of view, so he tied on a diver's belt weight to the stringer to keep the fish down. The plan was for Sandy to take the boat out the next morning with the bass attached, "catch" it, then bring it to the dock.

Everything seemed to work perfectly. The next morning when she paddled the boat out, no one saw her fiddling with the fish, and when she came back to the dock, everyone present believed she had caught it then and there. But one thing went horribly awry. Unbeknownst to Sandy, the fish had somehow swallowed the weight overnight, a very real possibility given the enormous size of its mouth. As the story goes, Sandy just assumed the weight had fallen off and was just as surprised as anyone else when Mike Butler pulled it out of the bass's belly.

DeFresco's bass, without the weight, weighed 19 pounds, 1 ounce, and is still recognized as the nineteenth-largest bass ever caught.

As if DeFresco's misadventures weren't bad enough, the story of Paul Duclos should serve as a cautionary tale to any would-be record chaser. Like a Greek tragic hero, Duclos had one of those days where fate seemed to intervene—first in a good way, then in a bad way—like it couldn't make up its mind. Duclos might not have been a true Basshole, but he paid a price for his naïvete and innocence.

On March 1, 1997, Duclos, who is the owner of a carpet-cleaning service in Santa Rosa, California, went fishing on Spring Lake (yep, the Trews' home water). He was using a large swimbait that was painted like a trout when he hooked into a bass. At first, he had no idea how big the fish was. It felt heavy, but it was coming to the boat with little resistance. As he got the bass in closer, he realized that the fish wasn't fighting because the treble hooks on his lure had clamped its mouth shut. He also happened to notice that the bass was the biggest he'd ever laid his eyes on.

Duclos unhooked the fish and brought it immediately in to shore, where he showed it to Lou Skorupa, a retired Coast Guard commander who was also fishing at the lake that day. Duclos knew that he had a special fish. He ran it up to the ranger station, but they didn't have a certified scale. So he called the Outdoor Pro Shop in nearby Rohnert Park. He asked—no, begged—the owner, Ken Elie, to bring a proper scale down to the lake. "He was in an absolute panic, stuttering and talking really fast," says Elie. But Elie was the only one in the shop that morning, and Federal Express and UPS were knocking on the door with their daily deliveries. "I told him I was really sorry but that I couldn't leave the store," he says. So Duclos, out of options, called his wife, Shelly, and asked her to bring down the scale from their bathroom. When she arrived, Duclos weighed himself on the scale first. It read 180 pounds. Then he weighed himself while holding the fish. It read 204 pounds, meaning the bass would have broken the record by almost two pounds. Shelly took a photo of him— wearing sunglasses and a black turtleneck underneath his button-down shirt—holding the massive fish. Then he released it. "I just did what I felt was the right thing to do," Duclos told me.

Word about the fish spread rapidly. His story showed up in the California papers, and *Outdoor Life* magazine put him on its cover. Most accounts expressed a fair bit of skepticism about Duclos's claim. Anonymous callers reached his home. They harassed his wife and cursed him and called him a liar.

Duclos, feeling he had done nothing wrong, was stung by the ferocity of the attacks on his character. He even went so far as to send his bathroom scale to the IGFA to prove that he wasn't a liar. Mike Leech, who was president of the record-keeping organization then, remembers receiving it. "We stood on the thing and it jiggled back and forth a pound or so," he says. "Then we put a dead weight on it, and it weighed a pound too heavy." Even if they had found it to be exact, bathroom scales are not certified by the IGFA for records. Leech says, given all the aggravation and bad press Duclos received, he eventually began to feel sorry for him. "His fish may have actually been the record," Leech says. "But the poor guy just didn't document it the right way."

Initially, Duclos saw nothing other than grief for the fish. "I wasn't looking for notoriety, or I would have killed the fish. Whether it's the record or not, I don't care," he told *Outdoor Life* in 1997. "I'm happy I let the fish go. If I had kept it, my life would have been a living hell. Worse than it has been. . . . I'm not a very religious person, but I was blessed by catching this thing. I got to hold her—and so did my wife. . . . Someday when we're old and gray, we'll have a fish story to tell."

But now, nearly eight years later, he says he's found some modicum of peace. "There were a helluva lot more positives than negatives" that came from the experience, he says. "I met some good people who helped me through this." Does he think his fish was the world record? "Absolutely," he says. And Duclos is still hard at it. "I just love to catch big bass," he says. "If another one like that happens to come along, well, then that would be great."

Duclos's scale still collects dust in an IGFA warehouse.

———

It's not hard to understand why some have been going to some lengths to "catch" the new record. Since the 1970s, the world-record bass has been called "the million-dollar fish," because, the reasoning goes, the lucky angler who hauls it in will be bombarded with tackle endorsements from companies eager to attach their names to the greatest bass of all time. That money, however, has always been hypothetical, never taking into account that the person who catches the new world record might just be using a cane pole and a cricket. But from 1998 to 2003, thanks to Mickey Owens and Bill Currie, founders of the Big Bass Record Club, that theoretical money was actual, to the tune of $8 million.

The six-year run of the BBRC was an exciting time for big-bass anglers. Folks like Mike Long made a decent side-living off the smaller checks that went out to the state winners. But the introduction of so much actual money—as it always seems to do—also had the effect of raising the lunacy of the entire world-record bass chase a few notches. Almost every month, it seemed, there was another con artist who called up the club or sent in photos of bass that were purported to be the next world record. In the second year of the contest, one woman e-mailed the BBRC to say that she had caught a 46-pound (!) bass that she had then put in her fish aquarium at home. She pestered the staff at the BBRC every day, almost to the point that some folks there started to believe her. But when she finally sent in a picture and measurements of the bass's length and girth, the fish turned out to be a measly 8 pounds. There was another guy that Owens heard about who had just gotten married near a lake in Florida. During his own wedding reception, as he was dancing and thanking the guests for coming to the festivities, he glanced out at the lake and saw a huge fish jumping. The man sprinted for the dock, found a fishing rod, and commenced trying to hook the bass that he was convinced was the world record, leaving behind a disbelieving wedding crowd and an unbelievably pissed-off wife.

In 2001, a man named Elmer Rodgers, who lived in the wooded countryside near Orlando, started calling the BBRC offices every day. He said that on a lake adjacent to his property, the world-record bass came up to feed every morning. Rodgers said he had yet to catch it and was afraid that his time was running out to do so. Elmer Rodgers had cancer.

After nearly three dozen calls from the sick man, Owens said he started to feel sorry for the guy, so he agreed to meet him at his lake and check out his fish. "I went over there, and the guy was in real badass shape," says Owens. "I mean his time was coming real soon." Owens and Rodgers, who was by then confined to a wheel-chair, went out to the lake to look for the fish one morning. And lo and behold, just like Rodgers said, an absolutely enormous fish rose from the depths. "The thing had to be close to forty pounds," says Owens. "The problem was that it was a catfish." Owens didn't have the heart to tell Rodgers the truth about his fish. As they wheeled back to his house, Owens told the sick man how grateful he was that he had shown him this fish, and that Rodgers should consider himself very fortunate to have seen the world-record bass. Owens never heard from Rodgers again, but hoped that he passed on with some semblance of peace.

But Owens would have his most memorable run-in with per-haps the most notorious of all Bassholes, a man named Phil M. Jay, the owner of the aptly named Outlaw Bait and Tackle store near San Diego. Rumors about Jay abound in the big-bass world. Just the mention of his name makes Mike Long roll his eyes and appear as if he is going to be sick. Phil Jay has been after the world-record bass since the late 1970s. He is a very good big-bass fisherman by most accounts, especially his own. He told me that he had landed thirty bass over 18 pounds and "three or four over twenty," which would make him a more accomplished big-basser than Mike Long. But, by those same accounts (excluding his own), it seems that Jay has a very hard time staying on the straight and narrow.

In 1981, Danny Angotti, a detective for the San Diego Police Department and a bass-fishing addict, got a call from Jim Brown, then the manager of the city lakes. Brown told Angotti that a man named Phil Jay claimed he had caught the world-record bass, weighing in at 24 pounds, 1 ounce, at the scene of so many other Basshole episodes, Lake Miramar. Jay didn't weigh the fish at the dock, which everyone knew had a certified scale. Instead he took it to the meat department of a local supermarket. According to

Brown, Jay was already under suspicion for illegally poaching bass at night. Rangers posing as fishermen had been tracking his every move on the lake for years. And this fish only seemed to amp up the feelings of distrust. Brown figured since Jay's claim might entail fraudulent behavior, he should get the police involved. So he asked Angotti, a fellow fisherman, to check it out.

Angotti called Jay the next morning. Jay explained that he didn't weigh his fish at the lake because he wanted to avoid the ruckus that the world record would certainly cause. "I asked him if I could see the fish and he said 'Sure,' " says Angotti, who has since retired from the force. "He told me that he had frozen the fish. I started to think this all sounded like a bunch of BS."

A week went by and Jay never called back to set up a meeting. During this time, according to Brown, a young man in a taxidermy shop, "really no older than a kid," broke down and admitted that Jay had paid him a couple hundred dollars to falsify the weight of the fish. Meanwhile, Angotti had placed another call to Jay. And Jay, perhaps sniffing danger, explained to him that his attorney had suggested that he not talk about the fish to anyone. Jay, who is now sixty-four, denies ever paying anyone to lie about his fish. "The city of San Diego just doesn't like me," he says. And though he eventually dropped his application to the IGFA after the organization demanded more evidence of his catch, he says: "I am sure that I am the world-record holder."

After that episode, Jay became very well known in the big-bass world, but for all the wrong reasons. When I contacted a southern California bait-and-tackle store in trying to track him down, the owner there told me, "I don't know why you would want to talk to that jerk." But Jay's tenacity and persistence is such that he almost seems to engender a bit of begrudging admiration from those who've been asked to verify or repudiate his catches and claims over the years. "You've got to hand it to him," says Jim

Brown. "Besides being a very good fisherman, he's been in the middle of some bizarre stories. Others may have caught more big bass, but Phil has probably raised more questions and eyebrows with his catches over the years than all of them combined. I'm not alone in regarding him as a kind of charming scoundrel." And apparently, Jay hasn't changed his spots.

Mickey Owens had heard the rumors about Phil Jay when he started the BBRC, but it wasn't until the club's fourth year that he would actually hear from the man himself. As 2001 drew to a close, Mike Long had the biggest fish of the year in California—his giant 20-12—and looked like a cinch for the BBRC's $25,000 state prize, which he had won for two years running. But in late December, just a few days before the deadline, the BBRC received an application for a bass that bettered Mike's by just a few ounces. The application came from Phil Jay. Almost immediately, calls started pouring in from other California fishermen and outdoor writers, who said simply that Jay was shady and that Mike Long was a better person, so Mike should get the money. "It's like there's a bass mafia out there that sticks up for each other," says Owens. Sound familiar? Perhaps Jay was the recipient of a "hit," and was getting "bitch-slapped" from one of those bassfellas.

Anyway, Owens said it didn't matter to him if everyone hated Phil Jay and loved Mike Long. "I didn't care who won," says Owens. "As long as the fish was legitimate, I had to give the money away anyway." But there was something fishy about Jay's application, including differing accounts of exactly which lake the fish had actually come from and accounts from eyewitnesses who said they had seen Jay pull the fish out a freezer (which must have piqued the interest of Danny Angotti). And though Owens says the calls didn't sway him, the announcement of that year's California winner was postponed a bit while he tried to gather as many facts as possible. In the meantime, he got a letter from Jay that threat-

ened to sue the BBRC if he was not declared the winner. Owens
didn't like being bullied. He wrote back to Jay and asked that he
take a polygraph test to settle this once and for all. Jay declined. "I
thought if I took one every one else should take one as well," he
says. A few days later, Jay became the first and only person to
be expelled from the BBRC, and Mike Long walked away with
$25,000.

As I read over these stories, it struck me that, despite their out-
rageousness, ethics in the quest for the world-record bass treads a
fine line, one that seems to be defined by each angler on his or her
own. Bob Crupi, with his black-and-white version of the world, is
sure that he's on the right side, and you're not. Mike Long is a perfectionist who seems to hold himself to a higher standard than
anyone else, yet he jumps at the chance to take advantage of his
own fame to fish lakes that are closed to everyone else. Mac Weakley and Buddha at least have admitted that their motive is big
money. But is attempting to grow the world record—whether
you're Porter Hall or the state of Texas—an ethical thing to do?
And even what goes on in the California reservoirs, where bass
grow to unnatural sizes because of stocked fish that are fed to
them like Chinese takeout, may not be something a purist could
stomach. Dazy Perry, the son of the record holder, even goes so far
as to say that if a bass from outside of its native range—Florida
and Georgia—were to break the record, it should have an asterisk
by it in the record books.

 Sure, stuffing a weight down a fish's mouth goes well beyond
the ethical pale. But perhaps it's just the darkest edge of a huge
gray area. And maybe these Bassholes are really just examples of
the broader reality of modern sports, where something is irretrievably lost from the purity—and enjoyment—of an activity when it

becomes a pursuit of records and riches. I mentioned Barry Bonds earlier, how we could watch his record-breaking home-run ball sail out of the park. But his records will always bear the stain of steroids. Is anything pure anymore?

These thoughts swirled around my head as I found myself doing something that many might find unethical. I was boarding a plane for Cuba, a country I wasn't legally supposed to enter, but a place that's been a fixed star in my imagination for years.

"And the best fisherman is you."

"No. I know others better."

"Qué va," the boy said. "There are many good fishermen and some great ones. But there is only you."

—Ernest Hemingway, *The Old Man and the Sea*

CHAPTER NINE
Castro's Bass

L ike its movies, television shows, and blue jeans, America's most popular fish has also been exported all over the globe. Largemouth bass are now found across Latin America and Europe; in Zimbabwe and South Africa; and in Japan. Generally speaking, anywhere in the world you find a mild climate and a dash of fresh water, you'll also find bass. And like those other American exports, nothing about the bass's arrival in a new society is ever neutral. Just as Nepalese children find themselves suddenly coveting American cars and hairstyles after watching reruns of *Beverly Hills, 90210*, fishermen the world over have become obsessed with catching bass wherever the fish has been introduced.

Perhaps predictably, in no overseas country has bass mania taken a greater hold than in Japan. The story goes that back in 1925, a Japanese businessman named Tetsuma Akaboshi procured four hundred bass from California and smuggled them into his home country, dumping the fingerlings into Lake Ashinoko, not far from Tokyo. The bass, as they always do, proliferated—moved either by migrating birds or fishing enthusiasts—and are now found in lakes from the capital to Kyoto, and even in eight of the thirteen moats that surround Tokyo's Imperial Palace. Some Americans may view this invasion of a foreign species as somehow fitting and just, given the takeover of so many American acres by invasive Japanese weeds like kudzu and knotweed. But the Japanese authorities don't find it so amusing. Fear of the foreign fish has even prompted an official government initiative to eradicate the bass over worries that the species will eat and eventually wipe out the nation's beloved ayu, chub, and crucian carp. In the Imperial Palace's moats, there is an even graver concern that the large-mouths will gobble up the native goby, a fish that Emperor Aki-hito, a trained ichthyologist, has a particular affection for. The bias against bass anglers also seems to have been exported. "Japanese bass fishing is a 'dark fishing' and cannot be called a sport," Minoru Sato, the director of the National Federation of Fisheries Cooperative Association, recently told the *Los Angeles Times*. "Bass anglers are very bad mannered—parking a car on a plowed field, interrupting traffic, cutting off lures if gotten caught in fishing nets. It is a lawless situation regarding a foreign fish."

But in the past fifteen years, despite (or perhaps because of) the emperor's and the government's best efforts, bass fishing has become the new Elvis in Japan, especially among the country's youth, for whom the sport taps into all of the outlaw, counterculture character (and growth) that skateboarding has in the United States. Japan-based tackle manufacturers, like Yozuri, Shimano, and Daiwa, now supply bass anglers all over the world. Record hunters Mike Long and Bob Crupi are worshiped by Japanese fishing nuts. And the country has two wildly popular bass-fishing TV shows, a pro circuit, and five magazines—with names like *Basser* and *Crazy Bass*—that are devoted to *dekkai* bass, the Japanese term for big, fat largemouths.

Takahiro Omori, now thirty-three, was one of those young

bass-obsessed rebels. In 1992, against his parents' wishes, he decided to forgo college and moved from his home in Tokyo to a small town near Lake Fork Reservoir in Texas, to pursue his dream of becoming a professional bass fisherman in the United States, He slept in his truck, washed dishes at night, and promptly finished 304th out of 308 competitors in his first U.S. tournament. But after a few painful years, he eventually caught on, and in August 2004, Omori won the Bassmaster Classic, becoming the first foreigner to capture fishing's most prestigious tournament. After so many years of struggle capped by the ultimate triumph, Japan's new hero reported that he felt "dizzy."

And of course, wherever bass and the bass-fishing culture have been imported, the story of George Perry and his world-record fish has always come along with it. Countries outside of the United States have shown big promise in growing huge bass, and it's very plausible that the next world record will not be an American fish. The biggest bass so far out of Japan is a reported 17-pounder. In South Africa, there have been a handful of fish that weighed in the mid-teens. And in the 1980s, the conventional wisdom in the bass-fishing world was that the next record was going to come from one of the clear, underfished reservoirs in northern Mexico—lakes like Guerrero, Huites, and especially Baccarac, where locals claim to have a found a 26-pound bass floating dead with a 3-pound tilapia stuck in its throat.

But while Japan may be bass crazy, no foreign land has captured the imagination of U.S. world-record chasers more than a little island in the Caribbean, the nagging thorn in Uncle Sam's side, the nation led by that charismatic, bearded man in military fatigues who has, at last count, outlasted the bungling diplomacy of nine U.S. presidents and has outlived four of them. Florida-strain bass were originally imported to Cuba from the United States in fifty-five-gallon drums by the United Fruit Company from 1915 to 1920, to provide a little sport for the industrialists. The bass have taken well to the island lifestyle. A school of thought suggests that Cuba's longer growing season has produced a genetically superior bass that matures faster and grows bigger than its American cousins. And the rumors about big bass have drifted with the (no) trade winds across the Straits of Florida. During the 1970s and '80s, stories circulated that eleven different fish caught in Cuba had topped the record. On Lake Hanabanilla, a 26-pounder was supposedly hauled up in a net. A few years back, a 28-pounder was said to have been caught in Lake Leonero. In each case, the record-breaking fish was eaten before it could be verified. Regardless of whether any of those rumors are true, the standing certified Cuban record of 18 pounds is enough to make American big bassers salivate over the possibility of it all.

Cuba was like a fever dream for me. In the weeks leading up to my trip, I would wake up in the middle of the night, startled and sweating. I worried about getting thrown in jail for going there. I thought about the intense summer sun. And I wondered if the country could possibly stand up to the dreamy notions I had concocted about it. I wasn't the only one who had been left fever-ridden by the country. Cuba had staked out its own prominent place in the mythology of the world-record bass chase. Sowbelly was swimming around somewhere in one of the country's Edenic lakes, that fact the record chasers knew for sure. But they also knew that it was unlikely they would ever get down there, which, of course, only made the country play an even bigger role in their own fantasies. But I decided in August 2004 that I *had* to get down there, to find out for myself.

Havana looked like the dark side of the moon as my Aerocaribe flight from Cancún made its descent into José Martí International Airport. Hurricane Charley had ripped through the country with 150-mile-per-hour winds just three days before my visit, and most of the Cuban capital was still immersed in a blackout. But the cover of darkness seemed somehow fitting, like it allowed me to sneak into this forbidden country, out of view of the brightly lit behemoth that lay only ninety miles north, across the perilous Straits of Florida.

As I drove through the darkened city that night, I passed hundreds of Cubans who had swarmed into the streets, walking, talking, dancing, and avoiding the gloom of their unlit houses. I arrived at the Hotel Nacional de Cuba, one of Havana's finest establishments. There was no blackout there—the lights of the hotel shone brightly to the seawall a hundred yards away. The tourists must remain happy.

The Nacional, coincidentally, was the hotel in which my grandparents had honeymooned back in the 1940s. The Spanish neoclassical structure opened in 1930, designed by the American architectural firm of McKim, Mead, and White, which also built the original Pennsylvania Station in New York City. The hotel had been a standard-bearer of Cuba's prerevolutionary excesses. In the late 1930s, the mobster Meyer Lansky convinced the Cuban leader and U.S. puppet, General Fulgencio Batista y Zaldívar, to let him build a grand casino there. In 1946, Lucky Luciano held the infamous summit of leading U.S. mafiosi on the hotel's roof deck (re-created in *The Godfather, Part II*) to discuss the carving up of the city. No, my grandparents weren't mobsters, but they enjoyed the charms of the Nacional, as have the likes of Winston Churchill, Marlon Brando, and Frank Sinatra. In a city of decrepitude, the Nacional remains a stately reminder of Havana's past glamour.

In the grand lobby of the hotel, I met Samuel Yera—daydreamer, successful fishing guide, fervent world-record chaser, and perhaps the best bass fisherman in Cuba. At the bar, as three fat men played guitars and sang tenor, Sammy and I had a ceremonial *mojito*—lime juice, mint, Angostura, soda water, and Cuban rum—currently the drink of the moment in Manhattan. Sammy, who is forty-three, was wearing a big shiny BASS belt buckle and a denim fishing shirt with a hand-sewn International Game Fish Association patch on the right breast. He was skinny and taut, with short oil-black hair and a salt-and-pepper beard. His wire-rimmed glasses, the slight hint of crow's feet around his eyes, and his generally quiet, thoughtful nature gave him the distinct air of an intellectual. Strangely, he also had broad and somewhat out-sized shoulders for his slight frame. Later on in the trip, I would find out why.

I wasn't the first person who had traveled to Cuba in search of an elusive prize. Ever since Columbus first laid eyes on Cuba on October 27, 1492, the world has flocked to her shores hunting for some sort of treasure. The Spanish originally came seeking gold, and finding none, settled for the island's abundance of to-bacco, sugar, and rum during their four hundred-year-reign. Pirates laid in wait in the island's protected coves, picking off galleons weighted down with New World booty. At the turn of the twentieth century, American industrialists, attracted by cheap labor and a year-round growing season, constructed huge sugar factories in the countryside. The island served up booze to slake the thirst of dry Americans during Prohibition, gambling when stateside casinos were shut down, bountiful game and fish for high-rolling sportsmen, and willing prostitutes for the legions of college kids on spring break looking to shed their virginity as easily as their winter coats.

One of Cuba's best-known treasure seekers was Ernest Hemingway, who spent the better part of the 1940s and '50s there. He wrote the first few chapters of *For Whom the Bell Tolls* at the Hotel Ambos Mundos near Havana and used the country as a backdrop for *To Have and Have Not, Islands in the Stream* and, most famously, *The Old Man and the Sea*. He sipped frozen daiquiris at 10 a.m. at El Floridita that "felt, as you drank them, the way downhill glacier skiing feels running through powder snow," then gulped down *mojitos* later in the afternoon at La Bodeguita del Medio. Hemingway loved Cuba because, as he bluntly put it, it had "both fishing and fucking." Clearly a man who had his priorities straight.

Fidel Castro's revolution in 1959 changed the island for good (or at least for a good long time), making it harder for foreign nations—especially its big neighbor to the north—to exploit it. His power grab also set the stage for Cuba's ascension into global prominence. The failed Bay of Pigs invasion, the missile crisis that brought the world within moments of nuclear holocaust, and Castro's continued defiance in the face of the U.S. trade embargo has turned Cuba into a pugnacious island that "refuses to accept its real size and weight in the world," as journalist Christopher Hitchens wrote.

Since the revolution, Cuba has basically been off-limits to Americans, which of course has only added to its allure, prompting hundreds of thousands to break U.S. law to travel there. What attracts them is the undeniable mystique of the sultry island—the warm sea breezes, the pulsating mambo, the fat cigars, the sweet rum, and the beautiful women. But to a certain subset of the American population, there is one Cuban jewel that stands out among all others: its forbidden—and possibly world record–size—largemouth bass.

On my first morning in Cuba, Sammy and I jumped into a rented Kia and started the three-hour southeasterly trek to his hometown of Santa Clara. As we left Havana, Sammy told me that he missed the lively Cuban capital "sometimes at night," but he was clearly excited to be going home to see his wife, Margarita, and his infant daughter, the only one of his three girls who still lives at home. We took the country's main thoroughfare, which travels the spine of Cuba, and is named—with typical Communist flair—the Central Highway. Sammy drove fast on the bumpy road, which would have been a six-lane freeway had the lanes been marked. Only a few humble houses dotted the sides of the road, and the rest was a lonely landscape of green grasses and the occasional royal palm tree. We passed just three billboards on the drive, all of which carried not advertising messages, but political ones like *"Patria o meurte!"* (Patriotism or death!). Some farmers had spread out a hundred feet of yellow rice on what would have been the right lane of the highway, using the sun and hot pavement to dry the grains. A few men with handheld scythes cut the overgrown grasses that encroached on the road. And dozens of Cubans stood fanning themselves on the side of the highway, either trying to hitch rides or sell the sweaty hunks of white cheese they held out hopefully to passing cars.

The preferred mode of travel on the highway seemed to be the *coches*, which are handmade horse- or mule-driven carts. Only a few other vehicles labored on the asphalt, but some of the ones we did pass were magnificent, and are another major reason that Americans travel to Cuba: to see what is perhaps the world's greatest collection of American cars from the 1940s and '50s, the gilded age of U.S. automobile manufacturing. On our way to Santa Clara, we passed a '52 Chevy Styleline Deluxe, a '53 Studebaker Starlight Coupe, and a '59 Fleetwood Cadillac, all with grinning grillwork, winking chrome, and stylish fins that tapered over the brake lights. These pre-embargo American cars are called *cacharros* in Cuba, which literally means "broken-down jalopies." But the Cubans use the term with affection, and some of the cars we passed had obviously been worried over lovingly, sporting refurbished engines and a brand-new sheen. But many others were literally broken down on the side of the road, with bodies that had been layered catastrophically with house paint.

As we drove, Sammy's passion for all things bass became quickly apparent. In his excellent English, he asked me about my research so far, if I had been out to Lake Casitas in California or to Lake Fork in Texas. He wanted to know what Bob Crupi was like as a person, about what I thought of Paul Duclos and the bathroom scale incident. In answering his questions, I felt the same way I did when I was interviewing Porter Hall: that here was a man who was so possessed by the chase for the world record bass that he craved any and all information he could gather about it. The difference, of course, was that for Porter Hall, the information was somewhat easier to come by. Porter could travel to California whenever he liked; he could buy the magazines, call his sources, or look up anything on the Internet anytime.

But for Sammy, the facts came from the snippets of stories told by his American clients, or from the back issues of *Field & Stream* or *Bassmaster* that those same clients smuggled down for him, or from the limited time the government allows him to surf the Web. He says he's learned all he could about the world record so he can be a better guide for tourists. "It makes it easier to talk to people," he says. "If I find out my clients are from California, I can talk to them about Casitas or see if they know Bob Crupi. I can start a conversation this way, melt the ice."

But clearly these facts and stories also nourished his dreams. Though his country is the place he is sure the world record can be caught, it was the American bass-angling scene that intrigued him most. Sammy told me that if he were ever free to travel that he would go immediately to the United States. "I would like to fish in California and in Texas and in some of the places that are less crowded, like Alabama and Florida," he says. And one of his first stops, he said, would be the Bass Pro Shops superstore in Springfield, Missouri. "I would go there and spend two days just walking around looking at things," he says.

It was somehwat sad irony that this man who could not leave his country knew so much about the rest of the world and that he wanted to be able to leave Cuba—if just for a vacation—when so many others wanted to get in. Sammy knew that as long as Castro was in power, he was prevented physically from going anywhere, which is why he disappeared so often into his daydreams, which always involved his passion and what he knew best: bass fishing and the quest for the world record. Living in one's imagination is a strategy of survival in this country of poverty and restricted freedoms, according to Wendy Gimbel, a Cuban American who wrote in *Havana Dreams* that after the revolution, "those who hadn't budged from their homes had fled in their minds instead." I couldn't help but wonder if Sammy would be disappointed if he ever confronted in reality the things that had lived so richly in his mind.

Sammy grew up in Havana among the mysterious and enchanting old buildings and boulevards. Like every other boy in Cuba he played baseball from the time he was old enough to swing a stick, just as most American youngsters once did, with dreams of success and fame dancing in their heads. But his most enduring childhood memories have to do with bass fishing. His father, Manuel, was a mechanic in Havana, and was one of the pioneers of largemouth bass fishing in the country, helping to start local bass organizations and tournaments in the late 1960s, roughly the same time that Ray Scott was putting together BASS in the United States. Manuel, now seventy-five and retired, was Cuba's national bass-fishing champion in 1971 and '72, pursuing the sport with dedication and spending most of his weekends fishing the half-dozen reservoirs near the capital. Sammy remembers as a very young boy running into his parents' bedroom on weekend mornings and looking for his father. If he wasn't there, Sammy would then scamper into the main room of the house to look for Manuel's fishing rods. "If they were gone, I would cry because I wanted to go fishing with him," Sammy said. His insistence eventually paid off. Manuel started taking his son with him on fishing trips when Sammy was just five years old. A few years later, his father actually let him cast a rod.

Like seemingly all of the record hunters I had met, Sammy had one seminal childhood moment that stood out among the others. When he was seven, Sammy went with Manuel and a few of his fishing buddies to a small stream-fed lake. The men waded out as deep as they could, some up to their armpits, so they could get their lures into what seemed to be the most promising water. They cast for hours without catching a thing. After a while, Sammy wanted to fish too, so Manuel placed him in the shallower water near the mouth of the stream, keeping him out of harm's way and, presumably, in a less desirable spot. Sammy took just a few casts when he hooked something, which stayed in one place long enough for him to think that he was merely snagged on the lake's bottom. Initially, he didn't utter a peep to the older men, who weren't paying much attention to him anyway. But when the lure started to move, Sammy gave out a yelp. All of the men looked over in utter disbelief as the huge bass attached to the end of Sammy's line jumped clear of the water and broke off. Sammy said he cried hard after losing the fish and sullenly spent the rest of the day in the car waiting for Manuel and the others to finish their fishing. But, he thinks now, "It was a sign." The one that had eluded him, the one that will forever exist only in his imagination, had also hooked him, deeply.

Sammy was ten years old when his father first told him the story of the world-record bass. Manuel knew all about George Perry from the American magazines he had read before 1959, and the record was a prominent topic whenever he and his friends went fishing, a tale told and retold many times with reverence. Sammy says that the story of Perry and his record, whether it's true or not, always had a special meaning to his father, a sentiment he passed down to his son. "I get very excited about the record still," Sammy said. "When you read that a poor person caught the world record, it gives you hope. When you read about Bob Crupi and the others with their technology on those lakes in California, the average person thinks that the record is only for those people, the top people with the technology. But Perry's story says it can be for everybody. When I picture the world record in my mind, I picture it happening to someone like me."

Bass fishing cannot properly be called a sport for Cubans, the majority of whom fish primarily for food, just as Perry did. In America, bass fishing is a technology-enhanced pastime that long ago outgrew its original purpose—the gathering of food. For world-record hunters, the pursuit has arguably even outgrown its secondary purpose of recreation, becoming an obsessive pursuit with unhealthy manifestations for most everyone involved. Very little about the way the American record hunters fish is relaxing. In fact, for most people the pursuit seems more stressful than their day jobs. Bob Crupi worriedly squints at his fishfinder. Mike Long nearly loses his face in the wind generated by the seventy-mile-per-hour speed of his boat. Mac and Buddha drive their Mercedes like madmen to be the first in line at the lake. The world-record chase is certainly a totem of capitalism—one man trying to outdo another, competing in a free market using wits, guile, and technology in pursuit of fame and fortune. But the flipside perhaps, was that the twisting of this quest, the hypervalue put on this one fish, was a sign of some sort of decadence. I thought back to the Perry story and whether or not it could be interpreted like a biblical myth-history, some sort of divine instruction. If the fishing gods are like the God of the Old Testament, bent on doling out harsh lessons and rewarding only those whom they see fit, perhaps it is not an American, but an impoverished Cuban whom they have in mind for the next record.

About halfway through the road trip, Sammy motioned to one of the few gas stations that we saw and said, "I want to tell you a story that involves the world record, but I must have a beer to make my English better." With that, he pulled over and bought a Cristal, the light lager that is Cuba's national favorite. He sat back down in the car, took a few sips, and we got back on the highway. "OK," he said, taking a deep breath. "First there is the background."

In college, Sammy studied civil engineering and was a member of the school's fencing team. But bass fishing still played a very prominent role in his life. "Most people thought I was crazy," he said. "I was very tired with my studies and my fencing. And I would still be fishing all of the time." When he graduated, he worked for a short while in Havana as an engineer. But in 1985 he was transferred to Santa Clara, a much smaller industrial city of 175,000. The move turned out to be serendipitous for Sammy's eventual career. "There was better bass fishing there than I had in Havana," he says. Santa Clara was just a half hour from the Sierra Escambray Mountains, home of the fabled Lake Hanabanilla, the body of water rumored to be the hideout of the next world-record bass.

Sammy worked hard in Santa Clara as a civil engineer, helping to design, construct, and repair the area's roads and airports. But he worked harder on his bass fishing. Following in the footsteps of Manuel, Sammy entered a few regional tournaments on the weekends. With some early success, he realized that he was ready for the next step, but not before some more preparation. Sammy started traveling on the weekends to lakes in different provinces, where he would seek out the best bass anglers and watch them fish or corner them and pick their brains about their techniques and methods. He says all of this work helped him become a more complete bass fisherman. "People fall into regular routines and approaches," he said. "Fishermen when I got here in Santa Clara were all using the same techniques on the water. I learned their techniques, but I also used the techniques I had learned from others and from reading magazines." His homework paid off. By the early 1990s, he, like his father before him, had qualified for the Cuban national bass-fishing championships. He went on to win in 1993, '96, and '97.

I had heard a little bit about the Cuban tourneys before my trip. I knew that the country's national championship was every bit, if not more, prestigious in Cuba than the Bassmaster Classic is in the United States. But I was curious about how they differed from the high-octane American affairs. Turns out that perhaps only the quarry is the same, and their striking contrasts are an illustration of the different economic realities of these two countries.

First off, there is the prize money, which in Cuba is nonexistent. While the winner of the 2004 Bassmaster Classic took home $200,000, the Cuban national champion receives no money and no product endorsements—not even some free fishing doodads. The winner (total weight of three bass wins) just gets a fairly small trophy and the honor of knowing that he is the best bass fisherman in Cuba. That prestige is nothing to sneer at in this small but sports-obsessed country where all national champions—whether in baseball, boxing, or bass fishing—are revered.

Then there is the technology gap. Almost all Cuban tournament anglers have graphite rods and decent reels, like their American counterparts. But the lures are a different matter. Instead of buying them at a Wal-Mart or from high-priced boutique designers like Mickey Ellis and Jerry Rago, most competitors hand craft their own lures. The crankbaits are carved from wood, the flashy spoon lures constructed from actual eating utensils and, perhaps most impressively, the big rubber worms are made from the soles of old tennis shoes, which they melt down and pour into a homemade plaster mold. The competitors don't have fishfinders, sonar, global positioning systems, or even livewells (all Cuban bass caught during a tournament are killed and eaten).

But perhaps the biggest difference is in the mode of transportation. Good boats are hard to come by in Cuba, so most used in the tournaments are old wooden and fiberglass ones, patched and repatched ad infinitum, as dissimilar to the sleek rockets used in the United States as an old balloon-tired single-speed bike is to an eighteen-gear composite thin-tired racer. Even more difficult to come by are the motors and the gas needed to run the boats. So all Cuban tournament fishermen row their own boats with oars. "The starter's pistol fires, and then you just hear the *chop-chop-chop* of people rowing as fast as they can to get to the good spots," Sammy said.

Some people assert that bass tournaments in the United States should not be considered a sport like, say, basketball, because there is no intense cardiovascular activity involved. Fishing, they say, expends about as much energy as watching basketball on TV. But those same people would have a hard time making the equivalent argument in Cuba, mainly because of the exhaustive rowing involved. Sammy trained for the national bass tournaments as if he were an Olympic athlete: eating right, running, and lifting weights for months beforehand. That physical preparation is vital: Sammy once rowed twelve miles in a two-day tournament, losing four pounds on the first day alone. The Cuban tournament anglers, as opposed to some of the beer-bellied U.S. anglers, are generally slim, but shaped like Olympic swimmers with powerfully splayed shoulders thanks to the rowing, thus solving the mystery of Sammy's physique.

By this time, Sammy had finished his beer and was on a roll. He steered the conversation back to the world record, something that, even during his tournament days, he never stopped pursuing. But he believes that Cuba's chances of producing the fish are not as good as they once were, thanks to some geopolitics. "There was a time in Cuba when the world record was swimming in many lakes—in the 1960s and '70s when the government was building reservoirs everywhere," he said. "With our weather and the Florida-strain bass, it was possible for some giant bass." But at that time, Sammy was just a kid, without the knowledge and skills and hard-core obsession seemingly needed to track the fish down. By the time Sammy entered his bass-fishing prime, Cuba was in the throes of a devastating economic crisis.

When the Berlin Wall fell in late 1989, the Soviet subsidies that had artificially propped up the Cuban economy for nearly three decades went with it, and Cuba plunged into its deepest depression, one that the United States was sure would prompt a dispirited and suddenly desperately poor populace to overthrow Castro. The food once guaranteed by the government disappeared. Citizens were forced to make do with what they had. They made their main courses from fried banana peels and grapefruit rinds. And they ate bass. Lots of them. The Special Period, as Castro called it, ran from 1991–1994 and was anything but special for the island nation's bass. The Cuban economy eventually recovered, ironically due in large part to the use of American dollars as currency. But according to Sammy, the big bass have never quite done the same.

But that is something that Sammy would like to rectify. In the mid-1990s, Sammy started a small bass-fishing guide service for Americans and Europeans, using his fame as a national champion to get it off the ground. He quickly realized just how profitable the enterprise could be for him and the government. But he also understood that at least a few lakes had to be better managed to give the bass the chance to reach the giant size that compelled those tourists to visit in the first place. Sammy lobbied the government to designate a few prime lakes as catch-and-release only, a management technique that was a hard sell in a country that is still so subsistence-based. But his efforts fell on deaf ears. "The government does not understand," says Sammy. "Bass fishing, they say? It is a big industry, I tell them. They say, OK, show us the money."

So Sammy decided to go all out, to prove that it could be a viable tourist industry. He quit his engineering job, which paid him $20 a month, to guide full-time in 1997. "It was a risk," he said. "Some of my friends asked if I was sure I wanted to do it." In order to make ends meet, he added a saltwater service as well, mainly targeting the island's plentiful and easy-to-catch tarpon (in general, the Europeans like the saltwater and the North Americans like the bass). He convinced a Canadian client to donate four old fiberglass boats for his fleet, and he trained a few guides and contacted the tourist agencies, offering his services. He's been pretty successful thus far. In a good month, Sammy says he can earn $200, all in tips. (To put this in perspective, a surgeon's typical salary is only $30 a month. Tourism is king in Cuba.) Despite his success, he still cannot convince the government to help out by managing a few lakes.

But Sammy holds out hope. And despite the fact that there is virtually no catch-and-release in Cuba, Sammy is sure about one thing: "The world record is still here swimming around, absolutely," he said. "And even if the record is broken in the States, we will be ready with a new one." And with that, we pulled into Sammy's hometown of Santa Clara.

On December 31, 1958, an army of rebels led by the Argentine doctor Che Guevera came down from their hideout in the Sierra Escambray Mountains and stormed the city of Santa Clara, attacking a troop train packed with reinforcements and American weaponry bound for General Batista's forces. Within two days, Che had taken the town, Batista had fled the island for good, and Fidel Castro's reign over Cuba had unofficially begun. The United States was uneasy with Castro from the start, a feeling that only grew stronger after Castro nationalized all of the country's industries in his sharp left turn toward Communism.

From the beginning, U.S. presidents have underestimated Castro, and every attempt to bring him down has only made him stronger. He has remained as confounding and hard to catch for U.S. presidents as the world-record bass is for its pursuers. On April 17, 1961, President Kennedy was absolutely confident that with the CIA's help, the people of Cuba would rise up and overthrow "El Jefe." But the repulsion of the Bay of Pigs invasion instead became Castro's shining moment. In 1962, the United States and the Soviets went head-to-head in a nuclear chess match, using Cuba as the pawn. Again, the Cuban missile crisis only served to solidify Castro's importance on the global stage.

That same year, the United States began its Cuban trade embargo that continues to this day. But the embargo has not had the desired effect of toppling Castro. Instead, it has provided him with a necessary counterbalance to his power, an easy enemy to energize the country against and an excuse for all of Cuba's ills, like its poverty and miserable economy. Castro has even occasionally shown uncommon tactical brilliance in dealing with American power plays. In 1980, President Carter announced that the United States would accept Cuban political refugees with open arms, thinking this would lead to a crippling exodus of her citizens. Castro didn't fight the measure. Instead he emptied out his jails and asylums and sent them north in what is known as the Mariel Boatlift. Even George W. Bush's tightening of the trade restrictions and tough talk about not tolerating Castro has had a galvanizing effect on the country, as evidenced by massive anti-Bush rally in Havana in 2004. Almost every Cuban I met asked me if I liked President Bush. It was very clear where they stood on the issue. Perhaps the only thing the U.S. government can take solace in is the fact that Castro, like the record for the largemouth bass, presumably won't last forever.

One of the United States's biggest failures in dealing with Cuba has been the travel ban, which was enacted in 1962. (In actuality, U.S. citizens are allowed to *travel* to Cuba. They just can't *spend any money* there. Go figure.) The ban is a failure because it is so often flaunted (an estimated 20,000 U.S. citizens travel illegally to Cuba each year, most flying through Canada or Mexico) and so rarely enforced. In fact, the only reported person in the history of the ban to be indicted, tried, and sentenced is a Texan named Dan Snow, who was down there searching for—you guessed it—the world-record largemouth bass.

For most of his time on earth, Dan Snow led a fairly pedestrian life. He was the king of the Bosse High School senior prom in

Evansville, Indiana. He enlisted in the Marines and then became an insurance salesman for Allstate. But more than anything else, he loved bass fishing, and he eventually made his passion into a career. In the 1960s, he founded what would become the nation's largest regional bass club, then used that experience to get a job with BASS itself. By the early 1970s, he believed that he was next in line to succeed that organization's founder and president, Ray Scott.

At that time, the rumors had begun to drift north about the huge bass in Cuba. Snow explored the island, and decided that he would start a company that would lead trips there for American bass enthusiasts who were titillated by the claims of bass of up to 26 pounds that would demolish George Perry's record. In 1976, Snow says, he beat out Ray Scott for the exclusive contract with the Cuban government to lead bass fishing trips. In retrospect, Snow says, it was this act that would land him in jail fourteen years later.

In 1977, President Carter eased the travel restrictions to Cuba just enough so that Snow's trips were completely legal. He ran his business for five years with no hassles from the U.S. government. Then in 1982, President Reagan once again closed the door on travel to Cuba, with only a few very restrictive exceptions, one of which was travel done in the name of scientific research. Since Snow had always brought along a number of biologists to study Cuban bass, he figured his operation was still legal. But all of that changed when the first George Bush took office in 1988.

Snow claims that it was none other than Ray Scott who initiated the sting operation that brought him down. Scott was a well-known fund-raiser and supporter of the Bush campaign and remains a friend and fishing buddy of the forty-first president to this day. Snow says that Scott was still angry about losing out on the Cuban contract and had notified the U.S. government of

Snow's dealings. In late 1988, Snow was indicted for trading with an enemy, and faced up to one hundred years in jail and $500,000 in fines. After his trial two years later, he was sentenced to ninety days in jail, a $5,300 fine, and 1,000 hours of community service.

Snow served his jail sentence and did his community service for Meals on Wheels, but says he never paid the fine. And he remains incredibly embittered by the whole experience. "It was all a fraud, a lie," he says, his voice rising a decibel or two. "Bush was just trying to get back at me for his buddy, Ray Scott." Snow says the episode "ruined my life. I can't vote, can't own a gun. I used to coach soccer and baseball, but now I can't work with kids. I don't even know how I will pay the rent at the first of each month." Yet he says he's traveled back to Cuba some fifty times since getting out of prison.

Snow has channeled his bitterness into a run for the president of the United States as a write-in candidate in 2004 on a platform that includes, among other things, legalizing prostitution, opening a Department of Making Friends, and demanding the resignation of all members of the House of Representatives and the Senate. His campaign Web site says: "Your vote for Dan Snow will return America to greatness with respect!" When asked whether he thought he had a chance of winning the election in November, Snow replied without hesitation, "You never know."

Snow believes that the world record is still in Cuba, and one of the most likely spots, he says, is Lake Hanabanilla, the place where the 26-pounder was supposedly landed. Hanabanilla also happens to be Sammy's home lake, some twenty miles from Santa Clara.

In the intense heat of a late summer afternoon, Sammy and I drove to Hanabanilla. At the lake we met one of Sammy's guides, a man named Mario, who was short and compact and had a thick brush of a mustache. Sammy introduced us. Mario turned to me and, in perfect English, said, "I don't think that anyone will ever break the record anywhere." It was as if he had been thinking for days about what he would say to me and wanted to make sure I knew where he stood on the whole matter. It was the only time he would not use Sammy as a translator when talking to me for the two days that we spent together. With that out of the way, Mario cranked up the rickety old Yamaha 20-horsepower motor, one of the treasured few that Sammy has access to for his trips, another gift from a generous Canadian.

Hanabanilla is a beautiful man-made lake, relatively cool, clear, and deep for a Cuban reservoir. It is surrounded by sloping, jungly hillsides whose foliage stops just short of the water, which was down thirty feet or so when I got there due to a summer-long drought. Construction of the lake was begun by American engineers just before the revolution, then completed by the Cuban government. The reservoir provided drinking water for Santa Clara and the province of Villa Clara. A few humble dwellings dotted its banks, inhabited by *campesinos* who farmed bananas, coffee, and tobacco on the steep hills abutting the lake. I told Sammy that I thought it would be nice to live on a lake this beautiful. He shook his head immediately. "No," he said. "There is no electricity here."

Sammy was decked out like an American basser, wearing a short-sleeved white fishing shirt with a Ranger Boats logo, a gift from an American client. The tackle boxes he had brought with him bulged with hundreds of lures—also gifts from clients—and contained only a few of the handmade worms that Sammy obviously no longer needed but seemed to keep around for sentimental reasons. He told Mario to stop the boat in the middle of the lake. He explained that we were above an underwater point, hidden to the naked eye, but a place that Sammy, in his years of scouting and fishing this lake, knew well. It was August. Not the best time to catch the big bass, he said. The bass were neither shallow, as they would be for the late winter spawn, nor deep, as they would be in the fall. Instead, they hung suspended, which made them harder to catch. "But this is one of my favorite lakes," Sammy said as he cast out a 4-inch-long crankbait and reeled it in, trying to get it into the zone. He was relaxed and fluid. There were no jerky movements in his cast or retrieve. During the day, he never seemed to strain or get too excited about a missed fish. "It is so beautiful here that I can come out here without a bite. But I know that the world record is here. And people don't know how to fish it properly, which gives me an opportunity. There is no real fishing pressure here at all." He was right about that. Had the 7,900-acre Hanabanilla been a reservoir in California, we might have been sharing the water with two hundred other boats. But we would see only one other boat the entire day, and its two Cuban passengers were fishing the shoreline, where Sammy says only the small fish reside.

Though my Spanish is pretty poor, I did overhear Mario ask Sammy a question about *béisbol*. Sammy turned to me and said: "Mario wants to know what you think of what the Yankees did with Contreras." Jose Contreras, a Cuban defector, had been a pitcher for the New York Yankees until just a few weeks before my trip to Cuba. But the team had lost faith in him, and he'd been traded to the Chicago White Sox. I told Sammy that I thought the Yankees had made an uncharacteristic mistake by giving up on Contreras, who had an excellent forkball. Sammy and Mario seemed pleased with that reaction. Sammy said that they both still liked the Yankees because they were the team of another defector, Orlando Hernandez, the great "El Duque," perhaps the finest pitcher that Cuba has ever produced. I asked Sammy how Cubans felt when their best baseball players, like Contreras, defected to the United States. "First it is surprise when he leaves," said Sammy. "Then we are happy for him. Then we are sad when the Olympics come around. Contreras would have been a good pitcher for the team."

The Athens Olympics were going on at this time, and the event served as a reminder of just how sports-obsessed this small country is. Cuban boxers, feared around the world, were pummeling athletes from the United States and Great Britain. And the baseball team was well on its way to winning yet another Olympic gold. Castro is among the country's biggest sports enthusiasts, and fishing—before age slowed him down—was long his favorite pursuit. He fished for both bass and saltwater species. Back in 1960, Hemingway invited the young leader to be the guest of honor at his tenth annual billfish tournament out of Havana. Castro instead entered—and won—the tournament.

I asked Sammy what Castro, as the nation's biggest sports cheerleader, would think if Cuba produced the world-record bass. "He is a very competitive man," Sammy said. "When he does something, he wants to be the best and he wants his country to be the best. So he would be very excited by the world record because it would be an achievement of the Cuban people." I noticed that every time Sammy spoke about Castro, he lowered his voice a little bit. It shouldn't have surprised me. It is illegal for Cubans to speak out against their government, so they are very careful when talking about their leader. In fact, many Cubans refuse to refer to him by name. Instead, they just rub their fingers on their chins.

Just then Mario, who had been fishing while Sammy and I were talking, hooked into a bass. He brought it in quickly. "Small one," Sammy said. And it wasn't very long—maybe only fourteen inches from head to tail. But what it lacked in length, it made up for in girth. The little fish looked like it had swallowed a grapefruit. Just like a California bass. Sammy explained that the main forage fish in Hanabanilla were bluegills and tilapia. They didn't have the stocked trout that the California bass fattened up on. But what made these bass so special was the fact that, relatively speaking, there were so few of them living in this huge reservoir. So they had little competition from other bass and could feed at their leisure on the abundant baitfish, becoming absurdly overweight in the process. The "dominion of the few" was the same management theory to which Porter Hall adhered. Mario kept the fish because he had hooked it deeply in the gills, which were bleeding. Happily, he had the main course for his dinner that night.

Sammy and I started casting with renewed hope. But the action remained slow, so after a while we started talking again. I wondered if there were any other Cuban record chasers. "Not really," he said. "There are many who would like to break the record, but they are not targeting the big fish as I am." And even Sammy, with his busy guiding schedule and Margarita and his daughter to take care of, doesn't fish for the record as much as he would like. He says that he maybe spends two days a week during the spawning season chasing the record—far less time than his American counterparts. Not that he has ever stopped dreaming of the fish that has lived in his imagination since he was bitten by the bug as a child. "I became obsessed with the world record from the first time my father told me the story," he said. But that obsession was not always a good thing, at least as far as his fishing was concerned. "My father was my first teacher of fishing," he said. "But there was another old man, a friend of my father who was also a Cuban champion, who taught me about fishing." The old man was impressed by Sammy's dedication at such a young age, but he warned him about becoming too fixated on the record. "He told me that to fish well, I couldn't be so obsessed with the record."

That lesson has stayed with him to this day and helps explain his calm demeanor on the water, so opposite from a few of the high-strung Americans I had spent time with. Sammy approaches his fishing like a Zen master. It's the quality of time spent on the water, not the quantity. He tries to keep everything in perspective—his family, his job, his passion. He had read in a magazine story about how solitary some of the world-record chasers were, how they seemed to sacrifice everything in pursuit of their goal. That surprised him. "I want to break the record badly, but to lose your family to do it is not worth it," he said. "I think it's harmony—I want my wife and kids and friends to share it with me, for all people around me to have a piece." Perhaps this reaction could be expected from someone who grew up in a Communist country. But to Sammy this detachment gives him a competitive advantage. "It's sometimes better to look at this from a distance, like when you watch other people play chess and can see so clearly the moves they should be making."

When I asked Sammy what catching the world record would mean to him, his answer was thoughtful and, in parts, stunningly candid: "I am a human and I have a sense of pride. I've won all you can in this country; I can say I've done it all. But after that, what's left? Just the biggest fish," he said. "This is my profession. The world record is the maximum. The Bassmaster Classic has many champions, year after year. But only one man can catch the biggest of all. That single fish means more than anything else."

And to Sammy, the world record goes beyond the personal. "Perhaps that bass could make life better for all Cubans," he said, pointing out the impact the fish would have on the tourist industry and the pride of the Cuban people. "That would be great. To be involved in that would be even better."

Certainly Sammy's reasons for wanting to break the record are not purely altruistic. If he were to become the new record holder, he would achieve worldwide fame that would allow him to make more money as a guide. But that money would be minimal compared to what his American counterparts could expect. No one would offer him a contract to endorse a tackle company, no producer would call to book him on a talk show. He covets the record mostly for the feeling of accomplishment that comes from reaching the pinnacle of one's passion.

"There is one other thing," he said, slowly taking off his glasses to wipe the lenses, like a college professor about to make a pertinent point. "We had four hundred years of Spanish rule, but we were influenced so much more by America." The two countries, he says, have so much in common. "We are both nations of mixed immigrants with proud, enterprising citizens. Almost eighty percent of the movies Cubans watch are American," he said, though he left out the fact that they are edited for political content. He continued: "We enjoy each other's music. The national sport of Cuba is baseball, not like other Latin American countries where soccer is king." And there is, of course, a mutual love of bass fishing. Maybe, Sammy thinks, just maybe, a world-record bass could be the tipping point that leads to better relations between the two countries, and the understanding that they are so alike. Cubans, he pointed out, like the American people. Their feelings for the U.S. government are another matter.

But Sammy also worries if this is the right time to break the record, the right climate for an event like that. "Americans in the South, they are not happy with Cuba, maybe," he said. "All those people might hate me if I catch the record." No, I thought, they wouldn't hate you. They'd just be jealous.

Sammy paused for a moment. "Do you know what I call the world-record fish," Sammy asked me, seemingly out of the blue.

I didn't. I knew that Cubans called big bass *trucha grande*, which literally means "big trout," a holdover name from the early bass-fishing days in the American South.

"I call her *Rompecorazones*," he said.

"What does that mean?" I asked.

"It means Heartbreaker," he said. "That fish, she will break the heart of all fishermen."

———————

The next day we were at Hanabanilla by 6:30 a.m. The sky was cloudy, and the breeze felt very cool for an August morning. We met Mario and motored out to the lake. When we stopped, Sammy opened up a bag he had brought along. It contained a fishfinder that a Russian client had purchased for him. It was fairly primitive as fishfinders go. The transmitter was attached to a suction cup that kept falling into the water, perilously close to the propeller. And the fish that blipped on the screen were only shown as black, fuzzy masses, unlike the newer American models that have such incredible detail on the monitor, you feel like you're playing a bass-fishing video game. But it was the one bit of technology that Sammy had, and he was proud of it.

Sammy admits that he wouldn't mind owning a few more of the fishing products that he reads about in the bass magazines, especially a trolling motor and maybe a livewell. But he also wonders if too much technology and information is always a good thing. "When you are a child and you catch one or two fish, you believe you can be successful all the time," he said. "Then you read about all the techniques and new gadgets that you don't have and you start to believe that you are far, far away from becoming a good fisherman," he said, perhaps unknowingly getting to the essence of the yearning desire that the advertising industry so successfully creates in the United States.

And Sammy has found, like many American anglers have, that using the fishfinder doesn't necessarily make him a better angler. "Sometimes I see fish on the screen and don't catch them," he said. "Other times I don't see anything and I catch one. The technology I feel is sometimes too much and you lose that natural feel that you had as a little kid that's so important." Then he added, sounding every bit like a man who has read and memorized dozens of back issues of *Bassmaster* magazine: "You need to use your confidence, which is the number-one lure in your box."

Sammy's fishfinder is almost certainly the only one used on the lake, which is one reason that American anglers find the prospect of fishing in Cuba so intriguing. The lakes here are basically virgin territory for their sonar, depthfinders, big boats and motors, and a new batch of hot lures. The feeling is that if they could just get down there on that untouched water and use their gizmos, the big naive Cuban bass would fall to them easily.

The fishfinder did reveal some interesting sights. Sammy jacked up the sensitivity monitor so that the screen would only pick up the biggest bass, those that weighed over 10 pounds. The finder blipped all day long, showing that the bass, as Sammy had said the day before, were indeed suspended in the middle of the lake, and thus nearly impossible to catch. But they were there, and that knowledge—brought to us by the technology—did make the fishing more exciting than it had been the previous day. I had gone to bed the night before wondering if all the rumors about Cuba and its big bass were really true, or if it was just the case that they had grown mythically large in the forbidden imagination of big-bass hunters. But the fishfinder gave a little more credence to the rumors about Cuba and big bass, not one of which I had actually seen yet. I had to take it on faith—from the fishfinder and from Sammy, who seemed to have faith in abundance, for his fish and his country.

We fished in the middle of the reservoir again, this time over an old riverbed. We changed our lures frequently, trying to find the magic one that would make the fish bite. The tactical aspect of it all is what made bass fishing so rewarding to Sammy. "I like to fish in saltwater. It is very, very nice. And the bass is not stronger than the tarpon, it doesn't leap like a sailfish or marlin," he said. "But the bass are so clever, so smart. I like the challenge. Here in Cuba we have tournaments for snapper and other fish. But the one to find the best fisherman, the hardest to win, is the bass tournament."

We had basically the same luck as the day before. Mario landed a few small fish, and Sammy and I lost a few more. When Sammy cast and got his crankbait hung up on a sunken tree, he pulled out a homemade contraption, a heavy concrete weight the size of a big pill bottle, attached to a thick string that was wrapped around a small handheld wooden wheel. He affixed the weight to his fishing line and let it zip down the line until it hit the lure and knocked the hook off the tree branch. He smiled as he retrieved his lure, as proud of his little contraption as he was of the fishfinder. Even though he has many lures now, each one remains precious.

In the afternoon, Sammy and Mario took me to the Rio Negra restaurant, tucked away on the banks of the lake in a protected cove. It was once a happening spot in the 1970s and '80s, where Dan Snow's clients would come off the water for drinks and lunch under the palm-thatched roofs and listen to Cuban musicians whose electric instruments were plugged into a small, water-powered generator. But like so many places I had seen in Cuba, life ebbed at the Rio Negra. When we arrived, the proprietor, a shirtless, potbellied man, was staring forlornly into the distance. His face brightened when we walked in, obviously the first customers he had seen in a long while. The Rio Negra was still subsidized by the government, still had beer in its coolers that remained unopened, still had a little food shipped in every day just in case, even though it has had virtually no business to speak of for the past decade and a half. We didn't even stay for lunch, leaving the lake a few hours later.

―――――――――――

Before we started the drive back to Havana, Sammy and I stopped by his house. He lived on a dusty street named Calle A (Road A), on a rundown block of dozens of side-by-side dwellings. It was what Americans would call a slum. The neighborhood was bustling with activity. Little boys flitted in and out of the street. Women fanned themselves while they gossiped in slivers of shade provided by awnings over the doorsteps. The occasional moped puttered by, spewing out black plumes of exhaust. The sounds of human activity could be heard ten houses down—voices, chattering televisions, clanging pots and pans.

Sammy's house was very humble. The three rooms had walls and floors made of concrete. There were no windows, only storm shutters. On the walls of the living room hung a picture of Sammy's eldest daughter, a print of a beatific Jesus, and a framed IGFA certificate that Sammy had received for a 12-pound bass caught in 1987. He is the only Cuban ever to be recognized by that organization. Perched on a small table were three modest trophies that all read CAMPEONATO NACIONAL DE PESCA DE LA TRUCHA.

Margarita, a petite blond woman, walked into the living room, holding Sammy's youngest daughter, the nine-month-old Claudia, on her hip. Claudia broke into a huge smile with her wide brown eyes when she spotted her father, and she tugged at the short whiskers of his beard. Margarita brought out the family's sole fan and placed it in front of the only Yankee present, who must have appeared to be on the verge of a heat stroke. She said something to Sammy in Spanish which made both of them smile.

"Margarita is afraid that I will show you my fishing closet, which is very messy," Sammy said. With that, he pulled back a curtain that revealed a little room that I had not noticed before. "I spend a lot of time in here," he said. It's the place he stores all of his fishing paraphernalia, the closet that was the keeper of all his daydreams, his own enchanted Narnia. Within, there were fishing rods in all shapes and sizes, messily splayed about the walls and stacked in the corners. Lure boxes bulged with hooks and rubber worms. Hats sporting patches from different American fishing organizations hung from big nails on the wall. And stacks upon stacks of *Field & Stream* and *Bassmaster* magazines fanned out across the floor. Sammy stood there holding the curtain open, smiling.

We drove into Havana, on the main drag known as the Malecón, that winds its way along the waterfront. We passed the American Interests Section (the United States has no formal embassy in Cuba), which was heavily fortified and well guarded. Maybe a hundred feet from the building there is the famous billboard that depicts a Cuban worker defiantly staring across the Straits of Florida at a menacing-looking Uncle Sam and shouting: *"Señores Imperialistas: No les tenemos absolutamenta ningun miédo!"* (Imperialists: We have absolutely no fear of you!) The waterfront buildings we passed—old Spanish colonial mansions that were once lived in by wealthy sugar barons but were now inhabited by three or more families—were tattered. The paint was cracking, the windows were smashed, and metal bars held up the crumbling foundations. I thought of James Michener's line in *Six Days in Havana*, when he first laid eyes on the Cuban capital: "This city needs ten million dollars' worth of white paint!" If there is an evolution to architecture that begins with finished buildings and ends with ruins, these old mansions are the missing links.

Before he dropped me off at the Nacional, Sammy began to grill me again about the research I had done for the book. He wanted to hear some of the stories once more, about Castaic Lake and the San Diego reservoirs, about Porter Hall and his attempt to grow his fish, about the rows upon rows of fishing lures in Bass Pro Shops, about Montgomery Lake in Georgia and what it looked like now. It was like he was trying to imprint these images in his mind. He desperately wanted to go see these places, but he knew he would have to settle for visiting them in his imagination and storing the little souvenirs away in his closet of daydreams back in that tiny, low-slung abode with Margarita and Claudia, places where, in some profound way, he might already have everything he needs.

AFTERWORD

One afternoon in the midst of my research for this book, I stood on a wooden dock that reached out into the swimming pool–blue water of a small reservoir near San Diego. The sky was cloudless, and the yellow rays of the sun felt soothingly warm—one of those perfect days when a T-shirt and jeans feels just right. I had spent a frenetic few hours on the water with some of the characters in this book, but they were gone now, leaving me behind. I needed some quiet time.

At the far end of the dock, a kid, maybe fourteen years old, was staring intently at something in the lake, shading his eyes with his hands. His body was ticking with excitement. Curious, I walked out to see what had entranced him so. He pointed to a black-and-green blob suspended maybe fifteen feet below the water's surface. It was a bass. "That's Bertha," the kid told me, moving aside so I could get a better look. The bass was enormous. She weighed at the very least in the mid-teens, and was possibly bigger than that. But it was hard to tell. The lens of water, like any account of a big one that got away, is always distorting in one way or another.

But she was certainly a smart old bass, or perhaps just blessed with the fortune of dumb luck. On this lake, fishing was prohibited within thirty yards of the dock. She was in a protected haven, at least for now.

As the kid walked away, I lay on my stomach and peered over the side of the dock to get a better look. I stared down and she stared right back, an easy feat for her to accomplish: Her stupendous girth had pushed her big bulging brown eyes unnaturally to the top of her head, like she was a flounder. I could see that her fins were tattered and bloody from the rigors of the spawn, from clearing away sharp gravel to make a bed and fending off insistent males, who repeatedly bumped her sides. But she was recuperating now, only recently removed from a brief moment in time when the weight of her tens of thousands of eggs would have made her a few pounds heavier. Maybe that extra weight had been just enough to push her over the edge. Maybe—just maybe—not too long ago, she was the one.

But no one would ever know. She was safe for the moment, sheltered by a set of man-made regulations. Safe from me as I gazed down from above, safe from the hooks of the hard-core record hunters, safe from becoming the bass that would turn an insular world upside down . . .

"Bertha," I said out loud, letting the name linger there for a moment. It didn't matter what they called you—Bertha, Cash, Big Muthafucka, *Rompecorazones*, Sowbelly. The names they provided for you were merely incidental to what you provided them. You had a profound effect on the lives of a few passionate men and women. You filled them with an overpowering desire, an impulse as mysterious as your own urge to spawn a few days ago, or to swim here today. You made people do strange things, like neglect both family and work, lie and cheat. But you also gave them hope, provided their lives with meaning and direction. This quest for you helped them whittle this big, distracting world down to a manageable size, even as you stayed, as you are now, just beyond their grasp.

Around you, Bertha, had blossomed one of those subcultures that, though it's now spread across the globe, seems uniquely American, with its blend of myth, ambition, optimism, technology, and competition. A subculture that has, at times, the languid feel of baseball (perhaps the reason for its many references within), the spontaneity of jazz, the ruthlessness of the high halls of capitalism, and even a dash of the corruption that seems to seep into anything that really matters to anyone.

Bertha, I thought to myself, you know not what you've done.

The ghosts of George Washington Perry and his fish haunt each and every one of the characters in this book. No one will ever know for sure if Perry really did catch a 22-pound, 4-ounce large-mouth bass on that rainy day in Georgia in 1932. But that mystery is the life-giving wellspring of each of their stories. Many of them believe that Perry's fish is a myth, but they all recognize it as the standing record. It's something they take on faith. "Myths which are believed in tend to become true," wrote George Orwell.

In this day and age when seemingly every fact can be tracked down with a keystroke in a matter of seconds, perhaps we need our myths and mysteries more than ever. Myths have always been a part of human life. They help explain the unexplainable. They provide us with hope, instruct us, fill us with awe. And those things that mean the most to us as humans—love, family, religion—all have their roots in mystery. As I worked on this book, I developed a greater appreciation for the role of myths and mystery in this record chase, and in the world in general. I began to admire the fact that these men and women were pursuing something with so much passion, without knowing for sure if the record they wanted so desperately to break ever actually existed. And even Sowbelly, for that matter, that would-be record breaker, lived only in their vivid imaginations and fantasies, at least for now. Somehow, I found that to be optimistic.

I don't know if spending so much time interviewing, thinking about, and writing about these people actually shed any light on my own mysterious passion for fishing. But, in the end, that self-knowledge became irrelevant. The stories of their lives, each so different yet all centered around a common point, are what I found to be far more intriguing.

If there is a golden rule in fishing, it is this: One should strive to cover the water and take a cast into every promising cove. In this book, I have utilized this methodology in attempting to provide what is in essence a snapshot of the present state of the quest for the world-record largemouth bass. I have gone back in time to some spots where I knew big stories could be caught, to George Perry and the genesis of the record chase, to the hoaxes and near misses that help make up this story. I have cast a line into some of the most inviting coves in covering the best of the modern-day record chasers, men like Bob Crupi, Mike Long, Jed Dickerson, and Porter Hall. And I have taken a longshot—always worth doing in life as in fishing—in traveling to Cuba, where I happily spent time with Samuel Yera, a keeper if there ever was one.

But it is impossible to cover it all. Somewhere out there, in some hidden place off the radar screen of the record chasers, someone is working a secret honey hole in total obscurity. I may have even laid eyes on that person and whizzed right on by to the next cove over.

In the years to come, George Perry's world record will face more pressure than ever before. Technology and tactics and information have improved dramatically and are being used by tenacious fishermen like Mike Long and Jed Dickerson, who will wear out their arms in their pursuit of angling's holy grail. The bass in California show no signs of abating their incredible growth. Texas continues to raise millions of dollars in its hubristic attempt to grow the next world record. Porter Hall's optimistic gamble may eventually pay off. And in Cuba, well, you never know.

The fact is that any of the people profiled in this book could break the world record at any time. Or—and I believe this gets to the essence of the chase and the stories within these pages— Sowbelly could be landed by literally anyone else. By the time you read this line, there may already be a new world record. After all, you just need a rod and reel, a lucky lure, and one cast. And another quest would begin anew.

ACKNOWLEDGMENTS

My first debt of gratitude goes to the characters in this book. Their passion was a pleasure to be around, and I tried my best not to get in the way of their stories.

Countless folks put me up on their couches, pull-out beds, and floors during my travels: Tyler and Bridgett Vadeboncoeur in San Diego, my brother Chris Burke in Atlanta, Princess Augusta Tickletummy and Bill and Bea Baab in Augusta, and Porter Hall in Mississippi. Mac Weakley and Mike "Buddha" Winn went so far as to drive me to the airport after a FedEx truck made a mess of my rental car.

The talented writer Jonathan Miles helped me find Samuel Yera and generously shared his own wisdom about Cuba. Bob Walz and Jose Fuentes at Last Frontier Expeditions & Safaris got me down there (and back) in one piece.

To the *Forbes* crew, a big thanks for letting me take the time to do this book. Editors Alan Farnham and Bruce Upbin encouraged the initial idea. Head librarian Anne Mintz and fellow reporter Rob Wherry turned over every rock in assisting me with my research. And the *Forbes* softball team ("Never Settle!") provided a welcome diversion on those beautiful spring evenings.

Mary O'Malley and Nancy Moore at the Anglers' Club of New York put up with my coffee slurping and general loitering among the splendid stacks of perhaps the finest piscatorial library in the world. Dana Gibson and Pat Smith provided essential software assistance in the home office. And the professors Thomas Near, an ecology and evolutionary expert at the University of Tennessee at Knoxville, and Steven Friesen, a "myth-history" sage at the University of Missouri, helped me keep my thoughts straight and true. Mike Leech and Doug Blodgett at the IGFA and Mickey Owens and Shirley Boykin at the BBRC helpfully fielded my questions. And Ray Scott enthusiastically doled out his nuggets of bass wisdom.

My dog, Murphy, lived for thirteen great years and sat patiently by my side as I wrote the first eight chapters of this book. I miss you terribly, old friend.

And I owe a great deal to the two men who have had the most influence on my life, both personally and professionally: my father, Donald Burke, to whose memory this book is also dedicated, and my uncle Charles Gaines.

The folks at Dutton made this happen, and I thank all of them for their hard work, but especially Gary Brozek, my brilliant editor, whose encouragement and gentle but firm editing touch are felt throughout the text. I knew from our first lunch together that we shared the same vision for this book. That's a treat to be savored.

To my agents: Dan Green, who gave this project an approving nod, and particularly to Simon Green, whose wise counsel, faith in a first-time book author, and indefatigable enthusiasm for this project—and life in general—buoyed me throughout. As Simon says, "*Feel* it!"

To my mother, Hansell, from whom I have learned the true meaning of unconditional and selfless love. And finally to my wife, Heidi, pregnant throughout my writing of this book, and in a beautiful way, my own obsessive quest. Except that I actually landed her.

INDEX